Flavors of Empire

AMERICAN CROSSROADS

*Edited by Earl Lewis, George Lipsitz, George Sánchez,
Dana Takagi, Laura Briggs, and Nikhil Pal Singh*

Flavors of Empire

FOOD AND THE MAKING OF THAI AMERICA

Mark Padoongpatt

UNIVERSITY OF CALIFORNIA PRESS

University of California Press, one of the most distinguished university presses in the United States, enriches lives around the world by advancing scholarship in the humanities, social sciences, and natural sciences. Its activities are supported by the UC Press Foundation and by philanthropic contributions from individuals and institutions. For more information, visit www.ucpress.edu.

University of California Press
Oakland, California

Library of Congress Cataloging-in-Publication Data

Names: Padoongpatt, Mark, author.
Title: Flavors of empire : food and the making of Thai America / Mark Padoongpatt.
Description: Oakland, California : University of California Press, [2017] | Series: American crossroads | Includes bibliographical references and index. |
Identifiers: LCCN 2017016679 (print) | LCCN 2017019088 (ebook) | ISBN 9780520966925 (ebook) | ISBN 9780520293731 (cloth : alk. paper) | ISBN 9780520293748 (pbk. : alk. paper)
Subjects: LCSH: Thais—California—Los Angeles—Social conditions. | Cooking, Thai. | Thais—California—Los Angeles—Social life and customs.
Classification: LCC E184.T4 (ebook) | LCC E184.T4 P33 2017 (print) | DDC 641.59593—dc23
LC record available at https://lccn.loc.gov/2017016679

Manufactured in the United States of America

26 25 24 23 22 21 20 19 18 17
10 9 8 7 6 5 4 3 2 1

For my parents, Nuttita and Vitaya
For all Robin Hoods, past and present
For Thai America

CONTENTS

ILLUSTRATIONS

FIGURES

MAPS

ACKNOWLEDGMENTS

It is quite remarkable to think about all of the people—activists, colleagues, friends, family, and people I barely even knew—who had a hand in helping this book come into being. I owe an incredible debt to Chancee Martorell and the Thai Community Development Center, who enthusiastically supported my research and gave me full access to every document they had on Thai Town. Chancee, who has been the bedrock and heart of the Thai community in Los Angeles for over twenty years, taught me about the issues confronting Thai Americans and the efforts to address them when I volunteered at the Thai CDC as a graduate student. I am equally indebted to Wat Thai of Los Angeles, especially the volunteers and monks who handed me materials about the temple's history. Thanks also to the Royal Thai Consulate Los Angeles for lending me rare books. A very special thanks to Barbara Hansen, Wandee Pathomrit, Urai Ruenprom, Jet Tilakamonkul, and Prakas Yenbamroong for sharing their stories with me along with photos, newspaper clippings, memoirs, and research leads. I am proud to be in community with you all.

   Flavor of Empire began when I was an undergraduate at the University of Oregon. Matt Garcia is responsible for its inception. He told me during an office hours meeting in my sophomore year that I needed to write a history of Thai Americans. I agreed. In addition to Matt, who remains a constant source of support and mentorship, Nerissa Balce, Arif Dirlik, Adria Imada, Fiona I. B. Ngo, Peggy Pascoe, Mario Sifuentez, and Martin Summers helped develop my ideas and molded me into a graduate student. Mario is a major reason why I am a professor. His mentorship, friendship, and love over the years have helped me and this project blossom. For that, I am forever indebted to him. I also owe an insurmountable debt to Fiona for working tirelessly with me to get the project off the ground. I would not be the scholar I am today had Peggy not taken me under her wing. I miss her dearly and think about her often.

The Department of American Studies and Ethnicity at the University of Southern California was a vibrant intellectual space where I was surrounded by brilliant and generous souls. Lon Kurashige was a fantastic dissertation chair. He read drafts carefully and provided feedback both small and large, none larger than pushing me to think deeper about the significance of Thai Americans to Asian American history. Thank you to Bill Deverell, whose genius and love of history have been a source of inspiration from the very first day I walked into his Los Angeles history course. Robin D. G. Kelley's imprints are all over this book. His scholarship, teaching, and activism have had the greatest influence on my thinking and approach to history. At USC, Robin was enthusiastic about my writing on the cultural politics of Thai food from the beginning (even in its early, incoherent stages) and was extremely generous with his time, energy, and knowledge. He is a model of the type of scholar I could only ever hope to be. George J. Sanchez provided invaluable insights, suggestions, and tough criticism. Above all, he recognized the potential and broader implications of this project and never allowed me to settle for filling a gap in existing scholarship. George continues to mentor me, a practice I am no doubt paying forward.

Ruthie Wilson Gilmore, Sarah Gualtieri, Jane Iwamura, Lanita Jacobs, Dorinne Kondo, Nancy Lutkehaus, Fred Moten, Viet Nguyen, Laura Pulido, David Roman, Leland Saito, Karen Tongson, and Janelle Wong were exemplary activist scholars. My cohort—Chrisshonna Grant-Nieva, Todd Honma, Abigail Rosas, Gretel Vera Rosas, Margaret Salazar-Porzio, and Terrion Williamson— carried me through the program. Many thanks to Adam Bush, Genevieve Carpio, Jolie Chea, Michan Connor, Robert Eap, Laura Fugikawa, Perla Guerrero, Kai Green, Christina Heatherton, Emily Hobson, Imani Kai Johnson, Priscilla Leiva, Sharon Luk, Celeste Menchaca, Phuong Nguyen, Anthony Bayani Rodriguez, and David Stein. My sincerest appreciation goes to Laura Barraclough, Wendy Cheng, Dan HoSang, and Laura Pulido for seeing the importance of the Thai American experience in Los Angeles. I also am thankful for Hillary Jenks, who provided much needed support at different times throughout the project. Thanks also to Alex Avina, Gilbert Estrada, Glenda Flores, Jerry Gonzalez, Rosina Lozano, Julia Ornelas-Higdon, Yuko Konno, and Go Oyagi. Equally important were Sandra Hopwood, Kitty Lai, Jujuana Preston, and Sonia Rodriguez for taking a bit of stress out of grad school.

The University of Nevada, Las Vegas has also provided a wonderful community of scholars who have been integral to the completion of the book. I cherish my colleagues in the Department of Interdisciplinary, Gender, and Ethnic Studies—Constancio Arnaldo, Erika Abad, Sheila Bock, Lynn Comella, Kendra Gage, Tim Gauthier, Joan Mann, Brandon Manning, Anita Revilla, Danielle Roth-Johnson, and Rainier Spencer—for cultivating a space that values excellence in research. I am grateful to have Anita Revilla in my life as a mentor and friend. Brandon Manning became one of my best friends immediately upon his arriving at UNLV. As a result, he experienced nearly every growing pain and milestone of this book. I appreciate him for being there through the good and not so good times. Thank you to Michael Alarid, Willy Bauer, Jiemin Bao, Raquel Casas, Maile Chapman, Xuan Carlos Espinoza-Cuellar, Georgiann Davis, Bob Futrell, Andy Fry, Marcia Gallo, Peter Gray, Greg Hise, Tiffiany Howard, Ranita Ray, Todd Robinson, Meño Santillana, Jeff Schauer, David Tanenhaus, A. B. Wilkinson, Doris Watson, and Tessa Winkelmann. Willy and Raquel deserve great appreciation for guiding me through my first years at UNLV and continuing to be part of my support system. Much love to A. B. for hashing out ideas with me, offering comments, and being a good friend. Last but not least, I thank Desiré Galvez as well as my interdisciplinary studies students for taking a vested interest in the project. It mattered.

This project benefitted from the kind and knowledgeable staff at the Los Angeles Central Library, National Archives and Records Administration in Washington, D.C., the National Agricultural Library, and the C. Erwin Piper Technical Center. Many thanks to Allan Goodrich, Michelle Gobbi, and Stephen Plotkin at the John F. Kennedy Presidential Library and Museum in Boston, Massachusetts and to Kerry Bartels at the National Archives at Riverside, California.

A number of institutions granted funding along the way. I am thankful for the assistance provided by the John Randolph and Dora Haynes Foundation, the Historical Society of Southern California, and John F. Kennedy Presidential Library and Museum. I want to express enormous gratitude to the University of California, Los Angeles's Institute of American Cultures and the Asian American Studies Center for granting me a Visiting Scholar award for 2016–2017, which pushed me across the finish line. UNLV's College of Liberal Arts, specifically Chris Hudgins, Chris Heavey, and Pat Loosbroock, also stepped up to provide financial support for my research endeavors as well.

It has been a pleasure to work with Niels Hooper, Bradley Depew, Renée Donovan, and the rest of the staff at University of California Press to get this book into peoples' hands. A special thanks goes to Niels for his unwavering excitement for the book, from beginning to end. Thank you to my copy editor, Cynthia Gwynne Yaudes, for improving the book's clarity and flow. Thank you to Catherine Ceniza-Choy and Natalia Molina for reviewing the manuscript and providing direction during the revision process. I also thank Sean Malloy for reading and commenting on key portions of the manuscript. I also want to express my deepest gratitude for George Lipsitz. George offered generative comments and suggestions on the original manuscript as well as on revised versions that ultimately made the book better. Getting to work closely with George was a big deal for me. Despite the fact that his work had profoundly shaped my intellectual development since I was an undergraduate, for some odd reason I had never met or communicated with him before this process. He is proof that one can be a powerful mentor to others without ever knowing them personally.

I have received substantive feedback from presenting at universities, symposiums, and conferences. I wish to thank all the participants who engaged my work, asked questions, and leveled critiques from the Eating Asian America Symposium, Asian American and Asian Diaspora Food Symposium, LA History & Metro Studies Group, the Asian American and Pacific Islander History Group, and the Food Across Borders symposium. I also honed my arguments by contributing to anthologies and readers. One of the best things about such projects, aside from the feedback, is getting to share my work with leading thinkers in different fields. I am privileged to have conversed with John Bukowczyk, Melanie DuPuis, Jennifer Jensen Wallach, Robert Ku, Dawn Mabalon, Martin Manalansan, Valerie Matsumoto, Don Mitchell, Leslie Mitchner, Becky Nicolaides, Jeffrey Pilcher, Lok Siu, Lindsey Swindall, Michael Wise, and Judy Wu.

Finishing this book took nearly everything out of me. I am just glad to have people in my life who have kept me whole. For their timely encouragement and camaraderie, I thank Jose Alamillo, Tim August, Jordan Camp, Melany De La Cruz, Matt Delmont, Rudy Guevarra, Javon Johnson, Mariam Lam, David Leonard, Nhi Lieu, Anthony Macias, Simeon Man, Mimi T. Nguyen, James Padilioni, Elliott Powell, Isabela Quintana, Ana Elizabeth Rosas, Catherine Schlund-Vials, Danielle Seid, Nayan Shah, Julie Sze, Danny Widener, David Yoo, and Nolan Zane. My deepest appreciation goes to Anita Mannur, who has opened so many doors for me in this profession and remains one of my biggest advocates. Thank you, Anita. Thank you to my crew from the University of Oregon, where it all started: Christina Finley, Maria Hwang, Angie Morrill, Kit Myers, Margarita Smith, and Ma Vang. The love and support from my Thai American studies family—Danny Dechartivong, Anny Dhamavasi, Jenny Ungbha Korn, Wanda Pathomrit, Chai Rounchai, Pahole Sookkasikon, Quincy Surasmith, Kanjana Thepboriruk—continues to motivate and sustain me. Finally, Keith Allen, Arthur Llanes, Alex Luu, Johnnjalyn Manning, Marina Ramirez, Ty Shaw, Brenda Sifuentez, Sarah Sifuentez, Shanté Stuart, Jordan Thierry, and Tremaine Thompson remind me that there is in fact a life worth living outside academia.

I want to thank my aunts, uncles, and cousins for their dogged support. My younger brother, Mike, has been instrumental to the completion of this book. He not only created the maps on short notice, but also kept me laughing and smiling as deadlines approached. He is easily one of my most favorite people on the planet. My parents, Vitaya Chalermkij and Nuttita Sangthongkum, to whom this book is dedicated, have instilled a work ethic and fighting spirit in me that has served me well in my work. While they were never quite sure what publishing a book meant in our crazy academic world, they recognized it was important to me, and that it was important for me to tell the history of Thai peoples' experiences in Los Angeles. I also think they are dying to show off the book to their friends. I adore them.

My partner, best friend, comrade, and heartbeat of struggle, Gloria Wong-Padoongpatt, along with our two Jack Russell Terriers, Puffy and Davis, have endured this journey with me. Gloria listened to me spit out ideas and helped brainstorm, read drafts, line edit, and storyboard. She watched me crumble. She watched me rise. Above all, she was the only person who truly understood that this was just a book and not just a book. I can't wait to experience more of the world with you—and to fight by your side for a new one.

Mark Padoongpatt
Las Vegas, Nevada

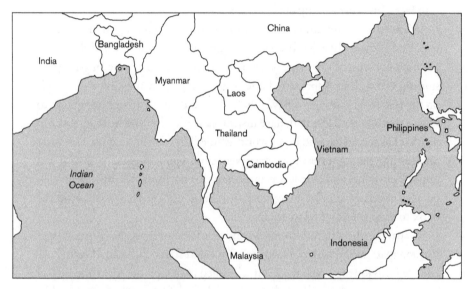

MAP 1. Thailand and Southeast Asia. Map created by Mike Padoongpatt.

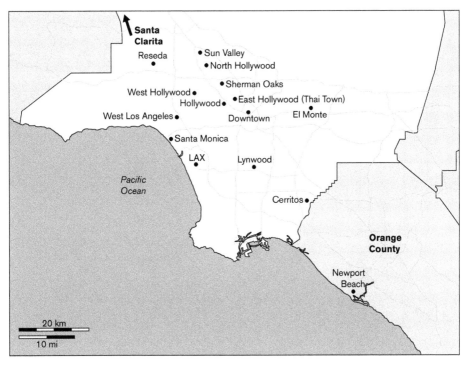

MAP 2. Los Angeles. Map created by Mike Padoongpatt.

- Asian - American Movement
- Multiculturelism
- American Imperialism

Introduction

FROM THAILAND TO THAI TOWN

FLAVORS OF EMPIRE EXPLORES THE rise of Thai food in Los Angeles and the way its hypervisibility shaped the racial and ethnic contours of Thai American identity and community. The interplay between food, identity, and community in Thai America began not with Thai immigrants bringing food practices with them to the United States, but instead years earlier with American intervention in Southeast Asia after World War II.[1] The informal U.S. empire in Thailand during the Cold War led to the migration of Thai foodways and, later, Thais to Los Angeles, where food became central to Thai American racial formation.

At one level, America's fascination with Thai cuisine resulted in Thais having to constantly remake themselves over the second half of the twentieth century in relation to the perceived exoticness and sensuousness of Thai food. I argue that this remaking produced "Thai Americans," which was not a cultural identity rooted in ethnic difference but a social and political relationship defined by U.S. empire, whiteness, liberal multiculturalism, and Los Angeles's racial geography. At another level, Thai foodways structured community dynamics and allowed Thais to distinguish themselves from others within and outside of their racial and ethnic group, especially other Asians. I contend that while food brought Thais together and provided a sense of pride and visibility, it also developed barriers to more radical community mobilization efforts to improve the lives of Thai people.

There is nothing natural or innate about why food became central to Thai American identity and community. A range of factors contributed to the growth of Thai cuisine in Los Angeles and turned it into an indelible and inescapable part of Thai American life. U.S. Cold War intervention made it possible for ordinary Americans (nonstate actors) to "discover" Thai food and introduce it to adventurous eaters back home before Thai immigrants arrived in large numbers. Next, as Thai food gained popularity through these acts of culinary imperialism, Thai Americans reinvented and repackaged it in a number of different "culinary contact zones"—homes, grocery stores, restaurants, food festivals, and "Thai Town"—throughout the city.[2] Thais and non-Thais used race, ethnicity, and nation in order to mark the novelty and difference of Thai cuisine in consumer culture. Thais, white food writers, and eaters relied heavily on human senses besides sight, namely taste and smell, to construct Thais as an exotic, nonwhite "Other." Thai Americans, in turn, also relied on flavors and tastes to distinguish themselves. Lastly, the rise of Los Angeles as a "global city"—a crossroads of the Pacific Rim economy characterized by increased discretionary spending, a growing service-sector industry, nascent multiculturalism, and major spatial transformations—made food inseparable from the Thai American experience. The production and consumption of Thai cuisine made it possible for Thai Americans to link identity and community to physical suburban and urban spaces and assert a right to live in and shape the city. As they used food to create place, however, such place-making practices fit within but also challenged dominant spatial imaginaries in the region.

This book contributes to the emerging scholarship on Asian American foodways by offering historical perspective on the relationship between food, identity, and community. To borrow from Rachel Slocum, I take food to mean a system that includes "all the processes that make animal, vegetable, or mineral into something to eat and then all that is involved in what happens next to bodies and societies."[3] I use foodways to refer to the network of activities that includes but is not limited to the procurement, production, consumption, and representation of a food. Food and foodways, then, must be understood as more than just a confluence of private practices centered on personal consumption but as a broader set of activities that involves multiple levels of interactions, public sociability, and community engagement. Drawing on this more expansive definition of food, I situate the procurement, production, consumption, representation, and dissemination of Thai food alongside the historical and material conditions of immigration and racialization in Los Angeles specifically and in the United States more broadly. I chart the transformation of Thai food culture alongside the history of U.S.-Thai relations, the emergence of Thai communities in the United States, and the consolidation of a Thai American identity at a moment of intensifying anti-immigrant sentiment and a blossoming multiculturalism in

American society. Taking this approach permits me to ground my theoretical analyses in the conditions that made Thai food evolve into an object of culinary diplomacy and how the meaning of Thai food changed in concert with immigration policies, movement and migration. In addition, while many food studies are focused on cooking and eating, this book considers the asymmetrical relations of power that allowed for access to and the consumption of Thai cuisine. Foregrounding political economy and social systems challenges the entrenched notion that Asian/Pacific Islander Americans are naturally or even culturally inclined to be good cooks and therefore spend their lives in restaurants and other food service work.

The story I tell demonstrates that racial projects emerge in seemingly mundane and unexpected places. I show how empire and war affect everything from the cuisines featured in restaurants and the identities of restaurateurs, cooks, and grocery store clerks to the makeup of entrepreneurship and the use and meaning of urban and suburban space in global cities. At first glance food does not seem a likely approach to studying the history of race and racial formation in the United States. For one, there are a plethora of other sites that have attracted far more research: immigration, housing, labor, education, and other forms of cultural production such as music, film, and literature. Second, food practices, specifically those of immigrant groups, typically get associated and framed in the context of ethnicity and culture. Overwhelming attention has been paid to the relationship between food and culture, with scholars treating foodways as a *reflection* or representation of ethnic traditions.[4] Much of this "food and culture" literature analyzes identity and community formation within older models of race, specifically the ethnicity paradigm. They provide insightful investigations into the way quotidian food practices, particularly cooking and eating, serve as powerful ways to affirm ethnic identity, preserve cultural traditions, and maintain a connection to the homeland in new and often hostile societies. So the question they are most concerned with addressing is whether food practices can tell us if ethnic groups are assimilating, acculturating, or maintaining their identities in relation to dominant American culture. These studies tend to advocate cultural pluralism and multiculturalism, arguing that ethnic groups should be allowed to maintain and celebrate their unique cultural traditions, values, and identities.

But as Anita Mannur, Robert Ku, and Martin Manalansan declare in *Eating Asian America*, "while race is often popularly understood as a function of skin color and other physical attributes, racial meanings and the processes of racialization permeate all facets of social discourse" and "this is especially true for food."[5] Placing race—as a social, political construction and not skin color, phenotype, or a biological essence—front and center turns our attention to the way food is embedded in the creation and maintenance of racial thinking and practice.[6] I explore the complex relationship between food and race because I am more concerned with power relations, political economy, and structural-based inequalities than I am with cultural heritage. Joining food and race analytically allows us to see more clearly the way the identities of people of color get structured in racial dominance—and not simply ethnic differences.

Analyzing food and race together also opens up new ways to theorize racial formation. It shores up insights from research on sensory constructions of race by illustrating the way social hierarchies of power have been inscribed on bodies by categories that are created and maintained by other human senses besides sight.[7] I draw on the work of scholars Mark Smith, Camille Bégin, and Emily Walmsley who demonstrate that taste, smell, and touch are not merely physical acts but also cultural acts infused with meanings that are socially constructed and historically specific.[8] Sensory experiences with cuisine are critical to processes of racialization in that they, in often visceral and emotional ways, draw boundaries around food and the people who cook and eat the food, distinguish between the foreign and the familiar, link cuisine and individuals to places, and inscribe relations of power onto plates and bodies. In this way, studying food provides a unique way to track the history of racial formation in ways different from analyses of photography, movies, architecture, literature, and music.

My approach to Thai food is also an attempt to chronicle the history of Thai Americans in Los Angeles. This book constitutes the first historical examination of a Thai American community. To date, the bulk of the scholarship on Thais in the United States is made up of a handful of dissertations and theses that are largely social scientific and explore contemporary experiences.[9] Anthropologist Jiemin Bao has written most extensively on the subject with a body of work highlighted by *Creating a Buddhist Community*, an astute ethnographic study of Thai immigrant community formation at a Thai Buddhist temple in Silicon Valley, California.[10] My work contributes to these studies by offering an in-depth historical narrative covering the Thai American experience from the 1950s to the 2000s. I trace the way Thai immigration and settlement patterns, identities, and community structure and dynamics changed over time in relation to Los Angeles's shifting racial, gender, and class order.

Flavors of Empire sets out to present a complex and nuanced history of the role of food in Thai American identity and community as a history of U.S. empire, race, and the city of Los Angeles and its suburbs. There is a great deal to be learned about postwar American culture and life through Thai food. It serves as a perhaps unexpected yet tangible entry point into major themes and larger threads in American history, including war, immigration, capitalism, border making, and urbanization and suburbanization. It helps us better understand the intersection of the social and the political as well as racial formation beyond U.S. national borders and the black-white binary. Thai food, as a research object, takes into account the intertwined nature of domestic affairs and foreign policy to provide a deeper and wider portrayal of the transnational character of many of the critical transformations in U.S. history.

THE EVERYDAY LIFE OF U.S. EMPIRE IN ASIA
AND THE PACIFIC

A history of food in the making of Thai American Los Angeles cannot be adequately understood without looking at America's global expansion into Southeast Asia after World War II. Today, Thailand has the distinction of being the only country in Southeast Asia to avoid formal Western colonization, a distinction in which Thais take immense pride. After World War II, however, the United States, as a new global leader, maneuvered itself into Thailand more intrusively than ever before, ushering in Thailand's "American Era." The rise of leftist anticolonial movements in Laos and Vietnam, coupled with China's Communist revolution, made Thailand a prime potential base to combat threats to the United States' global free-market capitalist aspirations. U.S. state actors began referring to Thailand as a pro-Western bastion of anticommunism in Southeast Asia deserving of U.S. support. The U.S. government provided Thailand with over \$2.2 billion of economic and military aid to combat the spread of communism.[11] In addition, the U.S. State Department relied on modernization projects, technical assistance, and a variety of cultural programs and exchanges to try and win Thai "hearts and minds" in pursuit of foreign policy objectives in the region. The intensified American presence in Thailand ran much deeper than U.S. state-sponsored dictatorships, militarization, modernization projects, and cultural exchanges; it insinuated itself into nearly all aspects of Thai society. With the arrival of

U.S. state actors came nonstate actors, which increased contact and interactions between Thais and U.S. citizens in everyday spaces and in everyday life.

This book joins insights from Asian/Pacific Islander American history, post-World War II American history, and food studies to deepen and widen knowledge of the way Asian/Pacific Islander American identities and communities were engendered by postwar U.S. empire. Robert Lee, Charlotte Brooks, Cindy I-Fen Cheng, Madeline Hsu, Christina Klein, Naoko Shibusawa, and others have documented that the racialization of Asian Americans happened in the nexus of Cold War global and domestic affairs and was thus intertwined with America's postwar ascendance as leader of the free world.[12] These scholars establish that in order to understand Asian/Pacific Islander America in the late 20th century fully, we must understand postwar U.S. expansion into Asia and the Pacific. Foodways provide a generative point of entry into that understanding. America was able to bolster its postwar global hegemony effectively through food in ways that informed Asian/Pacific Islander American racial formation.

Studies of food and empire have focused for the most part on labor, slavery, famine, foreign relations, globalization, world food systems, and single commodities like sugar to make sense of food's role in the rise of great empires.[13] Another approach, however, has gained momentum in recent years, one that treats food as a lens into the way imperialists, as well as their subjects, used food to imagine their relationship to empire and to others within it.[14] Uma Narayan's analysis of the role curry played in both the colonial British "fabrication" of India and in the diasporic Indian community in contemporary England best exemplifies this approach. She highlights the relationship between colonizers and the colonized, the different visions and uneven effects of the colonizing project, the way westerners' attitudes toward "ethnic foods" reflected forms of food colonialism and culinary imperialism, and the political and social meaning of ethnic food from the perspective of ethnic minorities in Western societies.[15] This growing body of work charts the centrality of food in the formation of European and Asian empires by exploring the way food shapes national and personal identities, enables empires to seep into everyday life, and sustains imperial ideology and practice.[16]

Flavors of Empire takes a similar approach in its exploration of the interplay between ethnic food, empire, and identity in postwar America. In Asia and the Pacific, the proliferation of a postwar infrastructure of U.S. military bases, embassies, financial institutions, businesses, private organizations, and aid programs established transnational pathways for U.S. citizens to engage new food cultures. At one level, this meant a saturation of American food products, such as Coca Cola and Hormel's Spam into the diets of local populations. At another level, it allowed hundreds of thousands of Americans to have access to "exotic" foodways for the first time. In Thailand, U.S. intervention created the conditions for American *farang* (whites), particularly women, to "discover" Thai food and introduce it inside the United States.

Thailand's effort to develop the country into a major postwar tourist destination spawned culinary contact zones that cornered Thais into a service-based economy, one catering to the desires of U.S. consumers and national wealthy elites at the expense of the basic needs of local Thais. In urban Bangkok, hotel restaurants and local eateries served as, in the words of James Farrer, sites of "social friction" and "social stratification" that brought together a diverse cast of producers and consumers face-to-face across race, gender, and class lines in ways that both undermined and reinforced power relations.[17] When Americans ate Thai dishes, they also consumed relations of power, devouring exotic representations of Thai food "in which the exotic element is partly on the plate and partly in the setting, extending to the racially marked staff serving the meals."[18] Thais certainly participated in the production of problematic representations and in the creation of flavorful cuisine, but not on equal terms. By the 1960s Thais on the lower end of the social order found themselves pressured to package and peddle their food culture to a growing number of American tourists as one of the few economic opportunities available. However, culinary contact zones provided spaces for Thais to openly resist, comply, and capitalize on the increased American influence in Thailand.

The everyday encounters that took place in Thai culinary contact zones shaped early Thai American racial formation. Thai foodways emerged as a potent site for producing and disseminating knowledge about Thailand, Thai people, and Thai culture in the United States. Alongside reports and ethnographic studies written by U.S. state officials and academics, culinary tourists constructed an idealized image of Thais for consumers back home. This particular expression of cultural appreciation, however, happened while U.S. officials attempted to modernize the country along American lines, which was consistent with the longer history of racial formation under U.S. imperial conquest in which nonwhites were hyperrepresented and even "celebrated" as they were subjugated, removed, or killed. Foodways helped sustain the development of the U.S. empire as a racial project that constructed and affirmed racial categories to subordinate nonwhite peoples and nations. Its history underscores Jodi Kim's contention that the Cold War in Asia must be considered "at once a geopolitical, cultural, and epistemological project of imperialism and gendered racial formation undergirding U.S. global hegemony."[19]

My emphasis on culinary contact zones and the everyday life of U.S. empire aims to show that food and empire is about more than just macro level global food distribution, agricultural systems, livestock and calorie counts, and aggregate data such as ratio of seeds to yield.[20] It is also about the micro level formation of personal and collective identities of both the "colonizer" and the "colonized" and their effects on the U.S racial order. The approach also underscores how the arrival and availability of ethnic food in America is not a global phenomenon but rather a phenomenon of U.S. global power. It sheds light on the intimate social and political connections that get food onto tables and the imperial structures underpinning these processes.

Flavors of Empire cuts against rigid generalizations of imperialism and globalization as all-powerful uniform systems of domination. U.S. empire, when viewed from below in Thai culinary contact zones, was far from totalizing and was a much more porous and complex structure of domination with room for negotiation and resistance.[21] Using Thai foodways to examine the history of American empire and diplomatic history allows for the nuances and contradictions, such as the use of hard and soft power, to be considered vividly and tangibly. The book's title has a double meaning that captures this approach. It refers more obviously to the flavors and tastes of many new cuisines that arrived and were made available by U.S. empire and neocolonialism. Yet it is also meant to highlight the different expressions and manifestations of the American empire—its various flavors—in the postwar world and the multiple actors who participated in it. Like other empires, to borrow from Julian Go, it was not a static essence but a nuanced formation made up of "sets of relations and forms involving multiple tactics, policies, practices, and modalities of power."[22]

LOS ANGELES AS A GLOBAL CITY

Examining the role of food in the making of Thai America also requires engagement with postwar Los Angeles history. In the 1970s, Los Angeles emerged as a full-fledged global city and developed into the nation's largest manufacturing center and service-sector economy.[23] It became a critical hub of a globalizing world economy, a crossroads where economic regions—in this case Asia and the Pacific—eclipsed local, regional, and national borders and a site of transnational circuits and flows of capital, information, goods, and people. As part of this larger "new global, flexible capitalism," the Los Angeles economy underwent a series of accelerated changes characterized by a complex pattern of deindustrialization and reindustrialization.[24] It led to the creation of distinct forms of low-wage labor and consumer services. Alongside the growth of relatively low skilled, low-wage manufacturing jobs in sectors like the garment industry, the service sector increased its dominance under these conditions.

"New" Asian immigrants played an important role in Los Angeles's ascendance into a global city. Postwar U.S. capitalist expansion and foreign policy, coupled with the passage of the 1965 Immigration Act, induced the arrival of thousands of newcomers. Immigrants and refugees from "new" countries—Thailand, Vietnam, Cambodia, Korea, and India—as well as familiar ones—China, Japan, and the Philippines—dramatically transformed the city, turning Los Angeles into one of the top immigrant destinations in the country. By the 1980s, Los Angeles International Airport supplanted Ellis Island as the main port of entry for immigrants from Asia as well as Latin America. The new Asian immigration was defined by a stark class bifurcation, included more women than men, and entailed settlement in both central cities and suburbs. In a sense, it consisted of both the "winners" and "losers" of global economic restructuring: well-educated middle class entrepreneurs, managers, and professionals as the beneficiaries, and low-wage, service sector and manufacturing laborers as the downtrodden. A number of Asian corporations, especially from Japan, infused Los Angeles with large capital investments—aircraft and computer manufacturing, financial institutions, medical facilities, and real estate—that spawned large-scale ethnic economies. At the same time, it contributed to the "racialized feminization of labor" as Asians and other nonwhite immigrant women became a desirable "flexible" labor force, particularly in service-based industries such as food service.[25]

Excavating the history of Thai food in Los Angeles is about more than commercial cuisine and what people ate. For one, it unearths the role that the food and restaurant industry played in the city's globalizing economy. My attention to procurement exemplifies the ways in which national borders still reverberated in global cities. It shows that the flow of Thai food imports across borders was not a result of softened or porous nation-state boundaries. Rather, it coincided with the expansion of import trade barriers and federal agencies along with an increase of border policing and enforcement.

At the same time, it is also about demographic changes, population shifts, and the hands that have been employed to create meals that arrive at restaurant tables. In Los Angeles, Thai immigrants entered an increasingly service-based economy. Having been primed by culinary tourism in Thailand, the food industry was one of the few appealing economic opportunities open to them. The restaurant business was especially attractive, as it was among the fastest growing service industries in the city and amid the top in employing immigrants.[26] Thais incorporated themselves into the food and restaurant industry as business owners and low-wage part-time workers, which contributed to the formation of both a Thai American middle class and a Thai American working class. Equally significant, many Thais who worked with food were outside of legal status. A product of U.S. intervention in Thailand and the "inclusionary and exclusionary features" of the Immigration Act of 1965, thousands of Thais entered the United States legally under temporary student and tourist visas but eventually overstayed to become what I call *exdocumented*.[27] Their stories are critical to understanding the meaning of citizenship and belonging under conditions of intensified global migration, especially for people who built lives and contributed to global cities through culinary practices despite their legal status.

While deindustrialization and reindustrialization led to the expansion of low paying food-related jobs, it also gave rise to ethnic grocery stores and restaurants, including the elevation of a handful of ethnic restaurateurs into the pantheon of celebrity chefs. Tracing the motivations, identities, and lived experiences of Thai food industry workers reveals that those employed in food service, often exploited laborers forced to toil away in demeaning low paying jobs, managed to find a semblance of pride and dignity. For restaurant cooks, preparing and serving Thai food to literally feed American society allowed them to not only maintain their "Thainess" but also establish a sense of belonging as contributors to the multicultural fabric of the nation. In the case of Thai restaurateurs, they were not merely economic agents who made decisions based on rational analysis of resources, profits, markets, and wages. They were, as Krishnendu Ray asserts, cultural producers with a passion and standard for taste, creativity, and innovation and a desire to share their culinary creations with others.[28] Additionally, restaurateurs, along with Thai grocery store owners, were also "place-makers" who left an imprint on the Thai American community and the broader metropolitan landscape.[29] By interpreting Thai restaurant and other food-industry workers as more than "creatures of political economy" who started and entered businesses strictly

multiculturalism 11-13
> avenue for people to form an identity
money > global market / cultural exclusion

for economic viability, this work contributes to the literature on ethnic entre-preneurship, and ethnic enclave economies.[30]

The transformation of Los Angeles's racial and ethnic landscape triggered anti-immigrant sentiment and anti-Asian racism. Asian immigrants (and Asian Americans who racially represented these groups) were yet again imag-ined as foreigners incapable of assimilating and therefore a threat to the whiteness of American society and culture. There was real concern about Asians overpowering white Americans with their cultural practices and tra-ditions.[31] Asian immigrants and Asian Americans also became the target of anxieties over economic competition from Asia, particularly Japan. The infu-sion of Asian immigrant capital into the city along with imported Asian products, especially automobiles, was seen as a foreign invasion that was destructive to the U.S. economy and (white) workers.[32]

At the same time, Los Angeles began celebrating its racial and ethnic diver-sity and cosmopolitanism. The 1970s marked the start of an era of multicultural boosterism championing its arrival as a world city and its connection to a glo-balized economy. The city presented its diversity as a positive transformation that brought an exciting array of new peoples and cultures. In doing so, Los Angeles proved that the changes brought about by postwar U.S. empire were not a one-way street, as new immigrants redefined what it meant to be an American and an Angeleno.[33] This permitted various racial, ethnic, and national groups to proudly display their identities and cultures. The city also witnessed a number of racial and ethnic minorities making historic strides in local government, most notably Tom Bradley, the city's first African American mayor. The inclusion of members of historically marginalized groups into the political power structure signaled Los Angeles's growing acceptance of not just different kinds of people, but of cultural pluralism—rather than assimilation— more broadly. According to Scott Kurashige, Los Angeles's shift from the nation's "white spot" into a "world city" involved global and local dynamics set in motion in the mid-20th century.[34] He explains that it grew out of an attempt to make Los Angeles a "capital of the Pacific Rim," which forced the city's elite to "develop a self awareness of its multiracial diversity and an interconnection to the peoples and cultures of the global community."[35] While U.S. Cold War intervention abroad compelled Los Angeles to embrace multiculturalism and orient its economic and cultural life toward the Pacific Rim, Kurashige con-tends that local conditions, particularly Bradley's liberal democratic vision of urban coalition building, also fueled the ascension of an "economically vibrant and multicultural 'world city' in postwar Los Angeles."[36]

Los Angeles's brand of multiculturalism, however, raised vexing issues. Several scholars have pointed out the problems with multiculturalism in Los Angeles in particular and multiculturalism in general as a strategy to lessen racism with the inclusion of cultural differences. It was more often than not capitalist driven, geared toward opening up new global markets and sites of economic investment.[37] It fixated on cultural purity, authenticity and, following the logic of commodification, separated groups into static categories as commodities in consumer culture. It also flattened important differences within and among racial and ethnic groups and thereby masked the unsavory and messy aspects of culture to present a safe, palatable version of "Others."

Above all, even though the city's commitment to liberal multiculturalism improved racial tolerance and led to new opportunities for nonwhites, it ultimately obscured and thus left unaddressed structural racial inequality. In *Immigrant Acts* Lisa Lowe argues that the "production" of multiculturalism in Los Angeles failed to "address the systemic inequalities built into cultural institutions, economies, and geographies" and leveled heterogeneity and material conditions "according to a pluralism that effectively continues to privilege the centrality of dominant culture—a pluralism that promotes a form of tolerance that leaves the status quo unthreatened."[38] Similarly, Kurashige demonstrates that the "qualified embrace" of multicultural diversity failed to achieve racial equality. Los Angeles, as he tells it, was committed to liberal multiculturalism and in doing so proved it had no viable solution to the long-standing problems facing racial and ethnic communities, especially African Americans, ranging from housing and schooling to employment and police brutality. What's more, celebrating multiculturalism allowed Los Angeles to feel good about itself in the wake of the devastating impact of deindustrialization and reindustrialization on the working class.

Flavors of Empire brings attention to the role food played in this blossoming multiculturalism. Doing so illustrates the way racial and ethnic identities and thus the U.S. racial order got defined in an age of flexible accumulation and mass migration. It also adds clarity to the way everyday people came to terms with increased immigration and racial and ethnic diversity during this period. I suggest that the history of Thai food in Los Angeles reflects the development of a "cuisine driven multiculturalism." Cuisine driven multiculturalism, which arose in the early Cold War period, refers to the belief among well-intentioned and well-meaning people that preparing and eating the cuisine of different, usually exotic, ethnic groups is an act of cultural understanding and by extension a challenge to racism. It is an articulation of race that pitches racism as a problem of prejudice, bigotry, and ignorance rather than a relation of power.

There are competing views among scholars about the effects of "cuisine driven multiculturalism" on race relations. Those who are critical see it as a superficial way of engaging racial and ethnic difference and an arms-length approach to inclusion. As Sneja Gunew and Frank Wu contend, a major reason why so many Americans have become obsessed with tasting diversity is because food is an "acceptable face" of multiculturalism. It is, according to Gunew, one of the few "unthreatening ways to speak of multiculturalism" and usually the "way in which diversity is acceptably celebrated."[39] They claim that ethnic food festivals, for example, flatten the intolerable and unpalatable to showcase cultural differences in a way that the mainstream finds pleasant and agreeable. Others who take a critical view, such as Lisa Heldke and Roger Abrahams, have argued that cuisine driven multiculturalism involves forms of culinary imperialism and cultural food colonialism that reinforces social relationships of power. Or as Abrahams writes, while it is tempting to view the consumption of another group's unique foodways as a sign of acceptance or positive feelings toward that group, "eating other people's foods has often been a sign of their having been subjugated."[40]

On the other side, the more favorable position sees cuisine driven multiculturalism as a positive alternative to the outright denigration of cultural differences and overt anti-immigrant sentiment. Uma Narayan, for example, has written that eating ethnic food generates positive feelings that contribute to a recognition and appreciation of racial and ethnic groups as part of the national community. Even if these feelings are visceral and do not reflect a deeper knowledge of the culture and history of the cuisine and the people it represents, she argues, it is preferred to the "unacceptable face" of multiculturalism that portrays immigrants as draining national resources, stealing jobs, contributing to poverty, crime, and tearing apart American culture.[41] So in this view, while eating ethnic cuisine may result in "shallow, commodified, and consumerist interactions with 'Others,'" it is better than no interaction at all that "permits the different foods of 'Others' to appear simply as marks of 'strangeness' and 'Otherness.'"[42]

This book expands on both of these positions. To build on Robin D. G. Kelley, I seek to "make sense of people where they are" *in addition to* "where we would like them to be."[43] The production, consumption, and representation of Thai cuisine in Los Angeles racialized Thais as an exotic nonwhite "other," which reinforced relationships of power established under U.S.

neocolonialism in Thailand. It further commodified Thai culture and masked the race, gender, and class structures that shaped the lives of the workers who cooked and served Thai food. Moreover, cuisine driven multiculturalism worked to naturalize the presence of Thais in the food and restaurant industry and thus their social position in U.S. society. In other words, as Thai cuisine flourished, so too did the idea that Thais possessed a cultural or natural ability to cook. As consumers celebrated Thai food, the social, political, and economic structures that pushed Thais into the food industry and service sector economy in the first place went ignored.

But cuisine driven multiculturalism also benefited Thais in Los Angeles. Thai Americans saw their exotification and perceived natural ability to cook as positive representations and participated in creating and perpetuating them. Being seen as exotic meant being unique and different, and in a consumer culture that often meant more customers. Being described as a "naturally" good cook was taken as a compliment to Thai culture. Thai Americans kept labor and gender exploitation behind the kitchen door hidden to prevent negative images of the Thai community from spreading in a way that might undermine these positive representations. They were also encouraged by America's curiosity and enthusiasm for Thai food. It gave them a chance to share Thai culture and interact with the mainstream at food festivals and inside restaurants. Equally important, the popularity of Thai cuisine became politically useful in Thai American community building efforts.

Still, my goal is to use cuisine-driven multiculturalism to extend our critiques of liberal multiculturalism in general, especially the notion that American society is willing to accept racial and ethnic diversity only when it is agreeable and unthreatening. The production and consumption of ethnic food in Los Angeles is a powerful way to expose, as Frank Wu asserts, the "dilemma of diversity" where Americans celebrate diversity but only up to a certain point. It permits us to think historically about the "carefully calibrated balance of acceptable multiculturalism" in the United States.[44] Although dominant society has certainly drawn the line of acceptability at specific ingredients, tastes, textures, smells, and preparation methods that are deemed too foreign and exotic—or "too ethnic"—and therefore intolerable, I argue that the threshold for acceptable multiculturalism is also based on how and where ethnic food practices take place. In other words, some sites of production and consumption, like restaurants and food festivals, are considered more acceptable or tolerable than others, such as street food carts. At the same time, I show that space also matters: ethnic food festivals, for instance, are considered more appropriate in the city than they are in the suburbs. It is imperative, then, to consider the way ethnic cuisine played out in different ways and in different places to better understand the limits of racial inclusion.

The global city experienced dramatic spatial transformations that also had a profound impact on food in Thai America. From the 1960s onward, the "fragmented metropolis" went through comprehensive urban restructuring that both intensified longstanding spatial patterns and changed the built environment. Suburbanization and decentralization continued in earnest with residential developments, jobs, and amenities pushing the edges of the sprawling metropolis further out. By 1992, Los Angeles almost filled in a 60-mile radius around downtown and was made up of five counties and over 160 cities and municipalities.[45] At the same time, the emerging "megacity" witnessed the urbanization of its suburbs as attributes typically associated with cities—jobs, factories, shopping centers, entertainment, class heterogeneity, racial and ethnic diversity, immigrants, gangs, and crime—accelerated at unprecedented levels in the suburban periphery. This new urban form, which has been dubbed "postsuburbia," "outer city," "urban village," "edge city," and "exopolis," to list a few, produced a situation where four of the city's outer counties eclipsed Los Angeles County in total population increase from 1970–1990.[46] At the same time, mass regional urbanization and decentralization coupled with deindustrialization wreaked havoc on Los Angeles's central cities. A wave of plant closures and industry flight to the suburbs and abroad led to population decline and stripped the urban core of resources and tax bases that led to the formation of new ghettos, barrios, and overall urban decay. Meanwhile, reindustrialization and post-1965 immigration spawned ethnic neighborhoods that revitalized others parts of the central city. Additionally, with the influx of foreign capital, the development of downtown Los Angeles accelerated in the 1970s and 1980s, marked by high-rise apartments and business office skyscrapers as well as immigrant street scenes. Finally, there was at least one other prominent feature of Los Angeles's spatial transformation over this span: the increased privatization of public space that turned Los Angeles into what Mike Davis calls a "carceral city" and "fortress America."[47] As Edward Soja contends, the eradication of public space and the growth of neoliberal privatization policies created a "most privatized urban landscape" of guarded gated communities, shopping centers, and financial districts.[48]

Los Angeles's spatial transformation was informed by what George Lipsitz has described as the "racialization of space and the spatialization of race."[49]

The changes perpetuated the region's long history of racial segregation and generated other spatial forms of racism in ways that tightened the links that connected race, place, and power. The suburbs and the central cities were not race-neutral sites. They were encoded with racial and classed meanings and moral assumptions about who belonged, what was desirable, and why "good" and "bad" neighborhoods came into existence. The concepts of "private" and "public" also emerged as racialized metonyms, in which private meant white and good while public meant bad and nonwhite, specifically black.[50] Racist policies and practices dating back to the early 1900s, such as housing discrimination and racially restrictive covenants, were key factors in the disproportionate concentration of whites in places with better school systems, amenities, and valuable personal networks—such as the Westside and in suburban neighborhoods and gated communities in "outer cities" in areas such as Orange County—and large numbers of people of color, often mixed together, in enclaves near downtown as well as suburbs with poor schools and more exposure to environmental hazards and crime.[51] In a post-civil rights color-blind era, structural racism in Los Angeles manifested in full force through physical segregation and spatial subordination. Decades after the passage of civil rights laws, race continued to matter because geography did the work of reinforcing white privilege and subjugating communities of color.

The entanglement of race and space in different neighborhoods produced different, racially specific ways of understanding the world and one's relationship to it through space, or racialized spatial imaginaries. Racialized spatial imaginaries function as common sense, saturating consciousness and influencing the way people interact with one another.[52] Los Angeles's post-1965 racial geography was influenced by a dominant white spatial imaginary, one that championed the suburban home as the "moral geography of the nation" and reinforced the rewards, privileges, and systemic advantages of whiteness through a commitment to color-blind policies.[53] Fueled by hostile privatism and defensive localism, it structured feelings and shaped public policy to exclude undesirable people of color, maintain homogeneous spaces, regulate behavior, control design and land use, and hoard amenities and resources. Without access to the places constructed by the white spatial imaginary, communities of color produced counter spatial imaginaries—in central cities and suburbs of their own - that valued different approaches to physical space and land use.[54]

As the "prismatic metropolis" became more complex with the movement of people of color into the suburbs, communities of color would pose direct

challenges to the white spatial imaginary. A growing number of Asian/
Pacific Islanders and Latinos were able to move into the region's variegated
suburbs during this period.[55] Immigrant suburbanization also intensified
and the suburbs gradually became the preferred gateway communities for
newcomers.[56] For Asian/Pacific Islanders specifically, gaining access to some
of these advantages and amenities often resulted in tension with white homeowners, especially in places with heavy immigrant clustering and visible
ethnic businesses and institutions, or ethnoburbs.[57] As the spatial imaginaries
of ethnoburbs make clear, the settlement of Asian/Pacific Islanders into the
highly racialized (white) suburbs was not indicative of assimilation or "whit-
ening."[58] On the contrary, it was a much more complicated process of ethnic
adaptation and retention that, combined with white resistance, reinforced
racial difference. The suburbanization of people of color turned suburban
spaces into heated battlegrounds over homeowners' rights, citizenship, and
multiculturalism that are best understood as confrontations over competing
racialized spatial imaginaries.

Thai Americans formed identity and community through foodways in different racialized spaces throughout the city. *Flavors of Empire* exhibits, to
borrow again from Lipsitz, how "the lived experience of race has a spatial
dimension, and the lived experience of space has a racial dimension."[59] During
the period of mass Thai migration from 1970 to 1990, Thais settled in both the
central city and the suburban periphery. They primarily moved to the poor,
predominantly Latino immigrant neighborhood of East Hollywood and multiracial and multiethnic middle and working-class suburbs like North
Hollywood. Thais made an immediate imprint on these spaces, establishing a
variety of physical culinary contact zones—the Bangkok Market grocery
store, restaurants, Wat Thai of Los Angeles food festivals, and Thai Town—
that reshaped the built landscape. A number of scholars have explored the
significance of "Asian" places in Los Angeles—from commercial shopping
centers, grocery stores, and restaurants to temples and ethnic neighborhoods
like Little Manila and Little Tokyo—as physical sites for Asian/Pacific
Islanders to negotiate racialized spaces.[60] While they have deftly illustrated
the way these served as arenas where contestations over community played out
and "contesting definitions, articulations, and representations of identities are
enacted," I assert that physical culinary contact zones acted as central places
for Thai Americans to form and express identity and build community and,
in doing so, put forth a spatial imaginary based on public sociability, collective
use of space, transnationalism, and liberal multiculturalism.[61]

Moreover, culinary contact zones allowed Thai Americans to claim a "right to the global city."[62] In this sense, my book attempts to understand metropolitan Los Angeles through the lens of identity and place but also democracy, rights, and justice. It draws on scholarship that has taken Henri Lefebvre's concept of "Right to the City"—a "cry and demand" for more democratic access to live and participate in the making of urban spaces and a citizenship in the city based on everyday inhabitance rather than legal membership or economic power—and expanded it to analyze the way various marginalized peoples have struggled for broader rights claims in different cities and sites of struggle: education, housing, health care, jobs, and, above all, public space.[63] More recently, researchers have applied the concept beyond the urban realm to examine struggles for a "right to the suburb."[64] Together, this rich scholarship has made clear that a right to the city is not merely about access and participation in urban life, but more importantly the right to remake and reshape the city. The right to the city/suburb, as Pauline Lipman writes, is an "imperative to transform oppressive and exploitative economic, political, and cultural arrangements and to build a new social order based on the full development of human beings in relationships of mutuality, respect, and collective well-being."[65]

Given that Thai foodways was a wider metropolitan phenomenon that took place in urban and suburban spaces throughout Los Angeles, I heed the call of Genevieve Carpio, Clara Irazábal, and Laura Pulido and adopt a "regionally oriented vision" of right to the city.[66] I use "right to the global city," a term coined by Mark Purcell, because it accounts for both the urban and suburban as intertwined yet distinct parts of the metropolitan geography as well as the rise of Los Angeles as a world city. Also, the concept is inclusive of Thais outside of legal status and sees them as inhabitants who make claims on space regardless of formal citizenship. The production and consumption of Thai food—its taste, flavors, smells—determined whether the right to the global city was expanded or constricted for Thais in Los Angeles. At the same time, Thai restaurants helped coalesce a "distinctive Los Angeles style" of cuisine, one that informed urban culture and the city's sense of self as a cosmopolitan place. Thai cuisine allowed the city to establish a unique gastronomic identity and gain some recognition as an exciting multicultural global kitchen. Thus, considering the role of food in struggles for a right to the global city offers a tangible entry point into the way people experience and perceive racialized spaces and a glimpse into the formation of metropolitan identity.

As the first historical investigation of a Thai American community, the pioneering nature of this book has required the collection and examination of a wide range of both conventional and original sources. No archive documented the lives of Thais in the United States in part because Thais left behind few written accounts. What little information did exist was scattered or buried in homes and community centers across Southern California. The dearth of materials written by and about Thai immigrants and Thai Americans forced me to be imaginative about evidence. Food offered a unique and effective way to expand my source base so that I could tell the story of how Thai America came to be. While dealing with an ephemeral topic such as the history of food practices demands an interdisciplinary approach, I relied primarily on a combination of oral histories and the historical analysis of archival materials.

From the outset I knew oral histories would be the most significant source of evidence concerning the inner workings of Thai foodways and of Thai American life. My capacity to communicate in Thai was invaluable. I conducted over a dozen oral history interviews in Los Angeles with Thai restaurateurs, food service workers, Buddhist monks, and community leaders as well as non-Thai food critics, workers, and others with knowledge of the Thai American experience. The interviews, all recorded, ranged in formality: a few took place in quiet meeting rooms, some in bustling restaurants. Most of the interviews lasted about an hour or two. I chose participants largely through personal recommendation, but I used the Thai Community Development Center in Hollywood and Wat Thai of Los Angeles in North Hollywood as my initial base for finding narrators.

I supplemented the oral histories with a range of original archival materials including untapped government preserved documents, and private papers gathered from interviews and site visits. While many government sources did not deal explicitly with food, they provided broader social, political, economic, and cultural context to understand the rise of Thai food in Los Angeles. To establish the nature of U.S. foreign policy in Thailand after World War II, I took a multiarchival approach and conducted research in Boston, Los Angeles, and Washington, D.C. I relied on returned Peace Corps volunteer papers and oral histories along with National Security Administration Files and presidential papers at the John F. Kennedy Presidential Library in Boston to serve as my eyes and ears in grasping the ways in which U.S. intervention affected Thai society on the ground. At the National Archives in Washington, D.C., I mined Department of State foreign relations papers and American University alumni records and photos. In Los Angeles, the Royal Thai Consulate lent rare books on U.S.-Thai relations published by both the United States and Thai governments. I also excavated the Los Angeles City Archives at Piper Technological Center and the Pacific Branch of the National Archives and Records Administration for reports, testimonies, and photos related to the zoning conflict at Wat Thai and Thai immigration and naturalization records, respectively.

Newspapers, cookbooks, menus, travel guides, magazines, and other materials that have yet to be officially archived allowed me to construct a more accurate and comprehensive portrait of the Thai food scene in Thailand and the United States. Newspapers provided plenty of coverage of Thai food and restaurants. I had to search diligently for any mention of Thais, but they were there and offered great information on the types of dishes served, names and brief histories of owners, décor, prices, and descriptions of taste, flavors, textures, and smells. Additionally, I analyzed Thai restaurant menus from the Central Los Angeles Public Library's menu collection. The Pacific Area Travel Association also published books and reports that were helpful in constructing the history of U.S. tourist development in Thailand from the 1950s to the 1970s and the way Thailand was advertised and marketed as a tourist destination to U.S. consumers. Cookbooks were particularly vital. In researching both Thai and non-Thai authored cookbooks I focused on the authors' life history and identified ingredients listed in recipes as a way of tracing the availability of foodstuffs during a specific time period. So rather than approach these materials as if they contained true or authoritative accounts representing Thais, I looked for small clues that allowed me to piece together the development and transformation of Thai American life. While it may be seen as problematic that a book on Thai American history relies heavily on written sources authored by white Americans and non-Thais, these accounts are valuable precisely because, together, they provide a glimpse of how U.S. citizens viewed Thais. Without them, it is difficult to grasp the larger social and cultural milieu that individual Thai immigrants and Thai Americans entered into and had to negotiate.

One of the more useful published sources was Benedict Anderson and Ruchida Mendiones' edited compilation of short stories written by Thai authors who witnessed the rapid social and cultural changes in Thailand in the American Era. The Thai Community Development Center in Hollywood granted me access to virtually every box and binder they had lying around that dealt with the formation of Thai Town, housing projects, and the many efforts they made to improve the lives of working and undocumented Thai immigrants between 1990 and 2008. The Wat Thai of Los Angeles handed me records related to the temple's history. I also discovered a trove of materials in the temple's small community library in the basement under the main temple hall. During my interviews, several narrators—especially elder Thais—also handed me newspaper clippings, photos, and self-published memoirs that included autobiographies, letters, and testimonials from family and friends.

CHAPTER BREAKDOWN

The book has five chapters that examine the role of food in the making of Thai America from the end of World War II to the present. Chapter one explores the blossoming of America's fascination with Thai cuisine during the Cold War. The informal postwar U.S. empire in Thailand vacillated between "hard" and "soft" power, consisting of state sponsored dictatorships, militarization, modernization projects, and cultural diplomacy. The chapter traces how this neocolonial relationship established circuits of exchange between the two countries, making it possible for thousands of Americans to go to Thailand and participate in U.S. global expansion through culinary tourism. Many, especially white women, treated Thai foodways as a quick and easy window into Thai history, culture, and the psyche of Thai people. I argue that these culinary tourists constructed an idealized image of Thailand and a neocolonial Thai subject by writing "Siamese" cookbooks and teaching cooking classes to suburban homemakers back in Los Angeles, whetting Americans' appetite for an exotic Other's cuisine.

In chapter two, I examine the origins of Thai foodways inside the United States, focusing on food procurement as a Thai American community building practice in Los Angeles before free trade. Before the 1970s Thai and Southeast Asian ingredients were not widely available, which led to a crisis of identity among Thai immigrants. The chapter follows Thai food entrepreneurs who resolved the crisis by developing a local supply of Thai ingredients, opening grocery stores like the Bangkok Market, and starting import/export companies. It also discusses the first wave of Thai immigration. U.S. cultural diplomacy in Thailand encouraged thousands of Thais to obtain student visas to study in the United States. These Thai college students were among the first to open Thai restaurants and food related businesses in the city. Many, however, ultimately overstayed their visas and became *exdocumented*.

Chapter three explores Los Angeles's Thai restaurant boom in the 1970s and 1980s to show how Thais grappled with U.S. racial, gender, and class structures through the food service industry. The boom, coupled with new patterns of discretionary spending, turned Thai restaurants into culinary contact zones where sensory experiences reestablished racial boundaries and sustained racial thinking and practices. To distinguish Thai food from other Asian cuisines, Thai restaurateurs along with white food critics used race, ethnicity, and nation to produce novelty and product differentiation in the marketing of Thai cuisine. In explaining to the American public how Thais were unique from other Asians based on what they cooked and ate, they relied on taste and smell to construct Thais as an exotic nonwhite Other. The chapter also discusses how Thai restaurants reinforced, created, and masked gender and class divisions within the community through labor practices in the kitchen.

The 1980s witnessed the growth of Thai American suburbanization, with large numbers moving to the working-class suburbs of the East San Fernando Valley near Wat Thai of Los Angeles, the first and largest Thai Buddhist temple in the country established in 1979. Chapter four examines food festivals at Wat Thai as a window to food, race, and place in the suburbs. It charts how the temple evolved into a community space that became popular for its weekend food festivals. The festivals, which attracted thousands of visitors, fostered a public-oriented Thai American suburban culture that was a claim for a right to the global city. The festivals, however, sparked complaints from a group of nearby residents who used zoning law to try and shut them down. I contend that the residents who opposed the festivals articulated a liberal multiculturalism to maintain the white spatial imaginary of the neighborhood.

At the turn of the 21st century, a significant number of Thais in Los Angeles lacked adequate housing, health care, and jobs, and they were victimized by human rights violations epitomized by the 1995 El Monte slave labor case. Chapter five explores "Thai Town" in East Hollywood, which was established in 1999, to highlight the role of culinary tourism in Thai American struggles for a right to the global city. It charts the history of Thai Town's development as a product of Thai community leaders, specifically the Thai Community Development Center, and Los Angeles city officials attempt to parlay Thai cuisine's popularity into political visibility, civic engagement, social justice activism and urban redevelopment. While playing on cuisine driven multiculturalism allowed Thais to use food, specifically culinary tourism, to root identity and community in a physical place, I assert that heritage commodification in Thai Town also constricted a right to the global city because it was geared toward a neoliberal vision of multiculturalism that sought to highlight Los Angeles's position in the global capitalist economy.

The conclusion explains why I wrote the book and how I came to study food. It also underlines the book's scholarly contributions and interventions into dominant narratives of postwar U.S. empire, race in America, post-1965 immigration, and metropolitan history. I end with a discussion of the larger goals of the book and the insights it provides into issues related to food and race in the United States today, including cultural appropriation, cultural food colonialism, and cuisine driven multiculturalism.

ONE

———

"One Night in Bangkok"

FOOD AND THE EVERYDAY LIFE OF EMPIRE

IN 1965 MARIE WILSON PUBLISHED *SIAMESE COOKERY*, the first Thai cookbook in the United States. As a self-described homemaker from West Los Angeles, Wilson wrote and illustrated the cookbook to encourage fellow homemakers to cook Thai food in their own kitchens. She assured readers that while "there is nothing plain about Thai cooking," the dishes are "not difficult to prepare."[1] Her cookbook included dozens of recipes collected over ten years of travel through Thailand. She also added a short memoir about her experiences with Thai people and culture. Her goal was simple and modest: "Thai food has found a permanent place in our home. I hope this little book will make it a happy addition to your household."[2]

To understand how and why a white suburban housewife from West Los Angeles like Marie Wilson became an authority on Thai cuisine in the United States during this period requires a look into the everyday life of U.S. empire in Cold War Thailand. U.S. intervention allowed white American women to taste Thai food for the first time and then become experts in it. They used foodways to build knowledge about Thailand and Thai people and disseminated it within the formal boundaries of the United States, especially in Los Angeles. Amid the development of Thailand's tourist industry and infrastructure after World War II, foodways emerged as the key site for constructing Thais as an exotic neocolonial subject. Yet white American women's fascination with Thai cuisine, part of a larger appetite for "Oriental" cuisine among suburban American housewives in the 1960s, did much more than foster attitudes and feelings that justified U.S. involvement in Thailand.[3] It also sustained the informal U.S. empire. These women's so-called discovery of Thai cooking practices, their role in transforming foods from sustenance to commodities, and their standardization of recipes in cookbooks all functioned as mechanisms of domination. Above all, U.S. neocolonialism in Thailand underpinned these intimate, complex encounters with Thai food culture and made their discoveries and representations of exotic Others possible.

The United States and Thailand enjoyed over a century of amicable relations before World War II, forging a positive, yet unequal, formal relationship primarily through commercial treaties and diplomatic, cultural, and educational exchanges.[4] Official relations had begun with signing of the Treaty of Amity and Commerce in 1833 (also known as the Roberts Treaty), the first ever agreement between the United States and an Asian nation.[5] American missionaries served as the first U.S. diplomats in what was then called Siam, and several became traders and printers. Americans believed in the superiority of Anglo-Saxon technology, intellect, and culture as well as the economic and moral necessity of free trade. Even the most sympathetic of American officials expressed negative sentiments about the "barbaric laws and customs" and the "outlawry and demoralization prevailing" in Siam.[6]

Of course, Siamese officials developed their own opinions about the West and Westerners based on interactions with Americans in Siam. King Mongkut of Siam and members of his royal court despised Christianity even as they accepted American missionary activity in the kingdom. They rejected Christianity as a "foolish religion" mainly because they considered it not nearly as rooted in a modern scientific, rational, and reasoned view of the world as Buddhist principles.[7] In addition, Siamese leaders opposed the Western notion that material and moral progress were intertwined, at times openly debating with diplomats and missionaries and criticizing them in print.

In spite of these qualms, at the turn of the twentieth century Siamese leaders became more deeply committed to Anglo-Saxon ideas of progress as they fixated on becoming a "civilized" modern nation-state. They adopted modern geography and its "indispensible" new technology of mapping and map making to discursively construct Siam's territorial boundaries, values, and practices—its "geo-body"—and made it legible as a modern nation to the Western world.[8] In addition, officials and various groups of elite in Siam embarked on a quest for *siwilai*, a transliteration of the English word *civilized* that expressed a desire to progress along Western lines in terms of material progress, etiquette, and everything in between.[9]

World War II both tested and strengthened U.S.-Thai relations. Shortly after bombing Pearl Harbor, on December 8, 1941, Japanese troops invaded

Thailand seeking safe passage to fight the British in Malaysia and Burma. Within a few weeks Thailand formed a military alliance with Japan. And on January 25, 1942, Thailand officially declared war on the United States and the Allied powers.[10] Thailand was not a passive victim of Japanese coercion. Prime Minister Plaek Phibunsongkhram believed Thailand could help Japan bring an end to white Western colonialism in Asia, and to possibly create a new world in which Thais and other Asians would not be "little brown brothers."[11] However, Seni Pramoj, the Thai minister in Washington, D.C., refused to deliver the declaration of war to President Franklin Roosevelt because he regarded it as illegal and against the wishes of Thai people. Pramoj, along with a group of Thai students in the United States, organized an underground "Free Thai" movement. In collaboration with the American Office of Strategic Services, the movement offered voluntary military support to the Allied powers, used political propaganda and public relations campaigns to persuade fellow Thai to resist Japanese forces, and performed damage control to reestablish good relations with the United States.[12] After Japan's surrender on August 15, 1945, Thai officials also issued a peace proclamation stating that Thailand's declaration of war was unconstitutional and against the interests of Thailand and Thai people. The arguments convinced U.S. officials. U.S. Secretary of State James Byrnes responded, "The American government has always believed that the declaration did not represent the will of the Thai people as it was under Japanese control. . . . During the past four years we have regarded Thailand not as an enemy, but as a country to be liberated from the enemy. With that liberation now accomplished we look to the resumption by Thailand of its former place in the community of nations as a free, sovereign, and independent country."[13] The end of World War II marked a watershed moment for U.S.-Thai relations: the start of Thailand's "American Era."

RENDERING THE THAI NEOCOLONIAL SUBJECT

The informal postwar U.S. empire created the conditions for U.S. citizens to get to know and experience Thailand, Thai people, and Thai culture. The new *farangs*, a diverse group of Americans ranging from social scientists and military officials to exchange students and tourists, produced and circulated representations of Thailand that attempted to establish sentimental bonds between Americans and Thais. They developed knowledge of Thailand and its people through popular culture and face-to-face encounters. Members of each *farang* category certainly had unique individual experiences and therefore interpreted Thai people and culture subjectively. Collectively, however, U.S. citizens put forth a set of overlapping and, at times, competing narratives. They familiarized other Americans with the relatively unknown U.S. client state, depicting Thailand as open and adaptable to global changes, such as the intrusion of American-style capitalism and culture, and describing Thai people as lazy yet friendly and naturally subservient to hierarchies. They saw Thai society and culture operating on a path of least resistance embodied in the *mai bpen rai* attitude, a widely used Thai expression variously meaning, "you're welcome" and "no problem" or "do not worry, just enjoy life," when applied to bad or unpleasant situations. These narratives justified U.S. intervention.

Immediately after World War II, U.S. businessmen and companies helped form the idea that Thais and Americans shared commonalities, giving the impression that capitalist development was in the best interest of both nations. Thailand's American era witnessed only a modest investment of U.S. capital in mostly mining, petroleum, hotel, silk, and shipping companies. Thailand remained too remote and too risky an investment. Still, some companies and their executives sought to expand and capitalize on Thailand's trade relations and historical pro-Western stance.[14] Among them was Jan van Oosten of San Marino, California. As an executive for a steamship line, he traveled to Bangkok for two months in 1949. A naturalized citizen from Holland, Van Oosten saw great similarities among Americans and "Thailanders," mainly because both championed freedom in "business and personal life" and had never been "conquered or exploited." "The Siamese intrigue me more than any other Oriental nationality," he observed. "They are adaptable and at the same time independent. Like Americans, they are democratic although the country is ruled by a king."[15] Before leaving Bangkok, van Oosten told Thai government officials that he wanted "to do something for your country." Officials obliged by honoring Van Oosten as Consul General, the first from Los Angeles and the second from California.

Thailand became a prime potential base to combat alternative political economies deemed threatening to the United States's global free-market capitalist aspirations. U.S. state actors began referring to Thailand as a pro-Western bastion of anticommunism in Southeast Asia deserving of U.S. support.[16] Edward F. Stanton, U.S. ambassador to Thailand from 1946–1953, described the country in a 1954 *Foreign Affairs* article as the "heart" and "citadel" of the region.[17] In February 1954 the U.S.-initiated Southeast Asian

Treaty Organization (SEATO), a security pact signed by eight countries to counter communist "aggression and subversion," was established and headquartered in Bangkok, which formalized American involvement in Southeast Asia as well as made clear Thailand's critical role in U.S. global communist containment.[18] In addition to Thailand's strategic geographic location for security, the United States was also interested in the country's substantial resources and similar free-market enterprise system that offered ripe private investment opportunities for U.S. corporations.[19]

Cultural producers also reinforced and distributed popular representations of Thailand as an adaptable nation in the service of U.S. intervention. Richard Rodgers and Oscar Hammerstein's 1951 musical *The King and I* was arguably the most far-reaching and influential narrative of Thai people and culture during the Cold War. *The King and I* opened on Broadway and played in New York through 1954 with Gertrude Lawrence starring as Anna and Yul Brynner as King Mongkut. After touring nationally and in London, the show was shaped into a Twentieth Century Fox film in 1956. It won six academy awards with a wildly popular soundtrack that stayed on the charts for 274 weeks.[20] The musical delivered an epic tale about a real yet Americanized nineteenth-century British schoolteacher, Anna Leonowens, who is hired by King Mongkut of Siam to teach and guide Siam along Western lines to avoid colonization. Rodgers and Hammerstein depicted Thailand as backwards but, if trained properly, a candidate for joining the civilized First World. Through the figure of Anna, U.S. citizens were encouraged to see modernization projects as anticolonial struggles for self-determination rather than acts of colonial domination. The musical put forth the idea that racial Others like the Siamese, "rather than being exterminated, could be modernized through an intimate embrace."[21] As Christina Klein has argued, *The King and I* functioned as a "spectacle of modernization" and captured the way the ideology of modernization extended beyond political officials and academics and became infused within middlebrow culture.[22] In other words, the film offered an opportunity for the average American to participate in the Cold War by way of consumption.

U.S. social scientists were part of the first group to produce "intelligence" on Thailand in the early stages of the Cold War. As students and architects of modernization theory, these well-funded researchers became fascinated with the decolonizing world and its potential for social, political, and economic progress along Western lines.[23] In 1947, the Southeast Asia Program at Cornell University pioneered investigations on Thailand under the leadership of

Lauriston Sharp and the initiation of the Cornell Thailand Project.[24] Sharp, who had spent a year as assistant director of the Southeast Asia Division of the State Department in 1945, launched the project (and later expanded it with a Rockefeller Foundation Grant in 1950) because, as he told the *Christian Science Monitor* in 1952: "Americans are just becoming aware of the political importance of the area. Yet our understanding of its peoples and cultures is far from adequate. There is a dangerous shortage of experts, and there are great gaps in our knowledge of even the most elementary facts."[25] The Cornell project, a hub of Thai Studies at the time, emphasized research, graduate education, and training students with a knowledge of the countries they will presumably work in via diplomatic corps and business. The Program disseminated this knowledge through the flagship "Data Paper Series," a collection that included social scientific studies on Thai culture, behavior, and social structure, focusing on political and ideological changes as well as "the social and psychological effects of technological change" in rural Thailand.[26] Anthropologist Ruth Benedict produced a notable ethnographic study of Thai culture during World War II, published posthumously in 1952, in which she concluded that the lack of Thai parental authority and discipline toward infants and adolescents led to "Thai cheerfulness, easy conviviality, and non-violence" and could explain why Thais "gamble with pleasure, are indolent rather than hard-working and accept easily subordinate positions in a hierarchy."[27] To be sure, the academic interest in Thais was minimal at the time, but the research did reflect the growth and legitimacy of area studies in the United States. With funding and support from a range of U.S. government agencies and programs—both overtly and covertly—the interdisciplinary field produced research that had intellectual value while also shaping global counterinsurgency and development programs to further America's Cold War policy objectives.[28]

Social scientists were not the only educators in Thailand. The Agency for International Development's (AID) University Contract program offers a vivid example of how U.S. education, as it insinuated itself into everyday Thai society, produced knowledge about Thais not only through academic research but also via personal interactions. U.S. educational programs were among the most impactful mechanisms of cultural diplomacy in Thailand.[29] On July 1, 1950, an educational exchange agreement was signed between the United States and Thailand that led to the development of the Fulbright Foundation, spearheaded by U.S. Senator William J. Fulbright. Shortly after, a number of American organizations, many private, began to appear, including the American University Alumni language center (AUA) in Bangkok funded by both the U.S. government and the private American University Alumni Association to help Thais develop English skills before leaving to study in the United States. Other organizations and programs included the Agency for International Development (AID), the Asia Foundation (TAF), the American Field Services (AFS), the Peace Corps, and the Rockefeller Foundation.[30]

During the 1950s and 60s, professors from thirteen different American universities—including Indiana University, Wayne State University, Michigan State University, and the University of Texas at Austin—traveled to Thailand as participants in the AID University Contract program. The goal was to modernize Thai faculty practices and institutions of higher education along American lines. As advisers, U.S. educators carried out modernization and extended goodwill on the ground, working with Thai professors to bring American solutions to Thai "problems." The process consisted of eliminating "authoritarian patterns of instruction," restructuring laboratories and libraries, and introducing new textbooks.[31] Advisers reported stumbling across numerous cultural barriers and difficulties in dealing with Thai cultural practices, specifically the Thai *mai bpen rai* attitude. From interactions at the College of Education in Bangkok, one frustrated counseling adviser from Indiana University believed that the Thai *mai bpen rai* attitude was a reflection of a deeply rooted Thai fatalistic approach to life that stood in stark contrast to American individualism. Other advisers took *mai bpen rai* to mean that Thais were much more leisurely than Americans and other "Orientals," evidenced by the way they did not take appointments, schedules, or planning seriously. U.S. educators also considered *mai bpen rai* to be a practice of avoiding confrontation and therefore saw the attitude as unthreatening.[32]

Another group of U.S. educators, U.S. Peace Corps volunteers, also drew on their first-hand experiences but constructed a more positive view of Thai people and Thailand as friendly, charming, and adaptable. The U.S. Peace Corps also sent volunteers to teach English, with other development efforts, across rural Thailand. John F. Kennedy spearheaded the Peace Corps in 1961 as a government cultural exchange program designed to induce warm attitudes toward the United States by fostering mutual understanding and peace through international development. The program shipped young, college degree holding Americans to participating countries around the world for various projects that included teaching English, malaria eradication, community development, rural health sanitation, irrigation building, and physical education.[33] Thailand welcomed their first group of forty-five Peace Corps volunteers on January 20, 1962.[34]

While the *mai bpen rai* attitude resonated with Peace Corps volunteers as it did with the AID program advisers, the volunteers interpreted it as an endearing cultural quality. Peace Corps director John McCarthy, a lawyer from suburban Claremont, California and a former World War II officer in the Pacific who oversaw 385 volunteers in Thailand during the mid 1960s, explained to the *Los Angeles Times* upon his return to Southern California that *mai bpen rai* was a lifestyle. He believed that while the attitude caused some irritation among younger volunteers who wanted faster results, understanding and embracing it was important if the United States was to continue Thai people's social and economic opportunities. McCarthy added that, as a whole, "Thais are a relaxed people" with a "highly developed sense of humor, using a play on words" and are "friendly, quick to smile, attractive with small features, adjustable, and are not rigid to strangers."[35]

Jerolyn "Jerri" Minor, a Peace Corps volunteer from Richmond, California, who taught in Chiang Mai from 1965 to 1967, recalled initially being attracted to Thailand only because her training for the corps was in the more familiar Honolulu, Hawaii. Minor was also intrigued because she had never heard of Thailand before the assignment—even pronouncing Thailand as "Thighland."[36] By the time her trip was over, however, her understanding of Thais mirrored the conceptions of her contemporaries. She fondly remembered Thais as "the epitome of friendliness . . . just lovely people . . . just beautiful people" and that "one of the things that made me so affectionate of the Thai people was this phrase *mai bpen rai*; it means you're welcome, don't worry about it, it's okay."[37] U.S. academics and Peace Corps volunteers understood that successfully negotiating these types of face-to-face encounters was necessary to counter the perception of the "ugly American" and maintain good relations between the two nations. But in the process they also defined in rigid and static ways what it meant to be American versus Thai based on cultural traits.

By the mid 1960s, U.S. military officials and American GIs constituted the majority of the rapidly growing number of U.S. *farang* population in Thailand. At least 45,000 U.S. military personnel were stationed in Thailand in 1969.[38] The influx and presence of U.S. *farangs* did not go unnoticed. A young Thai architect, Chumsai na Ayuthya, remembered first thinking that the growth in numbers of Americans was probably temporary—until he passed a fleet of U.S. Army trucks loaded with filing cabinets. "When the

American Army starts filing," he told a *New York Times* reporter, "it's there for a long time. You might as well get adjusted to it."[39] The boom was evident by the number of U.S. students enrolled at the International School Bangkok, which at the time was the largest school for U.S. citizens outside of the United States. The school, an eight-acre "piece of teenage America" in the heart of the Bangkok with palm trees, open-air classrooms cooled only by ceiling fans, and surrounded by a high hurricane fence, was initially established for the children of U.S. diplomats, businessmen, and military advisers living in Thailand. It opened in 1951 with an enrollment of seventy students who met inside an empty warehouse owned by the U.S. embassy. Ten years later, with the Vietnam War escalating, the enrollment rose to eight hundred and by 1966 the number was up to 2,700. The school was forced to open another campus on the outskirts of Bangkok to accommodate the growth. In 1968 school enrollment reached 3,600 students. Ninety percent were children of U.S. citizens—and overwhelmingly the children of U.S. military officials and diplomats.[40]

SEXUALIZING AND GENDERING THAIS

Compared to U.S. educators, American military personnel played a more major, or at least more explicit, role in engendering and sexualizing Thais. The construction of U.S. military bases in the rural backwaters of northern and central Thailand led to the proliferation of military towns, stimulating a gendered and sexualized service-based leisure industry, or what Teresia Teaiwa calls "militourism."[41] Next to the bases, clusters of bars, massage parlors, and other garish nightlife operations sprang up almost overnight. One of the most visible aspects was the GI bar scene. Established primarily for U.S. soldiers but frequented by other U.S. citizens as well as Thais, GI bars served as the hub of a military town's economy. The bars, some doubling as open-air restaurants, gave Thai villagers a chance to make money by offering services ranging from transportation to entertainment.

Inside the bars, customers indulged in alcohol, the latest U.S. popular music, and Thai women. GI bars either hired Thai women or the women simply freelanced in soliciting dances from patrons. Thai "women of the night" charged on average 50-70 baht ($2.50-$3.50) for up to an hour of dancing, handholding, and "necking," and 150 baht ($7.50) and higher for an "after-hours" engagement.[42] Peace Corps volunteer James Jouppi, who was assigned to Nakohn Phanom in northern Thailand, recalled visiting a GI bar one night with friends and watching a "train of fifty young women dance to a strange r[h]ythmical beat" called "the bump" where "the girls all held onto each other, each with her hands around the waist of the girl in front of her. . . . It wasn't rock and roll, and yet it was much too sensual to be a folk dance."[43] The money spent by a GI on this type of entertainment, whether in a crowded bar or an empty one, was reportedly enough to support "half of dozen Thais for a day."[44] According to Jouppi, Thai "bar girls," as they were called, made enough money to go to the movies, buy Panasonic cassette tape recorders, and afford a wardrobe of tailor-made clothes.[45]

Bangkok had transformed into a virtual playground for U.S. military men and tourists. GI bars with names like "Sorry about That," "Why Not?," and "Girl! Girl! Girl!" dominated Bangkok's streets.[46] Massage parlors targeting U.S. men also lined the streets. Although many of the parlors were located side by side along the street, they varied greatly in style. Some parlors operated out of small wooden houses on side streets. Others were large, air-conditioned establishments resembling gymnasiums. New Petchburi Road, a street filled with newly erected luxury hotels, offered Thai-, Korean-, and Japanese-style massages in over fifty massage parlors. Thai masseuses on display in storefront windows enticed *farangs* who, once inside, could choose a masseuse to fit his liking and would pay from 30 to 70 baht ($1.50 to $3.50) for her services.[47]

The U.S. military also designated different areas throughout Thailand as official rest and recreation (R&R) destinations for American GIs. R&R tours only added to the pubic brashness of the Cold War Thai sex industry. U.S. soldiers treated Thai prostitutes like girlfriends, whether strolling openly arm in arm or necking up and down the street. Between 1962 and 1976, at least 70,000 U.S. servicemen visited Thailand on three-day and seven-day R&R trips while taking a break from battle in Vietnam.[48] They spent an estimated total of $22 million per year in the Thai economy, making the tours extremely lucrative for the Thai government.[49] On New Petchburi Road in Bangkok (also known as the "American Strip"), U.S. soldiers entertained themselves at bars, nightclubs, strip clubs, brothels, and massage parlors catering to American GIs. Susan Cooper, a Peace Corps volunteer from 1969 to 1971, recalled in an interview that "a lot of soldiers came to Bangkok for R&R" and that the nearby Petchburi Hotel "was the scene of things that many of us have never seen before . . . and this was a hotel that was frequented by a lot of young ladies of the night."[50] One of the most popular destinations was Pattaya Beach resort, about one hundred miles southeast of Bangkok in the Gulf of Thailand.

During the late 1960s, the U.S. military selected the quaint fishing village and leased a large section of beachfront property on which to create an official R&R center. In addition to erecting new hotels, bars, and "rock and roll joints," U.S. officials also set up a daily hydrofoil service that brought GIs from Bangkok. When the servicemen arrived ashore, they were greeted by "Pattaya's Hawaiians"—Thai women dressed in hula skirts, bikini tops, and leis.[51]

Not surprisingly, prostitution thrived under these conditions. It is certainly true that prostitution existed in Thai society before the arrival of U.S. servicemen. GIs and other U.S. citizens, however, eagerly participated in the Thai sex industry. What's more, Thai prostitution became more lewd and gaudy during the American era, in that U.S. *farangs* and Thais approached prostitution quite differently. U.S. *farangs* searched for prostitutes in bars and massage parlors, but Thais searched out red-lighted brothels for their sex transactions.[52] The Thai government also played a role in maintaining gender and sexual norms, with Thai military commanders identifying Thai prostitutes—who doubled as bar girls, masseuses, and dancers—as "special job workers." The number of "special job workers" at Udorn Air Force Base for example, grew rapidly from 1,246 in 1966 to 6,234 in 1972.[53]

Hierarchy among Thai prostitutes was also informed by U.S. consumers' desires surrounding age and sexual purity. U.S. Peace Corps volunteer Mike Schmicker observed on one of his many trips to Bangkok that the "pretty girls" offered services to *farangs* at the large tourist and business hotels such as the Siam Intercontinental and Montien, earning several thousand baht a trick.[54] But when Thai prostitutes were "ruined," they ended up soliciting sex in Bangkok's seedier slum establishments such as the Mosquito Bar—a two-story concrete "dive dumped on the banks of the Chao Phraya River."

Most importantly, U.S. soldiers treated Thai women as little more than sexual objects. They often described Thai women in racial, gendered, and sexualized terms that projected Thailand as a dangerous paradise. The plentiful opportunities for sexual pleasure made Thailand a paradise for off-duty U.S. soldiers, yet a significant number of Thai prostitutes carried venereal diseases. Of the 100,000 Thai prostitutes working in Bangkok during the late 1970s, for instance, 70 percent suffered from a venereal disease.[55] U.S. soldier Gregory DeLaurier remembered being warned by his sergeant to "watch out for those LBFMs, son" as he first arrived in Thailand on an R&R tour. When DeLaurier responded to the acronym with confusion, the sergeant threw him a pack of condoms and spelled it out—"Little Brown Fucking Machines, buddy. You don't want your dick to fall off do you? These Thai honeys'll fuck your brains out but goddamn won't they give you the clap."[56]

In some cases, "one night in Bangkok" with Thai women developed into longer relationships and even marriage. Based on the accounts of U.S. soldiers at the time, U.S. servicemen went about getting a Thai wife in two ways. The first, and probably most common method, was to go to a GI bar or club, talk to an attractive Thai woman, and then ask if she had a husband or was in a relationship. If she was single, as was often the case since Thai men considered Thai bar girls to be tainted, then the U.S. soldier simply moved into her home (sometimes with her family members). They paid between 1,000 and 2,000 baht ($50-$100) per month for rent and all the services a woman, no less a wife, was expected to provide. The other option was for a U.S. serviceman to locate a Thai marriage broker. For around 1,000 baht ($50) the broker, typically an older Thai woman with an apparently steady supply of young Thai girls, introduced the GI to one of those girls. If he liked her, the GI then hired her as a *mia chow* or "rented wife" (also called a "duration wife"). This rental system was common practice in Bangkok but was even more prevalent around military bases.[57]

What did U.S. servicemen find attractive about Thai women, aside from their ability to "fuck your brains out"? They were physically beautiful and, particularly, exotic. Journalist Lloyd Shearer expressed these views in the 1968 *Parade Magazine* article "Thailand is a Man's World—and the G.I.'s Like It." Shearer described Thai women to readers as "in the main, lovely creatures of a delicate porcelain beauty."[58] He also said Thailand's Queen Sirikit and her physical beauty was a prime "reflection of the country's enchanting young women" because she was "petite, demure, shapely, reserved."[59] Shearer added that rural Thai girls, due to their lighter skin, were prettier than girls from the city. Moreover, he also revealed that American GIs believed that Thai girls found their flirty behavior and sexual advances irresistible.

Above all, U.S. servicemen sought out Thai wives because they could treat them as subordinates without consequence. U.S. servicemen credited Thai culture for preparing Thai girls through "tradition and training to treat men as superiors," which produced a "sweetly feminine Oriental subordination." A U.S. corporeal joyfully explained it to Shearer: "None of that equality of the sexes over here.... You tell your chick what to do, and she does it." A soldier from Oklahoma stationed at Udorn also described Thai wives as "honorable" and "pretty darn faithful" girls who "cook well, clean well, [and] sew well. They're industrious, conscientious, [and] easy to live with. They don't make any demands. This is a man's country all the way." In essence, Thai women became consumable objects—a national resource that made the lives of U.S. servicemen easier and more leisurely. Or as Shearer put it, "[Thailand's] most appealing, desirable commercial product is the native Thai girl."[60]

The number of GI children created personified the racial and sexual violence that U.S. militarization wreaked on Thai society, in addition to the fleeting yet frequent sexual encounters between U.S. servicemen and Thai women. By 1977, U.S. servicemen had fathered approximately 10,000 children with Thai women.[61] Most of these children were conceived on legitimate terms and not simply during a night of passion. At Udorn Thani, a province in northeastern Thailand that was the site of one of the largest U.S. air bases, Thais depended on exchange with the base for nearly a decade as they sold food, homes, and in many cases, daughters. Here, U.S. servicemen paid anywhere from $150 to $300 for a *mia chow* to sleep with them, cook their food, wash their clothes, and ultimately bear their children. Many Thai women believed they were married to U.S. servicemen because they participated in Thai wedding ceremonies together. They soon found that the United States did not honor such ceremonies or unions as their "husbands" simply left for America. But considering the number of Thai women who entered the United States as war brides, many GIs did try to bring Thai women back with them. Nevertheless, as GI children were put up for U.S. adoption, one American diplomat lamented the growing idea that U.S. military officials should be held accountable. "No one forced their girls to sleep with our boys," he said, "they did it voluntarily. Udorn wasn't our colony."[62]

U.S. military intervention paved the way for nonmilitary U.S. citizens to travel to Thailand and interact with Thai society. They shaped the cultural and social life of the informal U.S. empire in Thailand and influenced American perceptions of Thai people and culture. This happened not simply because of U.S. mechanism of power and domination, such as formal diplomatic policies and military strength, but also because of the postwar U.S. tourism boom. While many Americans worked as policy makers in Washington, D.C., and under the auspices of the U.S. State Department, they also wanted to experience adventure and see the world. U.S. militourism had such a profound impact on Thai society, especially in bolstering the "industrialization of sex," not only through militarization but because civilian tourism was used as a strategy for modernization and development.[63] Feminist scholar Cynthia Enloe has argued that when "tourism is imagined by local and foreign economic planners to be a fast road to development," it cultivates prostitution.[64] And this was precisely the case in Thailand during the 1960s.

U.S. TOURISM IN THAILAND

The knowledge about Thailand, Thai people, and Thai culture that emerged out of cultural productions, educational institutions and programs, and militourism was made possible by two related transformations during the 1950s and 1960s: The rise of post-World War II tourism to the Asian-Pacific region and the massive expansion of Thailand's tourism industry and tourist-based infrastructure.

Technological advances in aviation contributed majorly to U.S. tourism abroad. The postwar aerospace industry's reconversion of war aircraft into commercial airliners helped usher in the jet age, making U.S. travel more common. Yet technology alone does not cause human action. Many Americans became mass consumers with disposable income in the postwar era. By 1948 paid vacations had become standard in union agreements. With pent up energy for leisure, middle-class white U.S. citizens began embarking on getaways outside of the country for themselves and their children. In 1947 about 200,000 Americans had valid passports. In 1953 more than 1 million U.S. citizens traveled overseas and by the end of the 1950s roughly 7 million traveled abroad, mostly to Europe.[65] Although only a few visited Asia and the Pacific (only 2 percent of all travelers in 1959), the postwar period experienced a boom in the number of travel writers, newspapers, magazines, and films that featured places like Taiwan, Burma, and Thailand.[66] So contrary to standard historical accounts of Cold War American life that portray Americans as being bound to suburban homes and securing themselves in bomb shelters, U.S. citizens actually traveled abroad quite a bit during the postwar period.

U.S. tourism took on new meaning in the postwar world. U.S. state officials redefined the role of a tourist from just a sightseeing traveler to a bona-fide agent, representative, and diplomat of America. The U.S. State Department made a concerted effort to inform U.S. tourists that they were not merely travelers but U.S. ambassadors. With U.S. newspapers and magazines connecting increased tourism with anti-American sentiment and the ugly American epithet, the State Department encouraged American tourists to be on their best behavior overseas and to engage in meaningful exchanges to cultivate cultural understanding. In fact, in 1954 officials issued pamphlets and had them placed into U.S. passports to remind U.S. tourists to "act in a manner befitting their station" and to warn them not to "assume an air of arrogance" or violate "the common bonds of decency."[67] Violating those bonds could, the State Department argued, "do more in the course of an hour to break down elements of friendly approach between peoples than the Government [could] do in the course of a year in trying to stimulate friendly relations."[68] U.S. tourists had become, in essence, "millions of ambassadors." The new responsibility allowed everyday Americans to participate in the Cold War through travel.

The postwar period also witnessed the development of global tourist infrastructure designed to attract and accommodate travelers, which included the construction of airports, airstrips, paved roads, hotels, restaurants, shops, golf courses, and other entertainment venues. The U.S. travel industry lobbied for such development. Travel agents, for instance, realized that while U.S. tourists sought adventure abroad they wanted the exciting and foreign sights, sounds, and peoples to be kept a safe distance. Writing for the *Los Angeles Times* in 1958, Bert Hemphill, one of the leading figures in the U.S. travel industry and deemed one of the most traveled men on the planet, argued that tourist infrastructure was a necessity if nations wanted to profit from the postwar travel boom.[69] Hemphill claimed that hotel rooms, hotel workers, and travel agents were all critical to the U.S. tourist experience, as travelers spent most of their time in hotel rooms and dealing with hotel staff. Hotels in particular offered security and a haven from exotic foods, people, and languages. "The people won't come again unless they are comfortable," wrote Bert, "the very experiences they sought unsettle them."[70] U.S. tourists, it appeared, preferred to visit places only with proper amenities and palatable cultures.

Members of the travel industry believed that prying open foreign places for U.S. consumption with tourist infrastructure was an effective strategy for postwar modernization and development. On Bert Hemphill's trip to Guatemala in November of 1946, he described Guatemala City as a place that has "prospered greatly since 18 years ago when I first visited . . . streets are paved, buildings are modern and the city boasts the finest airport in Central America."[71] He added that the Pan-American Highway, which began its multimillion dollar construction during World War II, had yet to be completed, making navigation through the countryside difficult for tourists. Postwar tourist development also flourished in parts of Africa—a continent amid numerous anticolonial struggles. When Bert surveyed "darkest Africa" in 1949 he observed, "the final conquest of Africa has been made possible by the modern plane."[72] Moreover, Hawaii, a U.S. colony deeply entangled in U.S. militarization and tourism, underwent considerable infrastructure alteration as its tourist industry set travel records during the 1950s. As a popular destination for white U.S. travelers, missionaries, investors, and military officials fascinated by hula, the postwar period witnessed the expansion of Hawaii's tourist-based service economy.[73]

In 1952 the Pacific Area Travel Association (PATA) was established in Honolulu, Hawaii to help institutionalize tourist development and encourage U.S. travelers to "discover the Pacific." The association's objectives included professionalizing and consolidating roughly 2,200 worldwide travel organizations, strengthening relationships between travel agents and government officials, bringing together the public and private sectors, lobbying governments to ease regulations on travel, and modernizing tourist facilities. PATA saw Asia and the Pacific region as the next big consumer product. They believed the region could inspire transpacific travel that rivaled and potentially exceed the level and popularity of transatlantic travel to Europe. In essence, PATA's mission was to use tourism to help the people and cultures of Asia and the Pacific "move from post-World War II conditions of poverty to a position of global leadership."[74] This vision reinforced the U.S. government's view of tourism as well. PATA underscored the U.S. Secretary of Commerce Luther H. Hodges' view that tourists "bring wealth into a country . . . in the form of goodwill and understanding . . . [and] . . . wealth in the form of foreign exchange, vitally needed for international trade."[75]

There were enormous profits to be made in tourism. On June 2, 1959, hundreds of U.S. travel agents assembled at the Balboa Bay Club in Newport Beach, California for a banquet hosted by PATA and the American Society of Travel Agents (ASTA), a colorful affair that highlighted the cultural wonders of countries and peoples from Asia and the Pacific region. At dinner, an overwhelmingly white audience watched live cultural performances that played up the exotic magnificence of Asian and Pacific cultures and histories. The performances included singers and dancers, both men and women, from Hawaii, India, Japan, and the Philippines—all in their respective "traditional" regalia.[76] The banquet was an extended effort to discuss strategies to develop Asia and Pacific travel facilities, which began in 1950 when the U.S. State Department sent official invitations to all Asian and Pacific countries to attend a conference in Hawaii held by the Pacific chapter of ASTA (which became PATA). Bert Hemphill was in attendance, joined by prominent government officials of travel and tourist bureaus and representatives of ship and airline companies, many from Los Angeles.[77] The goal was to convince the most influential figures in the booming $2 billion dollar a year international tourist industry that even more profits awaited in the "Pacific Area."

PATA officials identified Thailand as a place with untapped tourist potential. The 1955 PATA handbook profiled the country and offered readers information on how to get to there, the climate, entry requirements, currency, language, and, of course, where to find clean, drinkable water. It informed travelers that a one-way sea fare via freighter-passenger service from a West coast port to Bangkok cost between $460 and $550, and would take a week or two.[78] A round-trip flight on Pan American World Airways, the only commercial airline that offered flights to Bangkok from Los Angeles, Seattle or San Francisco, cost $1,180 for a tourist-class ticket and $1,400 for a first-class ticket—with an elapsed flying time of fifty-six hours. These fares made a trip to Bangkok from a U.S. West Coast city, both by ship or plane, among the most expensive.

The handbook portrayed the country as a romantic, welcoming land occupied by friendly natives. PATA called Thailand a "sentimental favorite for world travelers," citing the "open-hearted charm and friendliness of the Siamese and the dreamlike fantasy of their capital city."[79] They described "the people of Thailand" as "Mongolian." The handbook also revealed that Thais had ancestral roots to China and were similar to the Chinese not only in terms of physical features but also in language and cultural practices such as food. In a section on "Food and Water," the agents wrote, "most restaurants serve 'Chinese Food,' including many delicacies from the land . . . a specialty is Siamese curries using Siamese rice, the finest in the Orient."[80]

At the time, however, Thai leaders and the Thai government had very little interest in tourism. An organized tourist industry did not exist. The country had a meager 871 tourist-standard rooms and roughly 50,000 visitors per year, with most staying in Bangkok for an average of two or three days.[81] Then PATA intervened. They worked with Thai leaders and the Thai government to make tourism one of the country's top priorities for postwar national development. In a 1958 report written for the U.S. Department of Commerce, PATA listed Thailand's location as the "air center" of Southeast Asia, its "raw materials" of spectacular temples, "exceptionally interesting classical Thai dancing," friendly people, and "colorful" way of life as key ingredients for a profitable tourist destination.[82] Someone, they urged, just needed to package and sell it.

PATA's efforts convinced the Thai government to jump-start the country's tourist economy. Prime Minister Sarit Thanarat established the Tourism

Organization of Thailand (TOT) as part of the development planning and the promotion of tourism.[83] Thanarat strongly supported PATA's suggestion for TOT to work closely with the Thai government and, most importantly, collaborate with outside specialists and business leaders holding private capital. Furthermore, PATA laid out guidelines and projections, based on empirical research, for Thai leaders to follow: (1) network with other Asian and Pacific nations to develop a regional plan for tourist development; (2) assure the construction of first class accommodations of 1,200 new hotel rooms totaling $18 million; (3) develop an effective, long-term promotional and marketing program; and (4) eliminate government barriers on travelers such as expediting customs procedures, reducing immigration paperwork, and liberalizing visa formalities. Finally, PATA recommended that Thailand "encourage the preservation of Thai art and customs" and that "further study will have to be given to ways and means of retaining their charm and preventing its deterioration and commercialization."[84]

The 1960s witnessed a frenzy of tourist infrastructure construction and the formation of a first-rate tourist industry in Thailand that catered increasingly to U.S. *farang.* In 1970, U.S. citizens constituted the largest group, about 150,000, of the total six hundred thousand visitors to Thailand.[54] The Thai government, through TOT, invested heavily in the capital and offered incentives to private investors to build new airport runways, highways, retail shops, bars, restaurants, R&R sites, and hotels. This rapid development turned a swamp rice field and fruit orchards into New Petchburi Road.[85] By mid-decade, about half of the nation's approximately 650 nightclubs, bars, and massage parlors could be found in Bangkok. In addition, Thailand built a majority of its tourist-class hotels in the 1960s. In 1966 alone, fourteen first-class luxury hotels opened in Bangkok, such as the Siam Intercontinental (cost of 500,000 baht to construct each room) adding 2,500 more tourist-standards rooms and raising the country's total number to 7064.[86]

The Thai government's investment in the tourist industry, which at its height from 1967 to 1971 generated 360 million baht ($18 million) in taxes to the Thai government, raised concerns among U.S. citizens and Thais.[87] In particular, both groups wondered whether the U.S. tourist presence constituted "progress" or an encroachment on Thai culture. As more and more U.S. citizens visited bars, coffee shops, hotels, and shopping centers, U.S. officials in Washington became increasingly concerned over their behavior. Yet, several American observers found Thais to be tolerant of U.S. visitors. "Americans were hated around the globe during the Vietnam War," wrote Mike Schmicker, "but not in Thailand.... The Thais I met were fascinated by America, its incredible wealth its anything-goes society and its technological prowess."[88] Others believed that Thais treated foreigners with more acceptance than other Asian nations because of Thailand's history as the only Southeast Asian country to have avoided Western colonialism. "The Thais," observed New York Times journalist William Warren, "have no colonial past to brood over."[89]

But U.S. tourism did in fact spawn criticism from Thais. The seemingly endless construction of tourist-friendly places made clear to Thais that an economy based so heavily on tourism was only going to focus on and serve outside interests at the expense of the local population. The money used to develop a tourist infrastructure complete with bowling alleys and luxury hotels had come to stand in for anything resembling an urban policy in Bangkok. Instead of using money to improve education, housing, and other public works, the Thai government and Thai leaders made the decision to transform Bangkok's urban landscape into a leisure getaway for U.S. tourists and wealthy Thai socialites. Those who spoke out against the negative social, cultural, or economic impact of tourism on Thai society were described as a small faction of traditionalists who stood in the way of modern progress in Thailand.

The U.S. tourism boom and the development of Thailand's tourist infrastructure enabled the leisure consumption of nearly all things Thai: manufactured goods, cultural performances, and women's bodies, to name a few. It gave rise to specific types of tourism. One of the more popular types was culinary tourism. Thailand's tourist infrastructure provided U.S. tourists, particularly white American women, with networks and pathways that allowed them to travel and move throughout the country and discover Thai cuisine. In the process, culinary tourism turned foodways into a site for the construction of the Thai neocolonial subject. In addition, U.S. culinary tourism altered Thai food culture as dramatically as it did the nation's urban landscape, countryside, and beaches. It would further corner Thailand and Thai people into a service-based economy.

CULINARY TOURISM AND THAIS AS AN EXOTIC "OTHER"

U.S. global expansion into Thailand secured and facilitated access to new markets, new people, and new foodways. On one hand, Thailand's rising tourist economy adapted Thai food culture to meet the desires and demands of U.S. tourists. Hotels and restaurants offering private dining experiences with a Western sequence of courses started appearing in Bangkok along with an assortment of foreign restaurants—Korean, Lebanese, Hungarian, Japanese, Italian, French, Mexican—in part to attract U.S. diplomats, businessmen, and military officials.[90] Several restaurants served hamburgers and chili con carne and were constantly filled with "homesick Americans" looking for food but also other Americans.[91] Newly created classical Thai dinner-and-dance shows also became popular, as they catered to more wealthy tourists and visitors who could experience a staged authentic version of Thai cuisine in the palace-like setting of "Old Siam."[92]

On the other hand, U.S. tourism in Thailand created less formal and less controlled social spaces that allowed tourists to have more intimate, organic interactions with Thai food practices. The experiences of U.S. Peace Corps volunteers provide a glimpse at how white U.S. citizens, especially women, approached Thai food with curiosity and excitement in culinary contact zones. Volunteers commonly made fond references to their first tastes and smells of Thai food when recalling their Peace Corps assignments during the mid to late 1960s.[93] Marianne May Apple, a volunteer from San Diego, California, assigned to Trat Province in southeastern Thailand, explained in a letter to her parents on May 24, 1966, that "the food really takes getting used to. It all has a distinctive taste and most of it is so hot that you think you're on fire."[94] In another letter to her sister later that year, Apple wrote: "My teacher ... usually invites me to lunch on Sat[urday] after I finish teaching. Last time we had crab eggs and blood—good[,] believe it or not! ... I think I will write a Thai cookbook ... because I have so many recipes that are of more a variety than those in the book at home." At the request of her parents, Apple also photographed Thai ingredients and dishes and suggested that the family plant a small Thai pepperbush, and find lemon grass and kaffir limes so that they could make "authentic" Thai food.[95]

Barbara Hansen first encountered Thai food in Thailand during the 1960s. Hansen, a food columnist for the *Los Angeles Herald Examiner* who was born and raised in Los Angeles, visited Bangkok twice during a three-month freighter trip through Asia in the 1960s. She stayed at the Royal Hotel in the heart of the city near the landmark Democracy monument. Here Hansen first tasted Thai food. She vividly recalls walking down from her hotel past the monument "to a restaurant called [Methavalai] Sorndaeng" that had "no air conditioning, no nothing, and nobody but Thais in there.

FIGURE 1. Peace Corps volunteers Bob and Barbara Drexler dining at a restaurant in Bangkok, Thailand, ca. 1969. Peace Corps volunteers in Thailand were among the many U.S. citizens to encounter Thai food abroad and among the first to introduce it inside the United States. Photograph courtesy of Granger Historical Picture Archive.

And the food, oh I was enchanted, oh it was so wonderful!"[96] Meda Croizat from Santa Monica, California also had her first encounter with Thai food around this time. The gourmet chef, home economics teacher, and "international hostess" traveled throughout Asia during the Cold War and became "Gung Ho for Oriental Cookery." She tried her first Thai dish in the 1950s in Bangkok where her husband, a U.S. Marine colonel, was stationed. By the late 1960s, Croizat had over twenty years of experience with Chinese cooking and developed a taste for and better understanding of Thai food. She described Thai cuisine as unique in comparison to other Asian foods because of the "spiciness of the curries and by the unusual and abundant fruits." Croizat especially liked mee krob, a sweet crispy noodle dish she said was a "favorite with all of us."[97]

Then there was, of course, Marie Wilson. Wilson became smitten with Thai cuisine when she traveled to Thailand in 1952 to marry her fiancé, who was teaching English in Bangkok as a Fulbright scholar. At first, Wilson recalled, "everything was so strange, I thought I would never get used to the very spicy foods, the humid, hot weather or the family customs."[98] The newlyweds, along with their newborn daughter Elizabeth, spent the next year and a half living in the country, of which she knew nothing upon arrival. But soon the "romance of Siam" swept her. She grew to love Thai food for its rich and highly seasoned dishes that "happily" combined Indian and Chinese origins. She found the greatest pleasure, however, in the cuisine's hot and spicy flavors: "we soon learned that hot food was only a Western idea but we never gave up trying to convince our cooks [hot] was better."[99]

New tastes, smells, sights, and sounds defined the encounters. The spiciness or hotness of some dishes awoke new parts of the palate for the culinary adventurers. Taste and smell informed Wilson's memory of Thailand or what she often, perhaps nostalgically, referred to as "Siam." In *Siamese Cookery* Wilson promised her readers that "new herbs and spices will fill your house with appetizing odors and make meal time an exciting adventure."[100] Jennifer Brennan, who first traveled to Thailand in the early 1960s to pursue opportunities for her [silk] business, fell in love with Thai food because of its "indescribable mixture of flavors."[101] As Brennan wrote in *The Original Thai Cookbook*, she was particularly impressed by the way Thai food awoke all the human senses: "elaborate preparation and decoration of each dish; unusual aromas; fragrant jasmine to pungent shrimp paste; a variety of textures and combination of finger foods; percussive musical sounds of fresh, juicy vegetables first contacting hot oil in a wok; and the rhythmic beat of a cleaver rapidly chopping on a board, counterpointed by the cadence of the 'thunk, thunk' of a mortar hammering a pestle—all climaxed by the incomparable, savory taste delight that is Thai."[102]

Within a few years, U.S. culinary adventurers like Wilson and Brennan developed an understanding of "authentic" Thai cuisine in the 1960s. They learned that unlike Western dinners that emphasized the main course, *khao* (white rice) was the centerpiece of a Thai meal. *Khao* was to contrast the highly seasoned and bold flavors of other, typically meat-based, dishes to be eaten with it, such as soup, curry, a steamed dish, or fried dish.[103] Sauces, like *nam plah* (fish sauce), accompanied these dishes. In addition, culinary explorers discovered that "Thais are very fond of sweetmeats" and dessert was "always special" in a Thai meal, which often ranged from sweet custards to fresh fruit—pineapple, mangosteen, rambutan, and durian.[104] They also found that Thais placed a great deal of importance on the decoration and appearance of dishes.

Wilson and Brennan also became experts on Thai ingredients, cooking methods, equipment, and the kitchen. In addition to rice, meat, fish, and vegetables, they familiarized themselves with fundamental ingredients in Thai cooking such as coconut and coconut milk, garlic, tamarind, coriander, lemon grass, and flower flavorings and essences.[105] They knew that chili peppers were a key ingredient used not just in the cooking process but also as garnishes during a meal. And both developed a working knowledge of the adobe-like stoves and charcoal pots inside Thai kitchens, along with woks, aluminum steamers, and, of course, the stoneware mortar and pestle used to pound ingredients like chili peppers, spices, and coconut flesh to "smooth, creamy substances."[106]

This growing fascination with Thai foodways embodied two different yet interrelated trends. First, it reflected Christina Klein's Cold War "global imaginary of integration"—a comprehensive framework that depicted the world as a place with porous borders and encouraged ordinary U.S. citizens to build cultural understanding in order to win the hearts and minds of peoples in Asia and the Pacific.[107] As the liberal counterpart to the culture of containment, such integration, ideally, would allow the United States to demonstrate to the world, especially amid rising anticolonial movements in the "darker nations," that it would lead not with force but by integrating Asia and the Pacific under U.S. influence and benevolence. Culinary tourists helped translate U.S. foreign policy objectives into sentimental and sensory bonds with Thailand for American consumers, breathing life into a broader "Cold War Orientalism." Second, it also reflected what Lisa Heldke calls "cultural food colonialism"—an "attitude problem" rooted in a colonial thirst for authenticity, adventure, and novelty among whites that could be quenched by finding and appropriating exotic cuisine. It was, in a sense, an edible version of "imperialist nostalgia."[108] This attitude justified U.S. political and economic forms of imperialism and neocolonialism in the region. Together, the global imaginary of integration and cultural food colonialism captured the way U.S. citizens participated in the drama of U.S. global expansion through everyday practices of food.

The more knowledge they gained, the more authority U.S. culinary tourists felt they had over not only Thai food but also the intricacies of Thai society. Thai food became a quick and easy window into Thai history, culture, and the hearts and minds of Thai people. Encounters with Thai food allowed them to play a key role in constructing an idealized image of Thailand and Thai people that appealed to the desires of white U.S. consumers. Brennan's narrative celebrated Thai cuisine as the embodiment of Thailand's history of political craftiness and flexibility. She considered Thailand's "bend, not break" posture in the face of "prevailing winds, whether political, martial, religious or cultural" as a "trait" that allowed the nation to maintain its independence and sovereignty amid European colonialism and war with neighboring groups in Southeast Asia.[109]

The result, according to Brennan, was not a mere regional adaptation of Chinese food, but a combination of indigenous T'ai, Chinese, Indian, and even Portuguese influences that evolved over thousands of years of "emigration, confrontation, and accommodation." The early Siamese, or T'ai, ate rice, fish, and game with sauces of garlic, peppercorns, and ginger. The Chinese contributed soups, noodles, other meats (duck), and stir-fry cooking methods. Indian and Arab merchants from the Middle East introduced cardamom, coriander, cumin, and other spices along with antecedents to Thai dishes, such as curries and *satay*. And the Portuguese brought small yet fiery chili peppers in the early 1500s, which flourished in Thailand's soil. For Brennan and others, one group's food culture did not obliterate another. Instead, the complex yet well-balanced flavors of Thai cuisine in the 1960s was rooted in one main characteristic of Thailand and Thai people: their ability to seamlessly "absorb foreign influences and translate them into something uniquely Thai."[110] In short, Thai food was testament to Thailand's history of foreign relations.

Thai foodways provided a gateway into the rhythm and pace of Thai life and society. With an ethnographic approach and tone similar to their academic counterparts, U.S. culinary adventurers painted a picture of a premodern, idyllic existence but also a modern "melting pot." Although seemingly contradictory, these visions together highlighted the rustic origins and unified elements of Thai cuisine that was to represent Thailand as a whole. In *Siamese Cookery* Wilson wrote based on her experience in Bangkok that "it does not take long to realize that the Siamese are a water people ... restaurant boats selling curries, coffee, and cake." "And on these boats," she marveled, "whole families spend their lives, selling, cooking, and eating, especially cooking and eating which the Siamese love to do. Everywhere, on water or on land, the charcoal stove on which rice is being cooked is fanned by a man, woman, or child. Every hour of the day I saw families squatting in a circle, laughing, talking, and eating their rice."[111]

Brennan observed a slightly different Thai population that was more demographically diverse. She described Bangkok as a city of contrasts filled with striking "kaleidoscopic" crowds of people: "Small, dark southern Thai, their flattened features showing a kinship to the Malays; paler skinned

Northerners; Chinese merchants; bearded and turbaned Sikhs; saffron-robed monks with shaved heads; aristocrats, whose aquiline features betray an ancient Brahmin heritage, and . . . school children in spotless uniforms."[112] All of these people, she believed, represented Bangkok. Yet from out of these differences, Brennan concluded, stood a distinct, one-of-a-kind Thai culture as these groups transcended racial, ethnic, national, regional, and religious lines and blended together to create a strong common identity. As if she formulated her view using contemporary U.S. assimilation theories, Brennan asserted that Thais, "as a race," have their origins "far from their present homeland. Their religion is an adaptation of Indian Buddhism. Their language is a synthesis of several tongues. Their culture is an amalgam of those of their neighbors—yet they possess an ethnic cohesiveness lacking in other Southeast Asian countries."[113] For U.S. culinary tourists, Thai food best exemplified this uniform Thai culture.

The romanticized view flattened power relations between white Western nations and Thailand. For instance, when Brennan applauded Thailand's ability to remain independent and sovereign, she implied that Thais were on an equal playing field and even had an advantage over Europeans. "In the winds of colonial wars," she wrote, "European oak could crack while the Thai bamboo would bend but, invariably, whip back to its firmly rooted, original posture."[114] The depictions also ignored power relations within Thailand. While culinary tourists acknowledged the history of political disputes and wars between the T'ai and other groups in the region—such as the Chinese, Burmese, and Khmer—they masked, under the veil of a harmonious multiculturalism, the process by which these groups became incorporated into the Thai nation and the subsequent social divisions and unequal positions they held in society.

In the mid twentieth century the heavily militarized and dictatorial Thai nation-state, bolstered by U.S. support, intensified efforts to craft a unified imagined Thailand out of its diverse citizenry as part of its pursuit of development and anticommunism. They demanded that all adopt the Thai language, convert to Buddhism, publicly display loyalty, and in essence embrace the national ideology of "nation, religion, and king." Thai leaders often resorted to violence and arrests to manufacture this homogenous Thai identity and culture, especially in areas with different religious, cultural, and linguistic traditions than what the Thai nation-state envisioned, such as in the southern provinces where the majority of people spoke a Malay dialect and practiced Islam.[115] They were consumed with trying to purge the nation and its history of all things Chinese over the fear of communist infiltration. In fact, food was a vehicle for extending nationalist ideology. In the 1940s, Prime Minister Phibunsongkhram's nationalist movement led to the creation of what would become the iconic wok-fried noodle dish, *Pad Thai*. Phibunsongkhram wanted a symbolic "Thai" national dish to counter the cultural influence of Thailand's Chinese population.[116] Thus, when U.S. culinary tourists celebrated Thais for their ability to blend differences and create a common culture they failed to recognize power, as it was a coerced movement into a dominant culture.

Cookbook authors had no reason or desire to highlight the history and violence of colonialism, nationalism, ethnocentrism, and social rifts. And culinary tourists did not want to confront any of it either. So the issue was not so much that Wilson and Brennan willfully ignored or misrepresented Thai society to build a romanticized version of Thailand. Rather, they believed, like fellow ethnographers and social scientists, that they were revealing the core of Thai history, people, and culture. The issue was that they, with some level of awareness, helped produce an idealized rendering they wanted to believe existed. As culinary adventurers, they enticed U.S. consumers to Thailand with the promise of an exotic paradise where local natives catered to all of the senses. For Wilson and Brennan, Thai food culture—its feel, sights, smells, morals, ethics, and behaviors—could best introduce this fantasy.

In a way, authoring and publishing some of the first Thai cookbooks outside of Thailand constituted a colonial practice that allowed white American women to become and act as authorities on Thai food. Taking cooking methods that were passed down orally and then publishing them in written form enabled these women to establish expertise and ownership of a food culture different from their own. Translating so-called inaccessible cooking methods into recipes during the Cold War standardized and thus "modernized" Thai food practices into a science in which ingredients could be measured, cooked, and replicated inside the home with new appliances. Also, being the first to present recipes in English turned them into authorities because they, by default, appeared to be the only ones with knowledge on the topic.[117]

Writing and publishing cookbooks meant more than introducing Thai cuisine, ingredients, recipes, and cooking methods. In her critique of the Indian-born food writer and actress Madhur Jaffrey, Parama Roy argues that the most compelling cookbooks are hardly ever utilitarian or simply just a collection of useful recipes for the home cook. On the contrary, they offer "autobiography rather than the recipe."[118] Thai cookbooks served as a platform for white housewives to present themselves as worldly, cultured individuals and explorers of foreign cultures with exciting stories to tell. As cultural outsiders, they had to convince their audience of adventurous readers that the collection of Thai recipes was indeed authentic and vastly different. To achieve this, authors almost always detailed their extensive travel through Thailand and submersion into Thai society and life. They demonstrated knowledge of Thai ingredients and mastery over cooking techniques. And they played up their personal relationships with "native informants" to not only authenticate recipes but also to show a willingness to accept exotic Others. Jennifer Brennan was skillful at using autobiographical narrative in her cookbooks to represent people and places as exotic. Yet, she was especially adept at supplying memories that spurred a sense of nostalgia among her readers—even for those who had never experienced the food firsthand.[119] For instance, Brennan's *Curries and Bugles*, a memoir-cookbook on Indian cuisine under British colonialism she published several years after *The Original Thai Cookbook*, was well received in Britain for the way it conjured a "Raj nostalgia" ethos. Britain's national newspaper described *Curries and Bugles* as "the perfect present for anyone who has had connections with the subcontinent, but for those who haven't she also manages to create an aching sense of nostalgia."[120]

So while American culinary tourists found excitement in getting to know an exotic culture, they also reinforced uneven power relationships and colonial dynamics. The insatiable appetite for Thai cuisine was at once a feeling and longing for colonialism, or imperialist nostalgia.[121] They received enormous pleasure in Thai foodways because during meals they got to experience what it was like to be truly revered, respected, and catered to by Others whose main goal appeared to be to service their every need. In *The Original Thai Cookbook* Brennan set an old colonial backdrop and invited readers to imagine themselves at the center of the story: "It is dusk in Bangkok and you are going out to dinner. The chauffeured Mercedes 280 sweeps you from your luxury hotel through streets lined with large, spreading trees and picturesque tile-roofed wooden shops and houses . . . Delicious smells of spiced, barbequed chicken and pungent curries assail your nostrils and sharpen your appetite as your car passes little street-front restaurants." "You pull up before a traditional teakwood Thai house," she continued, "greeted by an exquisite, delicately boned Thai woman, youthful but of indeterminate age." Brennan next walked readers through a Thai meal: "seated in these ornate chairs, you are aware of a soft voice at your elbow as another slender girl in traditional Thai dress offers drinks and places a bronze tray filled with an assortment of tiny hors d'oeuvres before you." She closed the narrative, "you rise at the behest of your hostess and are escorted into a steeply beamed, large room. . . . You try to sit down as gracefully as your tall, angular Western frame will allow" and are served "a parade of unfamiliar and exotic dishes."[122] So in addition to new flavors, tastes, and textures, a major appeal of Asian and Pacific food culture was the chance to experience being atop a global racialized social hierarchy—to be revered as colonizers of old.

U.S. global expansion in Thailand allowed white U.S. citizens to bring their Thai culinary discoveries back home, especially to Los Angeles. In addition to authoring cookbooks like *Siamese Cookery* and *The Original Thai Cookbook*, they also threw dinner parties and taught cooking classes to introduce Thai cuisine to other white suburbanites. When Marie Wilson returned home to West Los Angeles she regularly cooked Thai food for fellow housewives. The rave feedback she received after "enchanting" them with hot and spicy dishes inspired Wilson to publish her cookbook. When Brennan returned to Los Angeles in the 1970s she had accumulated over twenty years of travel experience in East and Southeast Asia, India, and Pakistan. She also taught Chinese and Indian cooking during her travels.[123] Brennan's sensory experiences and knowledge of Thai food compelled her to teach evening Thai cooking classes for white housewives in the recreation room of her Santa Monica apartment building. Her $30 courses, based on participation rather than typical demonstration, were often overcrowded.

The booming interest in Thai foodways was part of a much broader fascination with "Oriental" cookery sweeping white suburbanites during the Cold War. Although middle- and upper-class white Americans had been eating in Chinese restaurants since the late nineteenth and early twentieth centuries (when it was considered urban slumming with the dirty Chinese), the postwar period witnessed the increased popularity of Asian cuisine and restaurants. For suburbanites, spending a night out at an Oriental restaurant was a meaningful social and cultural experience. At the time most Chinese establishments served Cantonese and Mandarin dishes in addition to the more familiar "chop-suey"—a stir-fried dish of meat, eggs, bean sprouts, cabbage, and celery in a thickened sauce. Restaurant owners also catered to non-Asian guests, developing Western-style menus with combination dinners that had diners choosing a set meal from either column A or B. Owners also decorated their restaurants in ways that played up to white fantasies of Asia and the Pacific. In the 1950s, for example, Trader Vic's tiki-themed restaurant at the Savoy Hotel in New York City became a huge hit as customers came in droves for the tropical drinks, especially the *mai tais*.[124] Although Trader Vic's represented Polynesian fare, they mainly served Cantonese dishes including *rumaki* (Polynesian hors d'oeuvre usually made with water chestnuts and duck or chicken liver wrapped in bacon), crab Rangoon (deep-fried wonton with crab and cream cheese filling), and Calcutta lamb curry as well as egg rolls, fried rice, wonton soup, barbecued pork, almond chicken, and beef with tomato. Restaurants like Trader Vic's were so popular that they inspired copycats such as the Kon-Tiki Club in Chicago, which advertised "escape to the South Seas!" and offered a complete Cantonese dinner for $1.85 to $3.25.[125] The craze for Polynesian-style restaurants serving Cantonese food continued well into the 1970s, popping up in different parts of the United States.

Outside of restaurants, the growing interest in Asian and Pacific cuisine manifested in a variety of ways in lily-white suburbs with very few Asians or Asian Americans (and in many cases historically hostile toward Asians).[126] A number of white women authored cookbooks filled with recipes they appropriated from peoples they came in contact with. Many suburban housewives hosted dinner parties featuring foreign dishes and, for some, costumes.[127] Others displayed their expertise by teaching cooking classes and demonstrations for local civic organizations, church groups, and clubs. In Los Angeles' San Gabriel Valley in 1963, Margo Wells provided a cooking demonstration of "Oriental foods" to the Alhambra-San Gabriel Chapter of the Daughters of the American Revolution as part of their "Oriental Hour" themed benefit brunch.[128] The PATA banquet hosted in Newport Beach in 1959 also featured Asian and Pacific food as a one of the more delicious rewards of traveling to the region. Guests indulged in epicurean delights of Australian rock-shell oysters on the half shell, Indian spiced Mulligatawny soup, New Zealand lamb chops, Japanese sake, coconut sauce from the Philippines, and Kona coffee and fresh pineapple spears from the newly admitted state of Hawaii.[129]

White American women, particularly suburban housewives, were integral to introducing Asian and Pacific foodways to adventurous eaters inside the United States. Their access to and participation in food cultures was more than just an "attitude problem." It can be considered a colonial practice in and of itself, as they extracted recipes and culinary practices as raw materials and turned them into commodities to be sold in the U.S. marketplace. They benefitted by becoming authorities and in being recognized for their "discovery" of foodways that were not new—except to white American consumers.

Yet at the same time, the cookbooks, cooking courses, and dinner parties reflected their attempts to elevate their social status to challenge Cold War gender roles and suburban life. The "insatiable appetite" for Oriental cookery happened simultaneously with the postwar construction of suburban whiteness, characterized by intense cultural crackdowns and conformity, particularly around gender conventions. In a moment when nearly everything *looked* the same—houses, appliances, cars, and even the housewives themselves— one way they distinguished themselves was to deliver new flavors, tastes, smells, and stories. They relied on exotic tastes, smells, and problematic representations and performances of Oriental Others to make themselves appear more interesting, cultured, and unique to stand out from other suburban homemakers. But as white women used Asian and Pacific food culture to negotiate gender conventions, these acts of culinary appropriation also worked to construct and affirm their whiteness.

Most importantly, U.S. Cold War intervention in Asia and the Pacific allowed these women to move through and between the expanding U.S. empire to profit "at home." The U.S. global postwar infrastructure of military bases, embassies, financial institutions, businesses, private organizations, aid programs, and hotels led to the creation of transnational pathways, networks, and spaces for U.S. citizens to engage food cultures in different parts of the world for the first time. U.S. citizens devoured Asian and Pacific food with great enthusiasm as they traveled the Cold War world as volunteers, tourists, or simply to join spouses. It was under these conditions that white Americans "fell in love" with Oriental cuisine—and how others came to know and love food cultures of Asia and the Pacific. Foodways allowed white American women to participate in the drama of postwar U.S. empire.

NEGOTIATING U.S. EMPIRE THROUGH FOODWAYS

Thai food culture enlivened Thailand's U.S.-centered tourist industry and created the conditions for a neocolonial economy to flourish. The largely informal U.S. tourist encounters with Thai cuisine sparked a nascent culinary tourism in the 1960s that, even in its early stages, cornered Thailand and Thai people into a service-based economy. To borrow from historian Hal Rothman, the Thai government entered into a "devil's bargain," catering to the gustatory desires of U.S. consumers at the expense of the basic needs of local populations. Culinary tourism benefited interests outside of communities it was supposed to make economically viable in the first place. Fueled by the global imaginary of integration and cultural food colonialism, culinary tourism would alter the Thai economy and food systems.

Yet, Thais had their own goals and expectations of their encounters with U.S. tourism and culinary tourists. Adria Imada, Jana Lipman, and Dennis Merrill have illustrated that postwar U.S. tourism, as the cultural counterpart to U.S. political and economic imperialism, was not an all-powerful, uniform, or one-directional system of domination. It was a "textured and fluid structure" of inequality and resistance that hosts interacted with from the bottom up.[130] As the country's service sector economy boomed, Bangkok transformed into a playground for U.S. tourists (and wealthy Thai socialites). The development of hotels, restaurants, coffee shops and other leisure spaces attracted young Thai men and women from the rural countryside. They went to the city, learned English, and made money working service jobs—as waiters and waitresses, bartenders, hotel receptionists, tour guides, and souvenir shop clerks. Luxury hotels in particular provided a space for Thais to learn fruit, vegetable, ice, and butter carving to entertain tourists.[131] Thais on the lower end of the social order, especially Thai women, found that packaging and peddling Thai food culture to tourists was a viable economic prospect.

The intimate encounters that took place within Thailand's culinary contact zones also made it possible for Thais to negotiate and resist the increased American influence in all sorts of ways beyond formal commercial exchanges. One of the more typical forms involved Thai domestic servants who took personal advantage of American visitors—especially those who made the mistake of assuming that all Thais could cook good Thai food. To Marie Wilson, Thai cooks and servants were "indispensible" in helping with the adjustment to Thailand. During their time in the country, the Wilson family hired Thai domestic servants to shop at the local market and cook meals. However, Wilson recalled being "either 'squeezed' on the food money, or forced to care for dozens of the cooks' ne'er-do-well relatives, or fed poorly cooked food, or just not fed enough." The family, she wrote, "felt put upon, deprived, and bullied."[132] While her servants had introduced the family to Thai cuisine, they apparently (and quite literally) left a bad taste in the Wilsons' mouths.

Culinary contact zones also allowed ordinary Thais to meet American officials and distinguished travelers, especially in hotels. They struck up conversations and developed friendships. In some cases, Thais learned of new culinary opportunities in the United States. Above all, what happened in Thailand did not stay in Thailand. U.S. tourism and culinary encounters that took place within the context of U.S. intervention meant that the legacy of an intensive U.S. foreign presence would play itself out within the formal boundaries of the United States. The combination of U.S. Cold War politics and tourist culture paved the way for U.S. citizens to participate in the construction of imaginings of Thailand and Thai people, to have direct contact with Thai food, and to fuel the appetite for the exotic Other's cuisine. It also set the stage for Thai migration to the United States. The informal U.S. empire and immigration functioned as part of a "single global phenomenon" that stimulated the movement of both foods *and* people to the United States.[133] Upon arriving in Los Angeles, Thai immigrants negotiated the social, political, and economic consequences of U.S. empire through foodways.

TWO

———

"Chasing the Yum*"*

FOOD PROCUREMENT AND EARLY
THAI LOS ANGELES

IN 1971, THE GRAND OPENING of the Bangkok Market in East Hollywood, California, marked a watershed in the history of Thai food culture and Thai American community formation in the United States. Pramorte "Pat" Tilakamonkul, a Thai immigrant who arrived in Los Angeles at the age of twenty-six, opened a grocery store on the northwest corner of Melrose Avenue and North Harvard Boulevard. Inside, small checkout counters with conveyor belts partitioned the cozy store into two sections. Five aisles lined the west end, with a produce aisle stocked with, among other offerings, Thai basil, kaffir limes, golf-ball-sized greenish-white Thai eggplant, lemon grass, jackfruit, and green papaya. In the other aisles sat sixteen types of canned curry paste, different varieties of smoked, pickled, and dried fish in bags, cans, or freezer packs, and high-quality long-grain white and flavored rice in 20-, 50-, and 100-pound bags. At the east end of the store, customers could find Thai butchers behind a meat counter preparing cuts of beef, pork, chicken, and assorted organ meats next to a wide array of seafood imported from Asia and a variety of fresh fish not available elsewhere in Los Angeles.[1]

The Bangkok Market was the first of its kind. It was a major deal for Thais in Los Angeles. The acquisition of Thai foodstuffs, or food procurement, was an essential Thai American community-building practice in the 1960s and 1970s. For Thai migrants, tracking down and securing a supply of "authentic" ingredients was integral to the reconstruction of "wholeness" amid the physical, social, and cultural dislocation triggered by America's post-World War II involvement in Thailand.[2] Before the Bangkok Market opened its doors, Thai and Southeast Asian produce and ingredients were not widely available. Lacking necessary ingredients, Thai migrants turned to local vegetables, herbs, and other goods (mainly Chinese) to simulate Thai flavors at home and in restaurants. But as they tried to reproduce the complex and balanced Thai flavor profile of salty, sour, sweet, and spicy—known as *yum*—the absence of authentic ingredients led to a crisis of identity among a geographically dispersed Thai immigrant population. Taste and flavor thus played a critical role in early Thai American community and identity formation, both real and imagined.

A cadre of Thais, many of them first-wave migrants, resolved the crisis by first smuggling fruits, produce, and vegetables from Thailand and later working to establish a local supply of Thai and Southeast Asian ingredients by opening grocery stores and import/export companies that connected Thailand, Los Angeles, Fresno, and Mexico.[3] The Bangkok Market in particular helped create the necessary conditions for Thai food culture in the United States and the formation of a Thai American community. Because Tilakamonkul and his business partners negotiated the web of U.S. trade policies and barriers throughout the 1960s to the 1980s, the era before free trade under the North American Free Trade Agreement (NAFTA), the Bangkok Market came into existence, Thai restaurants opened, and Thai dishes were prepared without using too many substitute ingredients—all leading the Thai community to form around foodways. In addition, food procurement was a collective activity that brought people together and cultivated social and economic networks, and was crucial to the development of early Thai American life, because Thais had few formal organizations (labor unions, political groups, social clubs), cultural activities, or community spaces that could otherwise bring them together.

The history of Thai food procurement uncovers the way asymmetrical relations allow for such consumption and access to certain kinds of food. More specifically, attention to food procurement expands and nuances our understanding of the way borders shape social relations and impact people's lives. On the one hand, borders determined Thai immigrants' access to foodstuffs from Thailand and Southeast Asia. The U.S. nation-state, through a tangled network of import trade regulations, government agencies, and free-trade zones, regulated when, where, and how foreign foodstuffs entered the country.

On the other hand, Thai migration was also a product of the United States expanding its influence beyond its borders into Thailand. American intervention in Thailand during the Cold War, coupled with domestic immigration policies, directly shaped Thai migration patterns and Thai foodways. The restructuring of Thailand's education system along American lines allowed Thais, young and old, to learn about U.S. culture and society through first-hand experience in exchange programs. The experiences encouraged thousands of Thais to pursue student visas to study in the United States. However, many would eventually use "nonimmigrant" student visas, and then later tourist visas, as a way to bypass restrictive immigration requirements to join family members and friends already in the country. Thousands would overstay their visas, become *exdocumented*, and build new lives in Los Angeles. These Thai students were among the first Thai restaurateurs, opening makeshift Thai food establishments across the city to cater to fellow Thais.

THAI MIGRATION TO LOS ANGELES

Thais came to the United States in large numbers during the late 1950s. The first wave, between 1945 and 1965, was made up primarily of male government officials, political elites, and formally educated middle-class Thais from urban Bangkok. The second wave happened after the passage of the Immigration Act of 1965. This second wave altered gender and class dynamics among Thai Americans because it included a significantly higher number of women, younger migrants, tourists, students, and a lower number of professionals. Between 1965 and 1975, Thais arrived in more numbers than any other immigrant group, as the United States admitted a total of 25,705 Thai immigrants, 95,183 Thai nonimmigrants, and 396 Thai Americans.[4] By the late 1970s an estimated 100,000 Thai immigrants and Thai Americans were in the country.[5]

Unlike other Southeast Asians who entered during this period, Thais were not categorized as refugees fleeing war. Instead, U.S. cultural diplomacy and militarization facilitated Thai immigration. The U.S. presence in Thailand allowed Thais to learn about American society. Aroon Seeboonruang, along with other "Westernized" Thais who enthusiastically supported U.S. state-sponsored activities, was one of the first Thais to immigrate to the U.S. in the 1950s. His experiences reflect how U.S. cultural diplomacy won over some hearts and minds, influencing Thais to view America in a positive light. Seeboonruang helped train U.S. Peace Corps volunteers before they embarked on their assignments throughout Thailand. He remembered that the goal was "for Americans to go and help . . . those who haven't learned, to help the poor rural areas."[6] A volunteer himself under a two-year contract,

Seeboonruang taught thirty Peace Corps volunteers about Thai language and customs, earning an award for his help. Fondly recalling his service, he stated, "this is one example of how I helped America, because I volunteered to go help America."

Meanwhile, Cold War interests compelled the United States to make changes to its immigration policies. Congress passed an array of immigration legislation aimed at eliminating racial and ethnic bans to immigration and naturalization, in order to better relations with Asian and Pacific nations specifically and present itself as a true leader of the free world more broadly. U.S. international alliances during the Cold War, as Madeline Hsu has detailed, "improved acceptance of certain kinds of Asian immigrants and conditions for their permanent settlement" in ways that shifted U.S. immigration laws and ideologies and, as a result, transformed Asian American communities.[7] The passage of the 1952 Immigration and Nationality Act granted a quota of 105 for each Asian nation, removed restrictions against immigration from the "Asiatic Barred Zone," and did away with barriers that prevented Asian and Asian Americans from becoming naturalized citizens.[8] The piecemeal legislative changes culminated with the passage of the Immigration and Nationality Act of 1965, or the Hart-Celler Act, which eliminated the national origins quota system implemented in 1924 that had been based on a hierarchy of racial desirability that favored Northern Europeans and banned Asians. The 1965 Act also established a preference for family reunification and individuals with educational or job skills.

While the Immigration Act of 1965 liberalized immigration policies in ways that led to greater inclusions, it did not necessarily open the floodgates for immigration. Rather, the 1965 Act consisted of limitations, restrictions—notably the continued use and expansion of numerical quotas—and reforms that generated a dizzying web of statuses and gateways, each with their own path to legal citizenship.[9] For example, since Congress kept numerical quotas, student visas emerged as a pathway for permanent settlement for those who did not meet requirements or were excluded when quota limits were reached. In her study of Chinese student migration to the United States during the Cold War, Hsu revealed that new arrivals in this period gained entry through the "front gates" (preferential access as permanent residents eligible for citizenship), the "back door" (refugees and peoples entering unlawfully facing extensive barriers to legal citizenship), and what she calls the "side door" (migrants, such as students, using less scrutinized temporary visa statuses yet routinely gaining permanent status leading to citizenship).[10] Perhaps more importantly, foreign students were considered the right kind of immigrants. As conduits for the "improvement and strengthening of international relations through cultural exchange and understanding," students entering the country as "nonimmigrants" were now allowed to adjust their status to permanent resident without leaving the country.[11]

The combination of U.S. intervention in Thailand and the "inclusionary and exclusionary features" of the Immigration Act of 1965 led to large numbers of Thais entering the United States through the "side door" with student visas.[12] Of all the Thais who entered the United States during this first wave (pre-1965), 78 percent arrived with F-1 visas, which for Thais consistently ranked as the top choice of all possible visas.[13] In 1975 the number of student visas issued to Thai students ranked sixth behind only the totals issued to students from Mexico, Iran, Japan, China, and Nigeria. By the late 1970s, roughly 30,000 Thai students were enrolled in colleges and universities across the United States.[14]

Initially, Thai students did not intend to stay permanently. They planned on returning to Thailand equipped with more social and cultural capital. For some, Los Angeles was simply a stop on the road toward a degree that would be useful in the homeland—such as Surasak Wongskhaluang, who attended Bangkok Christian College in Thailand and participated in a four-year student exchange to India before arriving in Los Angeles to study accounting at Long Beach City College in 1969.[15] Wongskhaluang believed his U.S. accounting degree would hold more value and prestige than one earned in Thailand. A more typical experience was that of Urai Ruenprom. Ruenprom, who also attended Bangkok Christian College, and first arrived in Los Angeles on August 1, 1964, at age 36 with a nonimmigrant multiple status visa.[16] Ruenprom's family and friends had advised him to visit America to finish school. While in Los Angeles, Ruenprom attended Sawyer Business College in downtown Los Angeles and later took courses at nearby Los Angeles City College, always believing that his time in the United States would be brief.

Thai student migration had become so prevalent that in 1974 Thai writer Wanit Jarungkitanan wrote a humorous short story about it titled "Michigan Test." The story, set in 1970s Thailand, centers on a young man who scrambles to get a passport and visa to join his brother and sister in Southern California.[17] Knowing that his only chance to enter the United States was as a student, his brother sends him an immigration form to attend a "no-name" school. He takes the form to a crowded American embassy in Bangkok, where United States Information Service (USIS) and embassy officials tell him that he must pass an English-language exam known as the Michigan Test at the American University Alumni to be granted the visa. He arrives at the AUA a few days later, hung-over, and when permitted to start the exam stares blankly at it because, he realizes, his English had "gone to pot." Then suddenly, he kicks out his chair, stands up in the auditorium of two hundred students and yells (in Thai):

> "Every one of you here is applying to become a slave of American imperialism ... You're the ones responsible for implanting rotten values in our society and widening class differences! You're the ones who go off to bring back a degenerate culture from America to Thailand! Why are you all heading for America? Is there really no place in Thailand where you can study? Or are you planning to tear up banknotes for fun? Or dig for gold? Or come back home as academic diplomats? It's all a bunch of lies. The truth is you don't have the wit to make a living here in Thailand. So you want to get a whiff of snow and then come back and show off as if you now belonged to a different class of people. Isn't that so?"[18]

With the room in silence, he makes a mad dash for the nearest door and escapes.

Despite being a work of fiction, Jarungkitanan's story captured the experiences of real Thai student migrants and the way U.S. educational programs and organizations—the AUA—acted as a channel for their entrance into the United States. Drawing perhaps on his personal experiences and observations as a Thai student at California State University, Long Beach at the time, he offered a glimpse into Thai life under the American Era and the ensuing rifts that compromised notions of "traditional" Thai identity and stimulated Thai migration to the United States. Jarungkitanan explicitly referred to the United States an imperialist nation, one whose influence increased in Thailand with the arrival of U.S. citizens and organizations. His climactic ending makes clear that he is just as interested with the way Thais appeared to be smitten by American culture and their desire to visit and experience it for themselves. Using his main character to accuse Thais who wished to study in America of wanting to "come back home as academic diplomats" along with the claim that "it's all a bunch of lies," Jarungkitanan challenged both the Thai and U.S. government's attempts to use student exchanges as acts of goodwill and cultural understanding during the Cold War. In addition, he deplored Thais who studied in America for tearing Thai society apart because of their new sense of prestige and class status. His view was in line with many U.S. educators, state officials, and Thai academics at the time—many observing that "Westernized" Thais had little respect for many elements of their own culture.[19] Thai professor of public administration Amara Raksasataya wrote that these well-to-do Thais try to "imitate what they feel is the 'up-to-date' living style of those who have been "gilded abroad" and play a part in the "deterioration of our society—the weakening of our moral standards."[20]

More importantly, Jarungkitanan revealed an important fact about Thai student migration: that few Thais students actually cared about going to the United States to study. His protagonist represented a growing number of Thais who entered with valid, legal student visas without any intention of completing degrees. According to the U.S. consulate in Bangkok in 1971, 75 percent of all Thai students in the United States ended up staying. Just a decade before, only 7 percent of students told the consulate they planned to stay. Geographer Jacqueline Desbarats, who examined Thai migration patterns closely during this period, also noticed, "the occupational composition of the Thai group has . . . begun to register a gradual alteration, characterized by an increase in the proportion of unskilled workers and by the decline in the average level of English proficiency at the time of arrival. Curiously, this trend corresponds with the arrival of large numbers of Thai students."[21] Clearly, Thais were setting their own agendas and taking advantage of opportunities afforded by U.S. expansion without buying into U.S. propaganda about students as cultural diplomats.

Getting the U.S. embassy to issue a student visa required a great deal of legwork and coordination among separate entities in Thailand and the United States. In addition to obtaining a passport, the first step was to get an accredited institution in the United States to issue an I-20 form, which certifies acceptance for enrollment, and then to bring it to the U.S. embassy. Next, stricter English language requirements by American embassies in the 1960s meant Thais had to prove English competency by either passing the "Test of English as a Foreign Language" (TOEFL) or an equivalent examination. Finally, one had to show proof of financial support with a signed letter from a financial guarantor, along with a bank statement.

U.S. higher education became increasingly entangled with U.S. immigration law and policies. While the process of obtaining a student visa was easier than applying to enter as an "immigrant," it was still a messy process. Student migrations meant that the responsibility of enforcing U.S. immigration policy fell on U.S. embassy, consulate, university, and college officials. The U.S.

embassy in Bangkok acted like an immigration station. Embassy and consular officials had to assess the validity of I-20 forms, conduct background checks, process paperwork, and then issue visas. Embassy officials, often with little staff help, carried the burden of "playing god" by relying on their own instincts and assumptions about visa applicants to allow or deny entry to the United States every few minutes.[22] But university and college officials also got in on the act. Gloria Green of the Glendale College of Business and Paramedical, a private vocational school in Glendale, California, responded to accusations that her campus was a hotbed for counterfeit I-20 forms by saying, "I run a very tight ship here. . . if they come in this country and go to my school, I expect them to go to my school. We keep careful records, and if they don't attend the required 25 hours a week, I report them to the immigration service."[23]

As a result, Thai students often sought to attend schools that issued I-20 forms without very much discretion. These included places such as California State University, Long Beach; California State University, Los Angeles; Los Angeles City College; and private and trade schools such as Whittier College and Sawyer Business College in downtown Los Angeles. When embassies and universities implemented stricter enforcement of academic requirements for student visa applications, specifically command of the English language, Thais simply "black-marketed" blank I-20 forms.[24] More elaborate forms of fraud also appeared. For instance, to guarantee approval of a student visa, applicants had to produce proof of financial support with a statement from a Thai bank. Thais with modest to limited means worked around this requirement by having friends or employers deposit money into a bank account, printing the bank statement, and once the visa was granted, withdrawing the money and returning it before they departed for the United States.[25] So while Thai student migration appeared to be middle-class, working-class Thais also used student visas to bypass immigration requirements and settle in the country.

By the 1970s, Los Angeles became home to the largest Thai population in the United States and outside of Thailand. The number of Thais in Los Angeles (including those without legal status) grew from 300 to 400 in 1965 to an estimated 40,000 by the late 1970s.[26] Although some observers reasoned that Thais settled in Los Angeles because of warm climate "comfortable for Asian people" and the city's reputation for racial and ethnic diversity, it is more likely that Los Angeles' large number of colleges, universities, trade, and adult schools served as the primary "pull" factor.[27] Put another way, the top destinations for Thais after California were New York, Illinois, Ohio, Michigan, Connecticut, and Massachusetts—which were not necessarily places with warm climate or racial and ethnic diversity. What these states had were colleges and universities, some with long-standing relationships with Thailand. Thai settlement in Los Angeles also did not resemble an ethnic enclave. Rather, it was scattered, at times thirty miles apart, as Thai students lived mostly near their respective campuses and schools.

BECOMING "ROBIN HOODS"

By the early 1970s many Thai students soon found themselves outside of legal status—as exdocumented. Increased tuition costs for international students in California hurt Thais' ability to stay in good legal status.[28] It became a near-insurmountable barrier to the successful completion of their degrees within the time allotted on a student visa. They struggled to pay for school because they were ineligible for U.S. loans, granted limited funding from their home countries, and could work on campus for no more than twenty hours per week only after they had been studying for at least a year. Moreover, the recession reserved most jobs for students who were U.S. citizens. Urai Ruenprom's wife, Parsomsee, remembers how her husband helped fellow Thais not only obtain I-20 forms but also that "if anyone needed a job, and many of us did because we all came by way of student visa and were disparately [sic] poor, he would always find a job for them."[29] As a result, Thai students were forced to violate the terms of their visas and find work, which more often than not led them to drop out of college altogether and overstay.

It was right around this time that Thais in Los Angeles began using the slang term "Robin Hoods" to refer to Thais outside of legal status. Although the precise origin of the term is unclear, Jirah Krittayapong claims that it most likely originated from the famous English folklore tale of the outlaw character Robin Hood who stole money from the wealthy and gave it to the poor.[30] Krittayapong suggests that the tale "seems to parallel the situation of undocumented Thai immigrants who come to work in the U.S. (richer country) in order to collect money and send it back to help their families in Thailand (poorer country)." Yet it is more likely that Thais used the term to underscore the noble "outlaw" existence of Thai visa holders who broke the law (by overstaying) but for a greater moral good (to build a better life for themselves and their families). In this way, the Thai use of the Robin Hood image can be understood as a critique of U.S. immigration law, just as the figure of Robin Hood represented a critique of authority and laws that protected the ruling class.

Of course, there was an alternative to overstaying visas. One way to remain in the United States legally was to change one's visa status from "nonimmigrant" to "immigrant," and a good number of Thais did so. By the mid-1970s, 550 Thais had adjusted their status to permanent resident (out of 836 total adjustments within the population), including Urai Ruenprom and Aroon Seeboonruang.[31] However, in order to be eligible to change ones status, the Immigration Act of 1965 required that "an alien must be physically present for at least five years to prove a commitment to American society and the establishment of roots that would make deportation too harsh to endure."[32] More specifically, it was difficult for Thai student migrants to change their visa status because many had already violated the conditions of their visa by working but also staying longer than the time allowed (almost always less than five years).

The number of Thai Robin Hoods grew well into the 1970s and 1980s. U.S. consul officials in Thailand estimated that out of the 65,000 Thais in Los Angeles in 1980, more than half were undocumented.[33] But by the end of the 1970s more Thai Robin Hoods had entered with tourist or "temporary visitors for pleasure" visas, officially known as the B-2 visa. Tourist visas surpassed student visas as the top visa choice among Thai migrants in 1975. According to Immigration and Naturalization records, in that year 4,709 Thai nonimmigrants entered the U.S. for the purpose of "pleasure."[34] For the first time, the number of Thais who entered on student visas dropped to 3,340 by the middle of the decade.[35] Thai tourists accounted for nearly half of all nonimmigrants admitted.

As with a student visa, Thais had to apply for a B-2 visa at the U.S. embassy in Thailand and navigate U.S. consular and embassy officials. Since Thais saw a tourist visa as a method of immigration if they did not meet the criteria to enter as an "immigrant," they relied on a range of strategies to guarantee the approval of their application. When questioned by U.S. consular officials about why they wished to visit the United States (to which a wrong answer got the tourist visa application denied), Thais often lied about their intentions. When one Thai man was asked by a U.S. consular official if he had ever applied for a visa for the United States, the man shook his head and replied "No," despite the fact that he applied several years earlier and returned to try again under a different name, disguised in glasses. These failed attempts compelled the head of the U.S. consulate office in Bangkok, Richard Milton, to explain that "most of the people who come in here ... who lie about their intentions ... are people who need jobs and will work hard. But we don't grant visas to people just because they're nice."[36]

Another requirement, similar to that of the student visa process, asked applicants to show proof of financial support, property, and family ties as evidence that they had obligations to return to Thailand upon completion of their visit. For instance, U.S. officials demanded a statement showing no less than $15,000 secured in a Thai bank. This was a difficult task because Thais who sought to immigrate using a B-2 visa had only enough money to purchase travel fare. To circumvent the requirement, Thais would ask friends or employers to deposit the money in a bank, print the bank statement to show as proof, and once the visa was granted, the money would then be withdrawn and returned before they departed.

The numerous strategies, and in some cases multiple attempts, used by Thais to obtain a tourist visa were not unique to Thai people. However, Thais were perceived quite differently than other groups. "The nice thing about these people is that they don't argue," U.S. consul Donald E. Stadler disclosed to a *Los Angeles Times* reporter, "In Latin America, if you catch them in a lie, they start screaming about their human rights."[37] Moreover, state officials were more likely to overlook Thai "illegal immigration" because they were more concerned with Latinos. As one consular official put it, "why worry about 10,000 Thais when there are 600,000 Hispanics coming across the border?"[38]

The increased number of Thai tourist migrants coincided with the arrival of more women, which marked a pivotal shift in the gender dynamics of the Thai American population as a whole. In 1976 Thai women made up 74 percent of all Thai immigrants, a percentage higher than female immigrants in any immigrant group, including those from the Philippines, Korea, India, and China. In addition, Thai female immigrants also differed from their male counterparts in terms of marital status. That same year, 42 percent of Thai women entered the United States under the category "wives of U.S. citizens."[39] This significant portion of the estimated 100,000 Thai immigrants in the United States most likely married U.S. military officials and GIs and became war brides. While individuals of Asian ancestry were denied entry to the United States between 1924 and 1965, U.S. servicemen were allowed to bring their Thai war brides into the United States as nonquota immigrants under the 1945 War Brides Act.[40] As Susan Koshy reminds us, U.S. immigration law "served as a mechanism of selective incorporation of interracial sexual relationships" that continued to shape the lives of Asian American women well after 1965.[41] By 1980 the U.S. census reported that 40 percent of Thai women living in the United States were wives of U.S. military veterans.

Furthermore, a little over half had husbands who were veterans of the Vietnam War, specifically.[42]

The arrival of Thai war brides to the United States meant that the Thai American population as a whole continued to be geographically dispersed across the country and Los Angeles. Thai women married to American GIs and other U.S. citizens found themselves in large cities and small towns far away from other Thais and, in many cases, people of color in general.[43] In Los Angeles, the spatial dispersion of Thais across the region can also be attributed, to an extent, to the migration of Thai wives of retired GIs. Although some successful Thai businessmen and professionals became homeowners in suburban San Gabriel Valley, San Fernando Valley, and Glendale, U.S. veterans and their Thai wives who benefitted from the federal government's G.I. mortgage program were most likely responsible for the increased rate of homeownership for Thais at the end of the Vietnam War.[44]

Benedict Anderson and Ruchida Mendiones have argued that the impact of U.S. intervention on Thai society was "as much cultural as social," and that by the 1970s it had generated "something quite new in Thai history—the permanent settlement of large numbers of Thai in a California to which they were already culturally acclimatized before their departure."[45] While exposure to American cultural norms may have served as a primer for life in U.S. society, the migration experience and scattered settlement pattern led to a jarring sense of disjunction and fragmentation. Concerns over legal status only heightened the sense of dislocation and isolation. Exdocumented Thais lived in an in-between state—betwixt and between temporary and permanent, legality and illegality. In response, Thais created informal social networks as well as formal organizations such as the Thai Association of Southern California, established in 1961 (as Thai Student Association of Southern California) to help a promote a sense of unity and support.[46] Attempts to procure foodstuffs native to Thailand to prepare and cook Thai dishes also brought Thais in Los Angeles together.

"THAIS MUST HAVE THAI FOOD"

One of the most disappointing parts of life in the United States for Thai students was the absence of Thai food. Thai students found "American" fare—typically steaks, hamburgers, and sandwiches—to be good, but too bland. And even though many in Thailand associated the consumption of steak in America with wealth and high social status, the flavor profile of a grilled or pan-fried cut of red meat was relatively basic (seasoned mainly with salt, pepper, and butter) in comparison to Thai-style beef dishes, such as *sueh long hai* (crying tiger) and *nue nam tok* (waterfall beef). Malulee Pinsuvana, an "expert in Thai cooking" who traveled often from Thailand to the U.S. West Coast, including to Los Angeles, witnessed firsthand during this period the unsatisfied craving among her compatriots. In her cookbook, *Cooking Thai Food in American Kitchens*, Pinsuvana asserted: "I understand the longing of so many Thais living there [Phoenix and Los Angeles] for their native food. It is not that American food is not good, or that other types of food—Mexican, French, Italian and Chinese, to name a few—are not delicious, but their taste is not quite satisfying enough. In other words, Thais must have Thai food."[47] The closest the students could get to Thai food was Chinese food. But the flavor profile of most Chinese dishes at the time, which were Cantonese, was salty, sweet, sour, pungent, and sometimes bitter.[48] So while similar, Chinese food was distinctly different from the more expansive *yum* that typified Thai cooking: salty, sweet, sour, creamy, and hot/spicy.[49]

The yearning for *yum* reflected not simply a craving for better-tasting and therefore more satisfying food. It was also informed by a desire to reconnect with Thailand. Thai food represented a tangible way for Thais in Los Angeles to recreate and relive a familiar, comforting Thailand displaced in time and space. Most importantly, it had the power to aid this nostalgia neurologically through taste and smell. Meredith Abarca and others have demonstrated that while there is indeed a strong relationship between food and emotional memory, it is the combination and interplay of gustatory (taste, texture) and olfactory senses (smell)—what David Sutton calls "synesthesia"—that connects emotions and memories in the brain.[50] Drawing on recent studies in neurogastronomy, Abarca explains in her essay that the "sensory stimuli caused from eating or drinking affects the function of the hippocampus," a region of the brain that is critical to the formation of memories as well as "part of the limbic system responsible for the regulation of drives and emotions."[51]

The power of food to trigger emotional memories in the brain, according to Abarca, also cultivates the formation of individual "palate memories" and subjectivities that become central to a group's shared sensory collective memory and speak to "lived (hi)stories" and a "kind of intimate bond with food and diet molded by material circumstances."[52] Ultimately, the craving

FIGURE 2. Thai immigrants at a gathering in Los Angeles, ca. early 1970s. By the 1970s, Los Angeles became home to the largest Thai population in the United States and outside of Thailand. Photograph courtesy of the Tilakamonkul family.

for authentic Thai flavors captures the power and significance of the sensory experience of eating. Along with its social and symbolic meaning, eating evokes, neurologically, food memories from the homeland. It alleviates feelings of isolation, loneliness, and disruption caused by migration. Having the right ingredients and foodstuffs to recreate *yum* became extremely critical, as the craving could only be effectively satiated through gustatory and olfactory consumption.

Thus, even without Thai restaurants or grocery stores where the key ingredients to make Thai cuisine could be obtained, Thai students began recreating their own versions of Thai dishes at home. One of the more popular dishes was *moo tod gratiem prik Thai* (garlic and white pepper pork) over white rice. Another dish was boiled eggs with chili paste over rice. Soon, a number of Thai students started hosting Thai potluck dinner parties that allowed them to connect and socialize with fellow classmates and, occasionally, non-Thai English-language teachers whom they often invited to the gatherings.

A few capitalized on their culinary skills and the demand for Thai food. Some Thais remember placing lunch orders with a Thai couple, Arunee and Udom, who took phone orders during the evening, prepared the lunches, and then delivered them to worksites the next day. Thai college students, however, became some of the first to open and operate Thai restaurants in the United States. While no definitive record exists on when and where the first Thai restaurant opened (though it was in Southern California), we know that early restaurants were temporary, mostly small makeshift shops intended to serve a Thai student clientele who planned to return to Thailand once they completed their studies.[53] One example of these restaurateurs is Surapol Mekpongsatorn, who opened a noodle stand near the University of California, Los Angeles sometime in the early 1960s. His noodle soups sold well enough that he once boasted to friends that he made "so much cash he had to sleep on it under his bed."[54] Another student, Chow Buranasombati, first arrived in the United States in 1962 at the age of twenty-three to study design and photography at California State Los Angeles before he was asked by his parents-in-law to take over Tepparod Thai restaurant in East Hollywood in the late 1960s.[55] According to Buranasombati, he made the decision to stay permanently in the United States because it represented "the place to live if you want a house, a car, a place to grow."[56] Within a few years he was the owner of two Tepparod Thai restaurants. But where did they get the ingredients to prepare Thai dishes?

CHASING THE *YUM*

Anyone who created, or attempted to create, Thai dishes in 1960s Los Angeles procured ingredients in three main ways. First, they substituted Thai ingredients with what was available in local supermarkets. Marie Wilson's *Siamese Cookery* reflects this approach while underscoring the scarcity of Thai ingredients. Consider her recipe for khrung kaeng, or shrimp curry:

    1 tbsp. ground coriander
    1 tbsp. ground caraway seed
    1 tsp. turmeric; 1 tsp. pepper
    ¼ tsp. cayenne pepper
    ½ tsp. freshly grated nutmeg
    2 tbsp anchovy paste
    2 tsp vinegar

    Combine coriander, caraway, turmeric, pepper, cayenne, nutmeg and blend. Add anchovy paste and vinegar and mix well. Store in a small airtight jar in refrigerator.[57]

Here, Wilson's recipe suggests using anchovy paste to capture the saltiness of fish sauce and cayenne pepper for the spiciness of Thai chili peppers.[58] In addition, when she told her Thai friends in the United States about using sour cream in place of coconut cream for Thai curry dishes, she said they "approved enthusiastically as soon as they tasted a curry made with it."[59] Wilson's Thai friends however, had already been experimenting with cow's milk, sweet cream, and buttermilk to replace coconut cream or milk. Thais especially relied on Chinese ingredients to simulate Thai flavors. They shopped at Chinese groceries in Chinatown, such as the well-known and well-stocked Yee Sing Chong supermarket, to buy produce, sauces, rice, and other foodstuffs along with utensils and dishware. But while they could easily find soy sauce in stores, staples like Thai fish sauce and curry paste, which served as the base for all Thai curries, were not available.[60]

Another common practice was to pack dried and canned goods as well as fruits and vegetables and bring them into the United States—legally and illegally. Although the U.S. Customs Service did allow Thais to enter the country with certain foodstuffs, typically canned and processed foods, only a small amount intended for personal use was admissible. Almost all plants and produce were prohibited or required an import permit. Faced with these restrictions, small cohorts of Thai entrepreneurs began smuggling banned ingredients by traveling back to Thailand to collect plants, fruits, and vegetables native to Southeast Asia such as lemon grass, galanga, and Thai basil (and seeds) and sneaking them into the United States inside suitcases.[61] Therefore, producing the complex and balanced Thai flavor profile in dishes required more than just creativity, ingenuity, and a skilled palate; it also needed participation in unlawful activities. Yet attempts to smuggle Thai foodstuffs were difficult, in large part because the U.S. Customs Service had become increasingly concerned with the trafficking of narcotics and illicit drugs from Southeast Asia's "golden triangle."[62]

Lastly, the chase for *yum* ultimately led to the discovery of a small grove of kaffir lime (citrus hystrix) trees in the citrus town of Riverside, roughly sixty miles away from Hollywood. The kaffir lime, or *makrut*, is native to Southeast Asia and is an indispensable ingredient in Thai cuisine.[63] It is used not for its juice, which is very bitter, but for the pungent flavor of its zest and its aromatic leaves. Some makrut had made its way into the United States and was donated to Riverside's Citrus Variety Collection in 1930.[64] And in the 1960s, the collection, now part of the University of California, Riverside, was the only place in the country where one could find kaffir limes, as it was illegal to import Asian-grown citrus due to fears of the spread of canker disease. So when Thais in Los Angeles first learned about these makrut trees, they began organizing carpools to travel roughly 120 miles roundtrip—about two hours—in order to procure the prized ingredient. Once there, the group picked bunches of bai makrut as well as lemon grass shoots.[65] Upon returning home, they froze the leaves in plastic bags and preserved them for later use in making *nam prik pao* (chili paste) and *nam prik kaeng* (curry paste), the base components for spicy Thai stir-fry dishes, curries, and soups—namely *tom yum*.

There was a clear shortage of Thai foodstuffs in 1960s Los Angeles. One could argue that it simply reflected a lack of demand given that Thais had yet to arrive in large numbers. Yet the range of procurement strategies Thais performed—substitutions, smuggling, and a willingness to trek long distances—strongly suggests the existence of a passionate desire and a consumer base that included non-Thais.

No one responded to the demand for a steady supply of Thai ingredients more than Pramorte Tilakamonkul. When Tilakamonkul opened the Bangkok Market grocery store and import company in 1971, he had been living in Los Angeles for several years and knew firsthand the dire Thai food situation. There was only one Thai restaurant in the entire city and no grocery stores that sold Thai or Southeast Asian foodstuffs.[66] He also recognized that the Thai population in Los Angeles was growing and that it would continue to grow. Tilakamonkul's son, Jet, who grew up working in the grocery store, recalled nearly forty years later that his father "had the vision to say 'hey, there's a ton of Southeast Asian people here and we need to eat things like green papaya and long beans and jackfruit, [be]cause we don't have any."[67] From the beginning Tilakamonkul understood food procurement as a form of community sustenance.

Of course, Tilakamonkul wanted to capitalize on a potentially lucrative economic opportunity and business niche in an industry he knew well, and one that did not require formal education or English-language skills. He certainly had the pedigree to be a food-based entrepreneur. Tilakamonkul was born in southern China's Hainan Province. He spent most of his youth, however, in urban Bangkok after his parents moved him and his six brothers from China to Thailand in the 1950s to escape communism.[68] While in Bangkok, he grew up learning the food and restaurant business from his parents, who became restaurateurs after opening a Thai-Chinese shop house in a predominantly Hainanese section of the city, selling food and coffee to neighborhood residents.[69] He would model the Bangkok Market after this shop.

By the mid 1960s Tilakamonkul decided to leave Thailand for the United States with help from his brother and Mexican sister-in-law who were already living there.[70] He arrived in Los Angeles in 1966 and settled in East Hollywood, a neighborhood with a few other Thais and immigrants from Latin America and Eastern Europe.[71] For Thai immigrants, the local economy at the time offered mostly low-wage, part-time, unskilled jobs with no benefits in either the growing service sector or garment work for the apparel industry. Furthermore, East Hollywood was in shambles. Global economic restructuring, deindustrialization, and the continuation of policies that funneled resources away from urban cores and to the suburbs in Los Angeles helped to produce this cheap exploitable immigrant labor pool and created ghettos. These conditions were, however, ripe for establishing a small retail store. Small retail operations required minimal start-up capital, cheap rent, and less competition with larger chain supermarkets typically found in white neighborhoods.

CONFRONTING U.S. TRADE BARRIERS

The significance of Tilakamonkul's accomplishments and why and how the Bangkok Market even came to be cannot be fully grasped without knowledge of trade policies and conditions in the 1970s and 80s. Tilakamonkul and other Thai food-industry entrepreneurs confronted a number of problems as they tried to procure ingredients for Thai cooking to nurture Thai community formation in Los Angeles. To be clear, U.S. trade policy on imports during this period was not heavily restrictive. On the contrary, it was as liberal or "free" as it had ever been. In the post–World War II period, the United States joined other capitalist nations to reduce tariffs and nontariff barriers to trade. The group helped establish and participated in the General Agreement on Tariffs and Trade (GATT), a multilateral agreement that functioned as the main entity for the regulation of world trade.[72] By the 1960s, over eighty nations were participating in GATT as it governed an estimated 80 percent of world trade; Thailand was not a member but adhered to its principles.[73] However, Congress still placed barriers and restrictions on fruits, vegetables, and plants, banning some from entry altogether as they did with Asian-grown kaffir limes and leaves. Regardless of how liberal the trade policy, it was still necessary to have the wherewithal and knowledge to navigate the dizzying system of policies and procedures to make large and steady supplies of Thai and Southeast Asian foods available to consumers.

Importing goods from Thailand into the United States involved an intricate global distribution network and multiple players with different, often competing, interests. First, import companies such as Bangkok Market Inc. had to purchase foodstuffs directly from overseas companies or from agents of those companies with offices in the United States. Next, importers often hired a customs broker—an independent operator to handle the logistics of planning and orchestrating the entry of goods.[74] Once the goods crossed formal U.S. boundaries, the import company could either have the customs broker arrange transportation for delivery or hire a trucking firm to drive the goods to local warehouses, from where it would ultimately be distributed to retail stores or sold to other importers. Then there was the ship itself, which functioned as a "multimillion dollar floating business" that freighted goods stored in large containers across the Pacific Ocean.[75] From 1968 to 1977 the volume of Thai foreign trade grew from roughly $1.9 million to $8 million, with agricultural products accounting for 60 percent of total export value.[76] On average, Thailand shipped 11.5 percent of exports to the United States over this period.[77] The top export items included rice, tapioca, rubber, maize, sorghum, mung beans, tobacco leaves, shrimp, and other seafood.

To import foods for his market, Tilakamonkul and his partners had to deal with the intricate labyrinth of nation-state import-export policies in both Thailand and the United States. In Thailand, the National Economic and Social Development Plans (NESDP) set the guidelines for all of Thailand's foreign trade. In the 1970s the primary objectives of the NESDP were to increase export volume, seek new markets, and diversify production to create new export commodities.[78] In addition, the Ministry of Commerce was in charge of import-export control and trade promotion, while the Department of Foreign Trade dealt with export promotion, import-export licensing, and establishing standards for export products.[79] With few exceptions, Thailand's authorization system allowed companies to export commodities "freely" without undue restrictions.

The American nation-state depended on an equally complex web of federal departments and agencies to make sure importers complied with existing trade laws and regulations. Whereas Congress was largely responsible for setting trade and import policies, the Food and Drug Administration (FDA), the United States Department of Agriculture (USDA), and the U.S. Customs

Service were the key entities that administered and enforced the policies and therefore policed U.S. borders. The FDA monitored shipments of all drugs, cosmetics, and foods other than meat and poultry.[80] The USDA, on the other hand, oversaw only meat and poultry imports and in 1972, with the creation of the Animal and Plant Health Inspection Service (APHIS), also assumed the responsibility of "protecting and promoting" U.S. animal and plant health in order to safeguard U.S. agriculture from invasive foreign pests and diseases.[81] Lastly, the U.S. Customs Service, under the U.S Treasury Department, was in charge of classifying and valuing imports, determining rates and duties on imports, and collecting them. Customs also supervised the entry and unloading of vessels, vehicles, and aircraft, and enforced laws prohibiting the importation of restricted goods, drugs, and other contraband.[82] While these entities attempted to work in concert, each operated with different resources: U.S. Customs and the USDA had computerized management systems to expedite their efforts—the FDA did not; and the USDA had goods delivered to them whereas U.S. Customs and the FDA had to travel to inspection sites.[83]

Just as Bangkok Market Inc. was trying to get established, U.S. foreign trade policy swung to a protectionist stance amid rising anti-import sentiment in the United States. The post-World War II "golden age" of American capitalism came to an abrupt end as the country entered an economic recession. U.S. corporations saw their profits fall. Working-class living standards stagnated. At the same time, the rapid growth of capitalist systems of production around the world, particularly in Asia and the Pacific, exposed U.S. corporations to serious international competition.[84] In 1971, for the first time in the twentieth century, the United States imported more goods than it exported.

In response, support for "trade liberalization" waned among the business, labor, and agricultural community. These groups blamed imports for the recession, sparking an economic nationalism that historian Dana Frank has referred to as "one of the longest, deepest waves of Buy American campaigns in U.S. history," which encouraged U.S. consumers to buy products made only in the United States to help save jobs by fighting the encroachment of foreign-made goods at the border.[85] The debate over imported goods was also highly racialized. Asian imports, such as Japanese cars, came to represent the growing threat of Asian capital and Asian workers on the U.S. economy and the "native" (white) worker.

The protectionist sentiment sparked attempts to restrict, or at least slow down, the flow of foreign imports. But the United States could not impose higher tariffs to meet the demands for protection. Higher tariffs would have violated GATT regulations. Instead, Congress turned to nontariff barriers as the trade-restriction mechanism of choice: measures, policies, and practices other than a tax or duty designed to restrict imports and therefore protect U.S. companies and the domestic market from foreign competition. U.S. nontariff barriers included complex regulatory systems, quotas, bans, safety standards, burdensome customs inspections, and lengthy entry procedures. By the 1980s the United States witnessed a sharp rise in nontariff barriers that captured the total reappraisal of trade liberalization under GATT.

Unfortunately for Tilakamonkul and the Bangkok Market, the United States used nontariff barriers on food imports—especially fruits, vegetables, and plants. The amount of food imported rose incredibly in the 1980s, pushing the United States to rely more heavily on nontariff barriers to protect its borders. In 1983, approximately 32 billion pounds of foreign food entered the country. By 1988, 40 billion pounds of food was imported.[86] The nontariff barriers on foreign foods stemmed from concerns over the potentially destructive impact of imported goods on public and environmental health, specifically "native" species of plants, fruits, and vegetables vital to the U.S. agricultural industry.[87] It was at this time that the USDA, in addition to banning Asian-grown makrut from entering the United States, placed makrut under federal quarantine for canker because it did not trust the standards used by Asian nations to test for the disease.[88] Unlike cars, clothing, electronics, and other manufactured products, Asian food imports were not regarded with the same level of anxiety about foreign companies taking jobs or competing directly with U.S. agriculture and food companies. One would have been hard pressed, for instance, to find a grower in the United States who raised kaffir limes, lemongrass, or Thai eggplant to sell in the commercial market or to find a U.S. curry paste manufacturer. In other words, there was not a major agribusiness lobby working to keep out Asian foodstuffs because of economic competition. Instead of economic infiltration, foreign food imports represented disease and pest infiltration risks.

Along with quotas, bans, and quality standards, the U.S. Customs Service emerged as an effective and omnipresent nontariff barrier. As a federal enforcement agency the U.S. Customs Service was not a formal trade barrier, but its bureaucratic procedures and activities slowed the import process. In essence, U.S. Customs acted as a nontariff barrier, enlarging its operations dramatically during this period to keep pace with the rapid growth of food imports. It bolstered its personnel, invested in larger processing facilities, and implemented a nationwide computer network to expedite entry procedures and inspections. The agency spent roughly $900 million a year to accomplish this but generated a revenue of over $15 billion annually in duties, tariffs, fines, forfeitures, and seizures for the U.S. government.[89] As the bureaucratic and physical infrastructure of the U.S. Customs Service expanded, so did the responsibilities of U.S. Customs officers and inspectors. Typically, agents measured arriving shipments against quotas, subjected them to tariffs, and checked for narcotics, bacteria, and insects—"drugs and bugs."[90] These actions could be carried out in any place in the United States, within waters covered by the U.S. Customs Service, or within an authorized enforcement area. By the 1980s, customs agents also had to enforce over 2,000 regulations of more than forty agencies, including the FDA and the USDA-APHIS. For instance, even though 95 percent of the tonnage of imported food in 1988 fell under FDA jurisdiction, it all had to first pass through U.S. Customs.[91] Furthermore, Congress deputized customs agents by granting them the right to carry firearms, make an arrest without a warrant, and "perform any other law enforcement duty that the Secretary of the Treasury may designate."[92]

In a way, the U.S. Customs Service did more than just police the border by keeping out food at physical border spaces. It also participated in social and cultural border making: drawing stark lines between nonthreatening "native" foods and invasive "alien" ones to determine which foods belonged and which ones did not, at times using scientific research to justify the exclusion.[93] The U.S. Customs Service gave the impression that "foreign" foods were more dangerous than domestic foods. In doing so, it played a role in constructing and defining the U.S. nation-state as modern, safe, pest free, and disease free while constantly being under threat from the "torrent" of contaminated imported foods.[94] Bonnie Aikman, spokesperson for the USDA, revealed to the *Los Angeles Times* in 1987, "we [the USDA] worry a lot about this . . . for example, just one orange carried by an incoming passenger may have introduced the Mediterranean fruit fly to California in 1980. More than $100 million was spent by the USDA and the state of California before the fly was eradicated."[95] Aikman highlighted both the environmental and economic dangers of poorly inspected or uninspected imported meats and produce at a moment in which federal, state, and local governments became increasingly strapped for funds. A 1989 *Washington Post* article reported that the "rising tide of foreign foods," coupled with budget cuts on government agencies, put pressure on inspectors patrolling the nation's borders and "raised concerns about whether troublesome foods are reaching

American tables and if public health is being adequately protected."[96] The article also stated that about 40 percent of sampled imported goods (2 percent of all imports) did not meet FDA standards. In addition, U.S. Customs, the USDA-APHIS, and the FDA helped communicate these ideas by informing both importers and overseas travelers about the risks of foreign foods through pamphlets, booklets with lists of restricted items, and posters.[97]

For importers, the expansion of Customs operations and responsibilities meant cumbersome entry, inspection, and processing procedures for foodstuffs in transit. The ports of Los Angeles and Long Beach were particularly bad. With booming trade across the Pacific Rim, Los Angeles became a main hub for imports and Customs activity in the nation. It was the primary port complex for Bangkok Market Inc. The value of imports that came through the ports grew at a faster rate than at any other major U.S. port, reaching $48.7 billion in 1988. But the increased volume and value of imports at both ports burdened West Coast customs inspectors with a workload 50 percent higher than others around the country.[98] As a result, customs inspectors simply could not check and clear at all arriving imports. Instead, they inspected only 10 percent of all shipments (releasing 90 percent at the dock), relying on onsite import specialists and computers to determine which cargoes to examine.[99]

Not surprisingly, delays in processing and routine inspections also caused headaches for import companies. A 1986 study commissioned by both West Coast port authorities and shipping interests found that the Los Angeles and Long Beach ports had the worst processing delays on the entire West Coast: U.S. Customs only cleared 9 percent of imports selected for examination in less than eight hours; other ports on the West Coast had a clearance rate of 42 percent under eight hours. What's more, U.S. customs inspections were in no way uniform operations. The process was decentralized, and agents often had to make decisions on site, making for vagueness and inconsistency. The authors of the 1986 study noticed that importers were "increasingly selecting ports and carriers which offer the most trouble-free customs clearance."[100]

SIDESTEPPING TRADE BARRIERS AND FOREIGN
TRADE ZONES

Faced with these trade conditions and the discursive landscape around foreign foods, Tilakamonkul decided to sidestep the heightened barriers. He vertically integrated Bangkok Market Inc. and created new source regions to grow Thai and Southeast Asian produce. While Bangkok Market Inc. managed to import canned and packaged items like fish sauce, curry paste, and dried fish, it of course struggled to import fruits, vegetables, and plants. The USDA-APHIS banned Asian-grown kaffir limes and placed them under federal quarantine. They also started quarantining shipments of Asian-grown lemongrass because of rust disease.[101] In response, Tilakamonkul and his partners (some of whom participated in smuggling Thai foodstuffs) attempted to cultivate these and other crops in different parts of Southern California. It was perfectly legal to grow and sell kaffir limes and lemongrass domestically in California, so long as one could provide documentation to prove that they were, in fact, grown in the United States.[102] After failed attempts in Chino and San Diego due to inappropriate climate conditions, the group partnered with the wholesale company S.S.K. Produce Inc in Fresno.[103] Tilakamonkul discovered that California's Central Valley climate was ideal for growing Thai plants and produce.

As much as he cared about bringing food to his people, Tilakamonkul was just as driven to increase profits. He restructured Bangkok Market Inc. so that the company controlled the entire supply chain: production, wholesale, distribution, and retail. In addition to the retail store, Tilakamonkul opened two family-operated import warehouses, one in the northern California city of San Jose and the other in Maywood in Southern California's City of Industry. The warehouses opened up more ways to make money. According to his son, Jet, Pramorte was "a trendsetter" who developed multiple revenue streams and "monetized every segment of this business. Basically, our produce companies would support our markets, which would support our restaurants. And our import company would support our markets and our restaurants."[104]

In the mid-1980s Tilakamonkul expanded the operations of Bangkok Market Inc. even further. While the grocery store brought an abundance of locally grown Thai fruit and vegetables, much of it was available only seasonally. And with a growing Thai and non-Thai clientele, Tilakamonkul sought a year-round supply; he and his partners found it in Mexico. Bangkok Market Inc. applied for and was granted permission to establish, operate, and maintain two foreign trade zones (FTZs) in Sinaloa, Mexico, creating a global trade network across the southern U.S. border.[105] FTZs, also known as "free trade zones," are designated areas in or near ports of entry that, by law, are treated as outside of customs territory, in that they eliminate tariffs and other trade barriers and reduce bureaucratic regulations to expedite and encourage global trade.[106] In other words, FTZs allowed companies to effectively circumvent the regime of import control Customs was trying to maintain. Bangkok Market Inc.'s FTZs grew 90 percent of the Southeast Asian produce that came into the U.S. during the fall and winter seasons. Jet, who spent a number of his teenage years helping his father oversee the operations in Mexico, describes the conditions: "these are thousands of Mexicans that are growing our food. [They] don't know how to eat it, [they] don't know what the hell to do with it, and they're exporting it to us. It's really amazing to see."[107]

Besides a year-round supply of Thai and Southeast Asian produce, Bangkok Market Inc. found FTZs advantageous for other reasons. FTZs represented a "frictionless"—near magical—space of production, handling, and importing/exporting full of exemptions and special powers for U.S. businesses. Dara Orenstein contends that FTZs "deterritorialized rather than delineated the nation, creating archipelagos of murky sovereignty and unsettling what it meant to be or buy 'American.'"[108] This meant that U.S. import restrictions no longer applied to foreign, specifically Asian-grown, produce—because they were no longer "foreign," but American. U.S. Customs agents assigned to the zones also reduced the dutiable value of goods produced there, which helped to lower or eliminate tariffs. In addition, FTZs allowed businesses to avoid not only U.S. Customs oversight and regulations but U.S. labor and environmental laws as well.[109] As a physical site, FTZs were "isolated, enclosed, and policed" spaces with facilities for loading, unloading, handling, storing, producing, and shipping items by land, water, or air.[110] FTZs throughout the twentieth century were generally regarded as foreign land, although "foreign in a domestic sense," with "all the familiar trappings of a militarized national border: guards, customs agents, barbed wire."[111]

Establishing FTZs in Mexico was appealing because of changes happening in the country's agricultural sector at the time. The Mexican government enacted policies in the 1980s that altered the Mexican agricultural industry to be more privatized, market-oriented, and foreign-capital friendly, essentially prepping the country for the North American Free Trade Agreement (NAFTA). The support for increased commercial-based production of crops spawned an entrepreneurial class of Mexican growers looking for ways to tap into the capitalist marketplace, especially in the United States. From the perspective of the Mexican growers, investing in "exotic" crops opened a smaller yet more stable market that lessened the possibility of the glut that

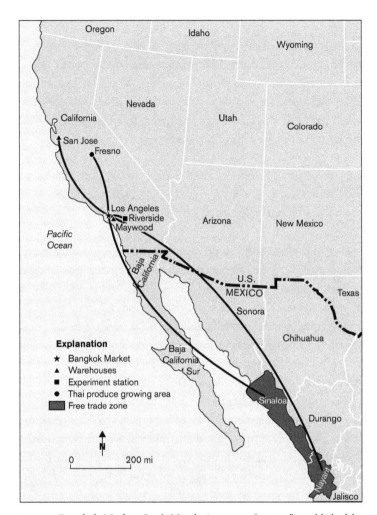

MAP 3. Bangkok Market, Inc.'s North American "empire" established by Pramorte "Pat" Tilakamonkul and his son Jet to overcome restrictions on the importation of Asian produce and the expense of importing processed Thai ingredients while profiting from the growing demand for Thai cuisine. The company also created a Thai import base in Houston for dry goods in the 1980s (not mapped). Cartography by Syracuse University Cartographic Laboratory & Map Shop. Courtesy of Rutgers University Press.

occurs in bigger markets. Such investment provided surer access to U.S. consumers, as Southeast Asian crops did not compete in the marketplace with crops produced by U.S. "big agriculture."[112]

Between the mid-1960s and the late 1980s, U.S. border practices through food trade policy had a profound impact on Thai immigrants' ability to procure and cook what they considered to be authentic Thai dishes. A complex regulatory system of government agencies acted as barriers to the importation of Thai foodstuffs as the U.S. nation-state tried to selectively benefit from and manage the increased flow of foreign foods. Tilakamonkul and fellow Thai entrepreneurs negotiated the hardening of U.S. borders in a range of ways, but perhaps most effectively by turning to FTZs where U.S. regulations and enforcement were not nearly as pronounced.

BANGKOK MARKET AND THAI AMERICAN COMMUNITY FORMATION

The opening of the Bangkok Market was a formative event that created the conditions for a Thai American community to take shape around foodways. Tilakamonkul and his business partners acted as, to borrow from Natalia Molina, "place-makers" who left a lasting imprint on the Thai American community and on the broader urban landscape.[113] Although they did not openly challenge social norms or participate in oppositional politics by way of formal political organizations or protests, their negotiation of complex nontariff barriers, from restrictions to enforcement agencies, allowed them to establish a central place to procure foodstuffs necessary to cook "authentic" Thai dishes at home while making it easier for Thai entrepreneurs to open restaurants.

But more than a place to buy food and ingredients, the Bangkok Market was a community institution. It provided a social space for the building of social networks and communal bonds that spanned gender, class, ethnic, generational, and national boundaries. The familiar food, language, smells, and atmosphere offered recently arrived Thais a much-needed buffer to build a new life in the sprawling, intimidating metropolis. The grocery store also fostered a working environment in which many of the employees—almost all family and friends, almost all immigrants—felt valued and took pride in their labor even if the pay was not always fair.

The Bangkok Market also revitalized East Hollywood and transformed the lives of people in the area.[114] It enhanced the neighborhood's identity as an ethnic immigrant space. Tilakamonkul and his partners were thus community builders and activists for not only Thai immigrants but also for the neighborhood of East Hollywood. The Bangkok Market became a magnet for Thai migrants. Within a few years of the store's opening, a majority of the city's Thai population moved to the East Hollywood area, near the intersection of

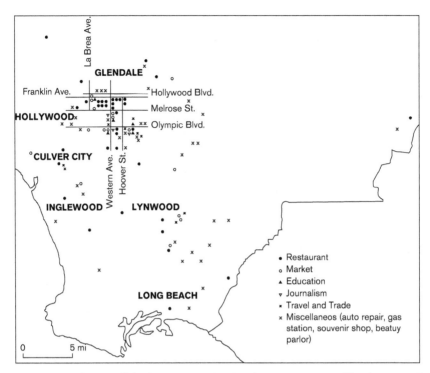

MAP 4. Distribution of Thai businesses in Los Angeles County in 1979. The clustering of businesses shows the formation of a Thai enclave economy in East Hollywood area. By the late 1970s restaurants constituted at least one-third of all Thai businesses in Los Angeles. Map based on Jacqueline Desbarats, "Thai Migration to Los Angeles," *Geographical Review* 69 (July 1979): 315. Map created by Mike Padoongpatt. Permission to reproduce courtesy of Wiley.

Hollywood Boulevard and Western Avenue.[115] East Hollywood, a predominantly white neighborhood just a decade earlier, was transitioning into a multiracial and multiethnic space. Thais settled there along with other immigrant groups from Latin and Central America and Armenia.[116] Although the area was in "decline" with "pimps, hookers, and drug dealers" mingling in and around blighted or empty buildings, the neighborhood surrounding the grocery store had developed into a small Thai enclave lined with Thai travel agencies, newspaper presses, auto shops, beauty parlors, and other businesses established to attract and serve Thai newcomers.[117] At least one-third of these businesses were food and restaurant related. Two interrelated processes were at work in East Hollywood: Thai businesses located to serve their clientele, and, in turn, the residential choice of Thai newcomers was influenced by these businesses as well as the location of earlier immigrants and employment opportunities.[118] Decades before nonprofit organizations and government agencies stepped in to enact official "community revitalization" projects, the Bangkok Market played a key role in enhancing East Hollywood in the 1970s.

Finally, the Bangkok Market fueled Thai American community development in Los Angeles by stimulating both a Thai enclave economy in East Hollywood and a Thai ethnic economy that reached beyond the neighborhood.[119] Although the Bangkok Market was physically located in East Hollywood, the store served those from inside and outside the neighborhood, which yielded bigger profits. The Bangkok Market quickly became a Thai business incubator, with Tilakamonkul providing financial backing to help launch Thai-language newspapers and community organizations. It also supported the growth of early Thai American community leaders, including Tilakamonkul himself, who was propelled into leadership roles in various Thai community building efforts. He would become a founding member of the Wat Thai of Los Angeles in 1979—the first and largest Thai Buddhist temple in the nation—and eventually served as its executive vice president.[120] In addition, the store led to the creation of other food-related businesses and import/export companies, such as Bangkok Market Inc., and encouraged food growing in California's Central Valley and later, FTZs in Mexico. Furthermore, Tilakamonkul expanded his enterprise to include Thai restaurants and helped several of his family members who worked at the grocery store get started in the restaurant industry.

THREE

Too Hot to Handle?

RESTAURANTS AND THAI AMERICAN IDENTITY

IN 1976 TOMMY TANG CAUGHT A BREAK. The manager of a Thai rock band landed his first restaurant gig as lead cook at the new Chan Dara in West Hollywood. Tang, who had been working dozens of odd jobs since his arrival in the city from Thailand in 1972, obtained the position after being recruited by a band member's girlfriend who was working at the restaurant.[1] Though he had only a fourth-grade education, Tang had cooking and restaurant experience—and a desire to "make a name" for himself. Back in Thailand he had worked as a busboy and later as a janitor at his father's café in Bangkok. Among his odd jobs in Los Angeles, Tang had taught Thai cooking to large groups and for lodges and clubs.[2] But he also possessed valuable experience in another area: entertaining Americans. He had learned to speak English in Thailand and worked as an R&R tour guide for American GIs during the Vietnam War. This particular skillset served him and Chan Dara well. Tang was quickly promoted to cook, then executive chef, and ultimately manager. At Chan Dara Tang first introduced his "not-too-spicy" brand of "Thai-Oriental-Western," helping the struggling business skyrocket in popularity with hip and trendy Angelenos.

Tang left Chan Dara in 1982 after he and his "fiery" Italian Jewish American wife, Sandi, opened Tommy Tang's Siamese Café on Melrose Avenue in West Hollywood. As owner and executive chef at the modern, neon-lit eatery filled with pink decor, Tang refined his culinary repertoire and perspective—what he later called "global cuisine with a Thai influence"—by continuing to fuse Thai and Western flavors that pushed the envelope of what was considered Thai food. He created a number of new Thai crossover dishes that struck a balance between the exotic and the familiar, such as Thai Risotto and Duck and Arugula Salad.[3] He continued to charm his mostly white clientele with his energy, charisma, and eclectic personality (and no doubt with his colorful bandanas, which he always sported as a nod to his younger days as a welder in Thailand). The restaurant was a hit. Customers—including Hollywood actors and actresses—lined up out the door to try his food. In 1986 the thirty-eight-year old Tang parlayed his success into another restaurant in New York City, Tommy Tang's, making him the first bicoastal Los Angeles chef.[4]

Tang's "new age" Thai cooking earned him both praise and ire. Some dubbed him a "pioneer" and an "improv artist" for his "accurate perception of what the American palate goes for, unlike many restaurateurs who miss by a mile when attempting to translate Oriental cooking to Western taste."[5] Others, especially those in the Thai community, viewed him as a sellout and accused him of corrupting real Thai cuisine. Tang, however, was not the only Thai person in Los Angeles to gain visibility because of Thai food, and he was not the only Thai chef and restaurateur who had to figure out, upon discovering that Americans enjoyed Thai food as much as did their fellow Thai immigrants, how to cook, sell, and serve Thai food to U.S. consumers. Hundreds of Thais joined Tang in the restaurant industry during this period. Many entered the U.S. food system and occupied a range of positions from owners of import-export companies, grocery stores, and restaurants to clerks, butchers, cooks, dishwashers, wait staff, and delivery persons. Most found work in Thai restaurants.

Tang's approach to Thai cuisine, which made him the face and personality of Thai food in the United States, was about more than modifying flavors to appeal to as wide a base of consumers as possible. It was more than just business savvy. Tang's dishes also symbolized his relationship with being a Thai immigrant in America. Interestingly, his style of Thai cooking matched his assimilationist views. In a 1982 interview with the *Los Angeles Times* Tang pointed toward East Hollywood and shared his views about a "whole Thai group" who act like "they're still in Bangkok." He accused Thai immigrants of not working to improve their life chances, claiming that "they stay together, they don't speak English, they only work where they don't need English—in sweatshops or restaurant kitchens. Those that go out and meet American society will be OK. Those that don't, won't."[6]

Tang's rise to celebrity chef status happened at a time when Los Angeles was experiencing dramatic transformations. By the 1970s the region developed into a critical hub of a globalizing capitalist economy oriented toward Asia and the Pacific. As part of this "new global, flexible capitalism," the city's economy underwent a series of rapid changes characterized by a complex pattern of deindustrialization and reindustrialization that led to the creation of distinct forms of low-wage labor and consumer services.[7] Thousands of newcomers, especially from Asia and Latin America, arrived to perform this labor and provide these services. They turned Los Angeles into one of the top immigrant destinations in the nation and fueled its ascension as a "world city."[8] The increased presence of Asian newcomers and growth of Los Angeles into a multicultural metropolis sparked anti-Asian and anti-immigrant sentiment. Yet at the same time it also led to a celebration of multiculturalism.

These transformations made food inseparable from Thai American identity formation. The angst and elation over racial and ethnic diversity in Los Angeles meant Thais encountered a society that was not entirely hostile toward immigrants. It was becoming increasingly open to the benefits of multiculturalism. Ethnic food became a tangible, fun, and unthreatening way to experience different cultures and to unite people across racial, ethnic, and class lines. Yet, even as American consumers became interested and willing to try new cuisines, they still used gustatory experiences to mark racial and ethnic boundaries.

For Thais, this happened mainly in restaurants. The Thai food boom during the 1980s, coupled with new patterns of discretionary leisure spending, turned Thai restaurants across the city into culinary contact zones that constructed Thai American identity. The production, representation, and consumption of Thai cuisine inside restaurants racialized Thais as an exotic nonwhite Other. Through decor and the food on the plate, restaurants provided a pleasurable and powerful way to make sense of Thai people—their history, culture, practices, and sensibilities—and how they were different from other Asians at a moment of increased immigration. The rise of multiculturalism in particular led to the further commodification of Thai culture through food. It rendered Thai food as a stand-in for the complexities and contradictions of actual Thai people and the Thai American community. Los Angeles's Pacific Rim oriented capitalist consumer society required its cultures to be distinct, neatly packaged, "pure," and "authentic" to fit its vision of multiculturalism. To this end, Thais and non-Thais used race, ethnicity, and nation to produce novelty and product differentiation in the marketing of Thai cuisine. The unique flavor profile of Thai cuisine—*yum*—was key to marketing this difference. The static and narrow version of Thai culture experienced through all the human senses inside restaurants came to dominate how Americans thought about Thais—and how Thais thought of themselves.

The commodification of Thai food culture produced, exacerbated, and masked gender and class divisions within the community. While many Thai women worked in restaurants to build social networks and create a pathway for upward economic mobility, they were also the main source of exploitable labor and were key to staging an exotic, sensual Thai experience. As Thais incorporated themselves into the U.S. economy primarily as small business owners and low-wage service workers, the restaurant industry contributed to the creation of a Thai American middle class and a Thai American working class. The history of Thai restaurants and Thai American identity formation in 1970s and 80s Los Angeles illustrates the way racial and ethnic identities and by extension the U.S. racial order get structured under flexible accumulation and mass migration.

ENTERING THE RESTAURANT BUSINESS

By 1975 restaurants constituted at least one-third of all Thai businesses in Los Angeles. The majority were low- to mid-priced establishments offering full table service with menus that required high-level food preparation skills. It is difficult to explain precisely why so many Thais entered the restaurant industry. In general, a complex interaction between structural, group, and individual factors made the cooking, serving, and selling of Thai cuisine one of the few viable economic opportunities open to them.

U.S. neocolonialism in Thailand played a role in shaping the contours of Thai restaurateurship inside the United States. Victor Sodsook's experience illustrates the interconnectedness of U.S. foreign policy, Thai migration to the United States, and the development of Thai restaurants and food culture in Los Angeles. Born and raised in the 1940s in the Thai suburb of Nam Buri, Sodsook knew from an early age he wanted to be a chef long before he ever stepped foot in America. Having grown up in the kitchen alongside his mother, he entered college to pursue a career in the hotel and restaurant management business.[9] After completing his degree in the early 1960s, Sodsook started working as a chef and organizing banquets for the well-to-do in the country's most elite hotels. His rapid success afforded access to not only state-of-the-art kitchens but also tourists and guests from around the world. More importantly, this happened during the ascendance of Thailand's American Era. The expansion of U.S. tourism and culinary contact zones allowed ordinary Thais like Sodsook to meet American officials and distinguished travelers. This led to conversations and friendships that, in some cases, allowed Thais to learn of new culinary opportunities in the United States. According to Sodsook, many Americans who indulged in his culinary creations strongly urged him to take his cooking talents to the United States. Confident that non-Thais would find Thai cuisine delicious and palatable given the rave reviews of his American customers, he saved his money and boarded a plane for Los Angeles.

Structural factors inside the United States also played a role. Thais faced barriers in the mainstream labor market and disadvantages due to their immigrant and citizenship status. This led many upper- and middle-class Thais to turn to self-employment.[10] Perhaps more importantly, Thais were also effectively barred from primary-sector jobs either because restrictions on student visas limited them to part-time work or their exdocumented status. Moreover, post-1965 Thai immigration exacerbated this problem. It included a significantly lower number of professionals and those without formal education from rural northern and central Thailand. Their low education levels, lack of English proficiency, and limited skill set restricted them to part-time, low-wage jobs in Los Angeles's booming service-sector economy.[11] Between 1969–1989, service sector jobs grew from 45 percent to 58 percent of all jobs in the city to make it "a more service-oriented economy than the nation as a whole."[12] Thais found plenty of work as office and hospital janitors, gas station attendants, auto mechanics, and hotel maids in this booming sector. However, the restaurant business was one of the fastest-growing industries in the service sector and one of the top in employing immigrants.[13]

At the group level, social networks helped steer Thais into restaurant work. Connections with family, friends, and coethnic acquaintances—relationships that reached beyond the region and the nation—provided Thais with information on how to start a restaurant, job openings, and other food-service opportunities. There was also a well-organized syndicate of Thai restaurateurs, a group of middle- and upper-class Thai male entrepreneurs (that included Pramorte Tilakamonkul) and others involved in the Thai food industry, which sought restaurant investment opportunities, scouted new markets, and opened restaurants. Though not an official organization, these "buddies" used their prowess as community leaders to recruit fellow Thais to work in their restaurant enterprises in an informal yet efficient way.[14]

Social networks also helped Thai entrepreneurs obtain start-up capital to open a restaurant. Very few Thais were able to finance a restaurant entirely with personal funds and it was difficult to secure startup loans from banks.

On top of that, unlike the Chinese, Japanese, Korean, and Vietnamese communities, Thais in Los Angeles did not have established loan clubs that could offer pooled cash to its members as seed money.[15] Thus, most Thai restaurateurs used a combination of personal savings, credit cards, and borrowed money from friends and family to get started.

A sense of responsibility among Thais to help other Thais most likely drove many of the restaurant employment practices and ventures. This "bounded solidarity," based on their collective experiences and marginalization as foreigners in U.S. society rather than a spontaneous feeling or innate primordial ethnic obligation, was quite clear in Thai restaurants where Thai employers and employees helped each other transition into U.S. capitalist society.[16] Thai owners expressed solidarity by hiring coethnics (in addition to family and friends) and through mentorship and informal training. While bosses were of course interested creating efficient and productive workers, they passed down cooking tips, food-service skills, and knowledge about the restaurant industry to workers under the belief that they were supporting the Thai community. For Thais who entered as low-level workers or did not have formal culinary training and food-service experience, learning and practicing lessons from owners often led to promotion and in some cases mobility into restaurant ownership. Thai restaurant workers were also motivated at some level by mutual support and reciprocity. Restaurant employment allowed them to feel like they were supporting, with their labor, Thai-owned businesses and therefore the development of the Thai community as well. Moreover, workers helped other coethnic workers develop restaurant skills and adjust to life in American society with informal instruction, guidance, and friendship.

Lastly, individual traits and demographic characteristics, which varied dramatically and had different effects, also influenced Thai restaurant employment in Los Angeles. The desire to make money and achieve the American dream was no doubt a major motivation. Chow Buranasombati, who came to Los Angeles as a student in 1962, operated two Tepparod Thai restaurants in the city, with his primary goal being upward economic mobility. Others, like Pramorte Tilakamonkul, decided to start a restaurant because cooking Thai food was the only skill and experience they had. Growing up in Thailand, Tilakamonkul was a "troublemaker" and "fuck up," so he arrived in Los Angeles with few resources and no formal education. But he knew Thai food culture. In addition to his Bangkok Market grocery store, Tilakamonkul opened a full-service restaurant, Royal Thai, in 1978.[17] The same was true for restaurant workers, as many turned to food service because they did not have the skills for other occupations open to them, such auto mechanic or garment factory work. Equally important, the Thai restaurant business was attractive because it offered cultural continuity. Thais were drawn because—socially and culturally—they could feel "at home" in a new home. For example, almost all the people working in Thai restaurants in Los Angeles were Thai and spoke the language. This created the conditions for Thais to feel and act as if they were, in Tommy Tang's words, "still in Bangkok."

It is important to stress, however, that Thai restaurateurs and employees were not simply economic agents who cared only about making money and made decisions based purely on rational analysis of resources, profits, markets, and wages. They were also cultural producers. Thai restaurant owners and employees, especially chefs, found pleasure in expressing their ideas of Thai culture and creativity inside Thai restaurants. They had a passion for and standards of taste and innovation as well as a desire to share their culinary creations with others."[18] Prakas Yenbamroong and his Talésai restaurant is a potent example. Yenbamroong left Thailand for the United States in the early 1970s to pursue an MBA at Cornell University. Immediately after completing his degree, he worked for Thai Farmers Bank in Bangkok and London before relocating to Los Angeles in 1979. While in Los Angeles, he noticed that only a few Thai restaurants catered to an "upscale clientele." So he called his mother, Vilai, in Thailand and asked her if she was interested in helping him run a high-end Thai restaurant. Vilai, an experienced cook who for a time prepared meals for heads of state in Thailand, agreed to help Prakas, her eldest son, by serving as executive chef. In 1982 Prakas left his job at the bank and opened Talésai—right in the heart of Hollywood's famed Sunset Strip.[19]

Beyond making money in an untapped market, Yenbamroong was inspired to redefine and advance the art of Thai cuisine. His culinary vision for Talésai, later described by his son, Kris, as "super progressive," was to improve Thai food by elevating and expanding Thai flavors.[20] Yenbamroong embraced change and adaptation, with the view that "food culture is, like everything else, is dynamic, it doesn't stay still, it's living, it's like organism . . . it changes with our community, our culture."[21] For him, it was important that Talésai keep evolving to be "relevant." In the kitchen, he and Vilai experimented with traditional, well-known Thai dishes, implemented modern techniques, and fused new ingredients into Thai cooking. Even though the experimental dishes did not appear on the menu until much later, the attempts to enhance the tastes and flavors of Thai cuisine cultivated a forward-thinking culture at the restaurant. It attracted the attention of *Los Angeles Times* restaurant critic Colman Andrews, who noticed that Talésai's approach and methods were different than those of other Thai restaurants in Los Angeles. Colman wrote in a review, "what really makes Talésai special is the cuisine. This is unusually delicate, careful, finely finished Thai food. It seems stripped down, simplified a bit, when compared to much Los Angeles Thai cooking—but the simplicity works in its favor, focusing attention on individual flavors. . . . Food tastes different here from most Thai restaurants, milder, more subtle."[22] Talésai's success can be attributed to Prakas's and Vilai's commitment to refined taste, culinary ingenuity, and treatment of the restaurant as a vehicle for the next step in the historical evolution of Thai food culture. Talésai was more than simply an economic enterprise.

THE LOS ANGELES THAI FOOD BOOM

Thai cuisine boomed in popularity during the 1970s and 1980s, and it happened with the explosion of Thai restaurants in Westside Los Angeles. In 1987 the number of Thai eating establishments owned and operated by Thais in greater Los Angeles swelled to more than two hundred.[23] While many sprouted in East Hollywood, the San Fernando Valley, and Orange County, neighborhoods in West Hollywood and West Los Angeles witnessed the greatest growth of Thai restaurants and quickly emerged as a hub of Thai cuisine. In fact, many Thais closed their restaurants in the Lynwood-Hawthorne area only to reopen them on the Westside. In 1978 Pramorte Tilakamonkul was among the first to locate a full-service Thai restaurant in this part of town when he opened Royal Thai restaurant at 10688 West Pico Boulevard near Overland Avenue. Soon, other establishments opened in Hollywood and West Los Angeles to rave reviews.[24] By 1977 the area had at least fifteen Thai restaurants, and possibly as many as fifty.[25]

The Westside was one of the whitest and wealthiest areas in Los Angeles. An unofficial designation, the label encompassed neighborhoods and cities like West Hollywood, West Los Angeles, Fairfax, Beverly Hills, Cheviot Hills, Westwood, Pacific Palisades, and Santa Monica. In the 1980s almost all of these neighborhoods were overwhelmingly white. This was true of the areas where some of the first Thai restaurants appeared. For example, the areas surrounding Royal Thai—Century City, Cheviot Hills, and West Los Angeles—were about 90 percent white.[26] Racist housing policies and racial

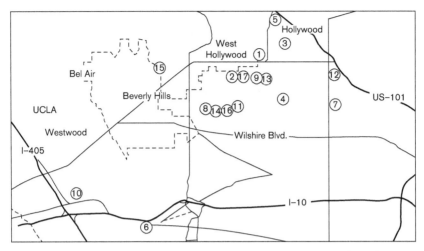

MAP 5. Popular Thai restaurants catering to non-Thais in Westside Los Angeles in the 1980s: 1. Bangkok 1; 2. Bangkok River Thai Cuisine; 3. Chan Dara Hollywood; 4. Chan Dara Larchmont; 5. Chao Praya; 6. Emerald Thai; 7. Pattaya; 8. Pink Marble; 9. Pintong Café; 10. Royal Thai; 11. Siam Mania; 12. The Siamese Castle; 13. Siamese Princess (Original Location); 14. Siamese Princess; 15. Talésai; 16. Tepparod Thai No. 3; 17. Tommy Tang's Siamese Café. Map created by Mike Padoongpatt.

restrictive covenants that barred the selling of homes to nonwhites in the early 1900s helped create these racial demographics. Yet, a sizable Jewish population also made up the whiteness of the Westside.[27]

Thai restaurateurs equated the Westside's whiteness with middle- and upper-class membership. In their view they were simply opening businesses in the middle of a potentially lucrative consumer base and profitable target market. Or as Jet Tilakamonkul remembered about his father's decision to locate the Royal Thai in West Los Angeles: "White people got money."[28] Geographer Jacqueline Desbarats also surmised that Thais opened restaurants in the area to "capitalize on the Thai food craze that is presently sweeping through the white middle class."[29] Thais were correct in their thinking. Income levels of Westside neighborhoods ranked as some of the highest in the county, far surpassing places where Thais lived and had originally opened up restaurants, such as East Hollywood and Lynwood. There was money to be made from white Westside Angelenos. Thai restaurant owners just had to find ways to get them to spend it eating in their establishments.

Fortunately, they opened their doors at the right time. The number of Americans who dined out gradually increased in the 1970s and 1980s. The growth of eating out represented a "new American eating pattern" that took place especially in global cities like Los Angeles. The rapid shift in eating habits fueled a flourishing restaurant industry. It generated demand for food service and thus expanded the market.

Several factors contributed to the swelling popularity of eating out, but none more than Americans' desire for the entertainment and social pleasures that came with restaurant dining. Industry experts attributed the popularity to the convergence of a greater number of working women, fewer members per household, rising income, later marriages, higher divorce rates, and more education, which to them meant "better-educated people tend to have higher incomes, to travel more, and become more adventurous eaters."[30] Yet, they also believed that the dining-out trend at its core reflected an emerging cultural and social transformation in which consumers viewed meals as a primary source of entertainment and recreation. A trip to a restaurant had become the "main event" of an evening's plans and where people did most of their socializing. In addition, diners craved novelty and change from the daily "humdrum" routine of their lives. Themed restaurants in particular offered the alluring "environment of a faraway place, a different time period."[31] American consumers were primed for the experience of eating more meals in restaurants, even in the face of an economic slump, rising inflation, and menu prices increasing at a faster rate than the cost of food at home.

Thai restaurateurs tried to take advantage of the desire for exotic Thai cuisine that had been casually spreading among the white middle-class since the mid-1960s. It was a risk. Thai food was still relatively unknown. It was, at most, one of the Westside's best-kept culinary secrets that appealed only to a subniche market of Thai food "lovers" and "freaks."[32] Before restaurants, Westside Angelenos learned about Thai foodways from other Westside Angelenos who published "Siamese" cookbooks and taught "Oriental" cooking classes. Marie Wilson, author of *Siamese Cookery*, was from West Los Angeles. So, too, was Meda Croizat, the homemaker from Santa Monica who was "Gung Ho for Oriental Cookery." And Jennifer Brennan, author of *The Original Thai Cookbook,* taught Thai cooking courses starting in the late 1970s using "proper" ingredients that began appearing in Los Angeles.

By the early 1980s, Thai immigrant women also helped fuel the appetite and expand the consumer base for Thai cuisine. Kamolmal Pootaraksa was one of the first Thai women to teach Thai cooking classes in the city. Pootaraksa, who learned Thai cooking and the intricate art of Thai vegetable and fruit carving as a teenager in Thailand before immigrating to Los

Angeles, taught her classes at Los Angeles City College. She actively reached out to local food critics and writers to help publicize them. *Los Angeles Times* food critic Barbara Hansen, who covered the Thai food boom, described Pootaraksa as "amazing" and the "real Thai pioneer" of teaching Thai cooking. In addition to her courses, Pootaraksa was also chef and owner of Krung Thai in North Hollywood and later Thai Cottage Restaurant in Studio City.[33] In 1986 she published the cookbook *Thai Home Cooking From Kamolmal's Kitchen*.[34] Yupa Holzner was another Thai immigrant woman who spread Thai food culture across Southern California. Holzner, who was raised in Bangkok, taught Thai cooking classes at Los Angeles Pierce College in the predominantly white West San Fernando Valley. Much like Pootaraksa, Holzner's target audience was white American women, and her recipes also called for the use of "authentic" Thai ingredients available in the area as well as substitutions, such as replacing fresh coconut milk with the canned version and Thai chiles with the more easily obtainable jalapeño and serrano chiles. Holzner also published a cookbook, *Great Thai Cooking for My American Friends*, in 1989.[35]

Aside from white people with exotic appetites (and money), the Westside housed the glitz and glamor of Hollywood and its world famous film, television, and music studios. Celebrities and others from "show business" quickly caught on to Thai food, helping transform it from a rare culinary treasure into a hip and trendy cuisine of Hollywood stars. Talésai had its share of celebrity diners. Chan Dara, a half-mile west of Sunset Gower studios in West Hollywood, was typically "packed night and day" with people from the "show biz and media worlds."[36] Royal Thai opened next to 20th Century Fox studio, a major complex that filmed and produced *Star Wars,* the *Six Million Dollar Man,* and *The Fall Guy.* On the grand-opening weekend, Pramorte Tilakamonkul placed a "Free Food" sign outside his restaurant and confidently told passersby, "You're going to love our food . . . and you're not going to pay anything." Allowing people to indulge in Thai food free of charge for two days straight got "everyone hooked," especially those from the Fox studio.[37]

Victor Sodsook's Siamese Princess epitomized Thai food's popularity among Hollywood's rich and famous that gave the cuisine a certain cachet. Sodsook, the chef who refined his Thai culinary skills working as a hotel chef during Thailand's American Era, first opened the Siamese Princess restaurant in Los Angeles in 1976. When he moved the restaurant to West Los Angeles in 1982, it quickly became a celebrity magnet. In his cookbook *I Love*

Thai Food Sodsook boasted "Hollywood stars love Thai cuisine" and listed his regular A-list celebrity customers that included Prince, Sally Struthers, Tina Turner, Jody Foster, Richard Dreyfus, and Warren Beatty.[38] Madonna, he claimed, enjoyed private vegetarian dinners in one of Siamese Princess's intimate booths.[39] Harrison Ford, a lover of hot and spicy flavors, ate at the restaurant whenever he was in town. The restaurant's popularity gained attention from California's culinary experts, who recognized Siamese Princess with a plethora of distinguished awards. By 1989, Siamese Princess and Sodsook had won approximately twenty-two dining awards, becoming more decorated than any other Thai restaurant or chef in the United States.[40]

Thai restaurateurs also exploited the growing obsession with healthy eating and healthy lifestyles.[41] The fitness revolution of the 1980s spawned an aerobics generation of mostly upper- and middle-class men and women fixated on weight and obesity. The health craze was especially strong in Southern California, where even an economic recession made little negative impact on the profits and memberships of private Los Angeles gyms and clubs.[42] When it came to eating habits, the demand for so-called weight-loss foods climbed rapidly. In 1984 Americans spent nearly $58 billion on "light" and "diet" foods, which made up about 20 percent of all retail food purchases.[43] Thai restaurateurs caught on to the trend. Thai restaurants advertised Thai dishes as a healthier and lighter alternative to other Asian cuisine, specifically Chinese.[44] Some provided lighter options and vegetarian dishes. For instance, Chan Dara allowed guests to substitute brown rice for white rice.[45] At Chan Dara's second location, owner Sukhum Kittivech observed that "people want less beef and pork," and so he offered tofu as a substitute. At the time, tofu was considered beneficial to both health and the environment.[46] Kittivech even created new dishes, like spicy tofu, for his majority health-minded clientele.[47]

The Thai food boom was part of the ascendance of ethnic cuisine in Los Angeles in the 1970s and 1980s—an ascendance that represented an immigrant-infused transformation of the city's food culture. Ethnic cuisine and eating establishments—especially Mexican, Chinese, and Italian—had long been part of Los Angeles' culinary landscape, dating back to at least the early 1900s, when local writers dubbed the city a "Mecca of foreign eating" and a "melting pot of epicures."[48] But 1965 marked a watershed. The thousands of people from Asia, the Pacific Islands, Latin America, Africa, and the Middle East who migrated to and settled in the city infused Los Angeles with new tastes, flavors, textures, and smells. Restaurants featuring the food of these new immigrant groups, like Vietnamese, Korean, Filipino, South Asian Indian, Greek, Ethiopian, Guatemalan, and El Salvadorian, opened in rapid succession. The number of Chinese, Japanese, Mexican, and Italian restaurants also increased. Taquerias started springing up on the street corners of South Los Angeles, a sign of the predominantly Black neighborhood's growing Mexican and Central American populations. The post-1965 arrivals did more than just expand the sheer quantity of eateries. They also added diversity, complexity, and depth. For instance, new immigrants from various parts of China introduced Szechuan, Mandarin, Hunan and other regional cooking styles to enhance the Cantonese-dominated Chinese cuisine. By the early 1980s, the city's ethnic food scene had become so vibrant that Lois Dwan predicted, "[ethnic restaurants] will be strong influences on what will, some day, be a distinctive Los Angeles style."[49]

One could argue that Thai restaurants influenced the maturation of a "distinctive Los Angeles style" that informed the city's identity as a cosmopolitan place. Alongside the rapid and jolting economic and demographic changes, Los Angeles emerged as one of the nation's most exciting, eclectic eating cities in part because of Thai restaurants. They helped the city, which for much of the twentieth century struggled to define and distinguish its food culture from renowned culinary cities like New York, establish a gastronomic identity and gain recognition as a rich, dynamic, multicultural global kitchen.[50] Thai food offered this distinction because of its exotic cachet and new and unique flavor profile. Food critic Ruth Reichl considered it "one of the greatest revelations" of the 1980s, describing it as "colorful and exotic, sweet and spicy with a tropical tinge that we all found overwhelmingly seductive."[51] Yet, it was also trendy, current, and in vogue. In a way, Thai food became synonymous with Los Angeles. It was associated with "all things L.A." or at least what the city imagined itself as or aspired to be: global, cool, hip, a seamless combination—or melting—of different cultural influences, and most of all, one of a kind.

STAGING "THAI"

The increased number of Thai restaurants on the Westside led to more contact between Thais and white America. Thai restaurants were not neutral spaces where food was just food—they were culinary contact zones where a diverse cast of producers and consumers interacted across race, gender, and class differences.[52] The naming of some of the first Thai restaurants in Los Angeles in the 1970s as "Thai-Chinese" underscored the saliency of race in American society. Faced with the challenge of introducing a new cuisine, Thai restaurateurs turned to names like "The Orient," "Lee's Thai and Chinese Food," and "Fortune Cookie" to use the familiar to draw customers.[53] Once inside the restaurant, Thais would try to convince them to sample Thai dishes. Thai restaurateurs racialized Thai food as "Oriental" to make it legible to U.S. citizens already accustomed to Cantonese-style cuisine and the "Far East." Aside from good business strategy, playing with the racial trope of "Oriental" and other Chinese signifiers that marked Asians as racially foreign points to the fact that Thais were acutely aware they lived in a highly racialized society. More specifically, it shows that ethnic and national categories from Southeast Asia were collapsed into dominant racial categories inside the United States.

Thai restaurants catering to whites (not the "trimmed-down, every penny-counts family restaurants") emerged as primary sites for the construction of Thai American racial and ethnic identity.[54] They contributed to the racialization of Thais as an exotic Other through the staging of authenticity via décor, menus, and the racially marked bodies of Thai workers.[55] The production and consumption of Thai restaurant settings and ambience, however, simultaneously worked to differentiate Thai cuisine—and by extension Thai people—as unique and novel in consumer culture.

By the late 1970s Thai restaurants started moving away from Chinese names in favor of "Siam" and "Siamese" as well as feminized verbiage to communicate the exoticness of Thai food. Places such as Sodsook's Siamese Princess, Flower of Siam, and The Siamese Castle, played up exotic expectations and evoked a bucolic image of Thailand and Thai people as "traditional": a premodern kingdom with royal dynasties, ancient temples, fertile river valleys, and beautiful arts and crafts. This signaled to customers that the restaurant's food was "authentic." In addition, restaurateurs also used words like "lotus," "orchid," and "flower" to market Thai cuisine as delicate and graceful. In doing so they strengthened long-standing racialized, sexualized, and gendered ideologies of Asian and Asian American women as "lotus blossoms" who were beautifully exotic, gentle, demur, submissive, nonthreatening, and, most of all, hyperfeminine and hypersexual objects of white male desire. In fact, the trope had been applied directly to Thai people during this period. "One of the first things that strikes you about Thai people," observed wife and husband travel writers Beverly Beyer and Ed Rabey in 1987, "is a likeness to their favorite flower, the orchid: beauty, grace, color and a delicacy that all add up to a blossom unlike any other in its appeal to the eye and sense of the exotic."[56]

Menus also purveyed exotic Thainess. Typical images and text that adorned Thai restaurant menu covers in Los Angeles included teakwood art designs, floral patterns, Siamese headdresses and dancers, and Thai-style font. Above all, menus sold the idea of Thai restaurants as an exotic and authentic culinary adventure for white diners. A few places made sure to emphasize certain items as classic Thai dishes, such as pad Thai, with notes like "very traditional Thai dish" and "Thai famous dish."[57] Some restaurants were more explicit about marketing the novelty of Thai food. Pin Tong Thai Café's menu had an "Adventure" section that listed *nam sodd*, *larb*, and *yum woon sen*. Café '84's, too, had a "For Adventurers" section that included mint leaves and chili (*grapow*), spicy garlic, and *prik king*.[58]

Victor Sodsook's Siamese Princess menus, however, stand out. They were, in essence, guidebooks. Inside the menu at the first Siamese Princess location, the list of dishes, written in transliterated English, did not include prices for each item but instead came with jovial descriptions to teach non-Thais about the dish. The description for "Yum Nua (Green Salad with Beef)" read, "crisp greens, onions and tomato are served with a Thai salad dressing that's heavily laced with lemon and other goodies. Atop, shreds of delicious sliced barbecued beef. A new salad for American taste."[59] For "Kaeng Karee Kai (Yellow Chicken Curry)," the menu decoded the color, texture, sourcing of meat, and even issued a warning for the dish: "the color comes from makrut leaves, the horapa and a wafting of fresh green chilies. That creamy quality is from cream that's made from coconut meat. The chicken comes from California. A caution note: know your tolerance for 'heat' and tell the waiter where it is on a scale of one to ten." When he changed locations in 1982, Sodsook altered the original menu by adding a brief entry defining Thai cuisine and another on "How to Order a Typically Thai Dinner." So more than just a list of dishes, Thai restaurant menus helped sell the journey and experience of a Thai restaurant.

Inside, the setting and ambience of Thai restaurants presented an idealized Thailand as a timeless, exotic land of colonial enchantment. It was common for restaurants on the Westside to be decorated with a combination of teakwood carvings, large mural paintings of rural village life, mini Buddhist altars nestled high on rear walls, a framed image of either King Bhumibol Adulyadej or King Rama V (or both), and Thai artifacts. Inside the Royal Thai in Newport Beach, for example, was an "exotic atmosphere" featuring "huge paintings of tropical flowers on silk" that contrasted the deep green walls and a displayed collection of antiques from Bangkok including Thai xylophones, golden Siamese temple dancers' headdresses, and wood carvings.[60] For restaurant reviewer Charles Perry, it stood out as a "sterling example" of a Thai restaurant that could take customers on a culinary and cultural exploration. It was "the kind of place where you get a dose of foreign culture with your food."[61] Like the Royal Thai, a number of other restaurants did such a good job of creating a "tropical/colonial" setting that they ignited white colonial desires and the colonial gaze.[62] In a 1988 review of the Siamese Princess, *Los Angeles Times* food writer Rose Dosti asked readers to "picture yourself in the drawing room at some faraway exotic colony at the height of British Empire glory. Bangkok, maybe, at the turn of the century. There is a bit of musty-dustiness in the air still, the kind British live with so comfortably. Threadbare elegance."[63]

The racially marked bodies of Thai workers were an important part of a restaurant's setting and experience. Chefs like Tommy Tang, Victor Sodsook, and Kamolmal Pootaraksa, with their charisma and bold personalities, often traversed the front and back of the house to entertain as native tour guides and cultural brokers. As living, breathing, walking, and talking embodiments of Thai culture, they bolstered authenticity and exoticness through their service. In addition, Thai waiters and waitresses, often outfitted in colorful and regal-looking *chut Thai* (Thai outfit), attracted much attention from diners as well. At Royal Thai, customers received service from "waiters in their traditional Thai shirts" who were "efficient and caring and write the orders in Thai for the kitchen workers."[64] At Chan Dara, diners could expect to be treated "by gracious Thai girls" and the "handsome, young crew of Thais whose serving manner is obliging, airy and pleasant."[65] As a result, Thai restaurants became spaces for crossracial and crosscultural interactions.

Even though it was a role and responsibility they could not escape because of their racialized bodies, acting as unofficial cultural diplomats gave Thais a sense of empowerment. It offered them a chance to foster positive relations between Thais and U.S. citizens in Los Angeles. Prakas Yenbamroong, for example, saw Thai eating establishments as gateways to Thai culture and cultural understanding: "I look at Thai restaurants and Talésai as cultural ambassadors ... whether or not we like it we represent Thailand, culturally ... automatically ... I try be a good window or ambassador to Thai culture."[66] Furthermore, restaurants allowed Thais to receive crash courses on Americans—and how to deal with them. At Tepparod Thai 1, owner Chow

Buranasombati learned to acquiesce to white customers who were "sometimes in a very bad mood when they come in" but "after they have eaten they turn into very nice people."[67]

It is important to note that a few restaurateurs tried to move away from the "traditional" Thai restaurant setting and its static representation of Thai culture. At Talésai, Prakas Yenbamroong opted for an original, modern design because he wanted an atmosphere that aligned with the innovative Thai food he served. After purchasing the existing restaurant on the property in 1982, Bangkok No. 2, Yenbamroong was initially set on naming his new place "Heart of Siam." He even had a $2,000 sign made. Soon thereafter, he hired an Italian designer, Nini, for $10,000 to help infuse the restaurant with contemporary flair. The designer convinced him to scrap "Heart of Siam" (and the $2,000 sign) for a name that would better reflect what was going to be a nontraditional Thai restaurant. Nini asked Yenbamroong, "what is the Thai name for desert?"[68] After Yenbamroong responded, "Talésai," Nini said "That's it!" Yenbamroong liked the new name because it sounded stylish and, more importantly, was aimed at his target clientele: the "blue eyes."

On one of this first visits to the restaurant in 1983, Colman Andrews described Talésai as "something special," adding, "it doesn't look like a Thai restaurant to begin with. It's more California-contemporary than Bangkok traditional in appearance—spare, white, clean-lined, cool. Accents of color and soft shape are added by the handsome graphics, sculptures and glass room dividers of Thai artist Kamol Tassananchalee. If you went by décor alone here, you'd expect to get hot goat cheese salad and grilled Sonoma lamb, not *thom yum gai* and *yum goong chiang*."[69] Despite such attempts by Thai restaurateurs to define restaurants on their own terms and in their own vision through setting and ambience, sensory experiences with Thai cuisine would effectively reinscribe Thais as a racially exotic Other.

SENSING "THAI"

Whereas restaurants helped shape Thai American identity through names, décor, and ambience, the production and consumption of Thai cuisine contributed much more powerfully to the racialization of Thais in Los Angeles. American diners did not go to Thai restaurants for the ambience. They went seeking a sensuous experience with the food on the plate. Thai cuisine satiated that quest because it awakened new parts of the American palate. "I have yet to meet a Westerner," claimed Rose Dosti, "who is not absolutely enthralled with the taste of Thai food. Spicy, yes, but tasty beyond words."[70] Ruth Reichl also captured Angelenos' affair with the pleasurable gustatory experiences of Thai food in an end-of-the-decade piece for the *Los Angeles Times*—in which she declared, "when it comes to eating, the '80s were L.A.'s decade" and "people in Los Angeles proved they were exceptionally adventurous eaters."[71] Reichl reflected on Thai food: "we loved the heat, we loved the sweet, we loved the coconut flavor that bound so many of the dishes together. We loved the way it looked and we loved the way it tasted. Most of us couldn't get enough of it." For Reichl, Thai food offered an exciting explosion of flavors for Los Angeles' sensation-seeking "adventurous eaters." Fellow restaurant reviewer Charles Perry agreed, proclaiming, "there may be no more appealing cuisine in the world than Thai."[72]

Sensory experiences with Thai food emerged as an incredibly useful and effective way to construct Thais as an exotic other. They marked racial, ethnic, and national difference—and thus produced racial knowledge and perpetuated racial thinking—through other human senses besides sight. Taste was particularly key to Thai American racial formation. Taste, in visceral and emotional ways, drew boundaries around food and the people who cook and eat the food, distinguished between the foreign and the familiar, linked cuisine and individuals to places, and above all inscribed relations of power onto plates and bodies. The sensory construction of Thais inside restaurants rendered Thais visible and legible to American society at a moment of intense social disruption in Los Angeles caused by increased immigration and multiculturalism.

Of all the flavors in Thai food, spiciness became most strongly associated with "Thai." By the mid 1980s, Thai food had solidified its reputation as a spicy cuisine, evidenced by restaurant critics' consistent mention of an establishment's propensity for heat in their reviews. After Dick Roraback and his friends sampled the food at four different Thai restaurants in the San Fernando Valley, all within a ten-mile stretch, Roraback announced that what they ate "further confirmed an old suspicion: For the Thais, spice is the variety of life."[73] Thai restaurants across Los Angeles gained recognition for serving up "spectacularly spicy food" similar to the kind on the "sidewalk cafes of Thailand."[74]

Thai cuisine was synonymous with spicy. The notion that Thai cooking was inherently spicy, and that eating fiery hot food was some immutable feature of being Thai, became so entrenched that critics considered nonspicy and even mild Thai food to be inauthentic. If a restaurant served "gently spiced" dishes, it was seen as an attempt to cater to the American palate and betrayal of "true" Thai taste. Mild Thai was "tourist Thai."[75] On the other hand, critics acknowledged that not every Thai dish was supposed to be spicy. They did this to challenge misconceptions but also to alleviate fears about whether Thai food was palatable. In her review of Siamese Princess, Barbara Hansen assured "those who dread the intense heat associated with Thai cookery can get through an entire meal without encountering a chile."[76] Hansen also informed her readers that Thai restaurants would tone down the heat of dishes upon request. At SukoThai, she reported, the waitresses will "obligingly" explain "the dishes and may ask you how hot you want them, as most Americans cannot take as much chile as the Thais."[77] Despite the fact that not all Thai food was spicy, and that Thai restaurants tried to make this clear by using asterisks to identify the hot and spicy items on their menus, the view that spiciness was fundamental to and ubiquitous in Thai cuisine persisted.

While spiciness got much of the attention, eaters picked up on the fact that spicy heat was simply one element of Thai cooking. Their palates recognized that the spiciness from chilis—fresh and dried—gave Thai dishes not just a sharp and intense heat but also immense flavor, especially when combined or blended with sour, salty, sweet, and creamy flavors. As Rose Dosti enthusiastically expressed, "It's hard to tell what chemical reaction takes place in the mixing and melding of chiles, ginger, coriander, fennel, garlic, herbal laos root, and mint in the hands of a Thai cook, but what a taste it is."[78] Lemongrass was another defining component of Thai cooking that eaters stumbled upon. The fragrant herb, specifically the lower part of its stalks, contained an essence of lemon that provided a subtle sour flavor to Thai soups, curries, and salads. Dick Roraback first learned of lemongrass and its permeating quality during a meal at Bangkok West: "shards of tasty greens bobbed in an opaque broth the color of prepubescent salmon, and under it all, a gently insistent taste of . . . ? 'Lemon grass,' said our waiter."[79] So rather than spicy heat alone, it was the perfect balancing of flavors—*yum*—that made Thai cuisine original and distinct.

Yum distinguished Thai food from other types of Asian cuisine, namely Chinese. When early Thai restaurants advertised their food as "Thai-Chinese," they made it seem as if Thai food and Chinese food were similar, perhaps even the same. Yet Americans learned that while many Thai and Chinese dishes may have appeared similar, the flavors of Thai cuisine were far different from the Chinese (specifically Cantonese) flavors that had become familiar to many in the United States. Food critic Colman Andrews teased out the difference between the two food traditions in 1976:

> "Some influences from the Chinese exist, of course, but most of the ingredients and cooking methods Thais use derive from quite another tradition—that of Indonesian and Malaysian food. Chicken and various meats are marinated and barbecued. Noodles appear in dozens of guises, hot and cold, thin and thick, crisp and soft. Curries, usually made with coconut milk, are popular. Cilantro seems to get thrown into everything. Other staples of Thai cooking include laos (a root similar to ginger), lemon grass, dried lime leaves (called makrut), mint, cucumbers, peanuts, anchovy sauce, rice vinegar, garlic, tamarind, and a variety of chili peppers—each one hotter than the last (All Thai dishes aren't spicy hot, but a good many of them are.)."

As a final note to underscore the difference, Andrews added, "One other thing: The right way to eat Thai food is with a fork (and, if necessary, a spoon). Only turistas use chopsticks."[80]

Taste proved to be a reliable way to identify and differentiate Thai food especially since all "Oriental" food seemingly looked alike. For example, Beverly Bush Smith described the ginger chicken with "julienne of fresh ginger, strips of black funghi and mushrooms" at Royal Thai as "Chinese in appearance" but "Thai in its seasoning." "Similarly," she noted," the shrimp with cucumbers, tomatoes and green peppers is prepared in a sweet and sour sauce, but it is not as syrupy as most Chinese sweet and sour sauces and is much more intriguing."[81] Dick Roraback also experienced a "Chinese puzzle" at Krung Tep. "On first impression, fairly ordinary Oriental fare," Roraback said of the dishes at the "least exotic" Thai restaurant he tried during his brief Thai food tour in the San Fernando Valley. But "then the subtleties begin to sneak up," he revealed, with Krung Tep's cooks doing "things with thin sliced beef that may look Chinese but shifts Thai-ward with every bite, nudged by a sprig of cilantro, a mellow sauce, a chorus of odd little mushrooms fresh from 'Fantasia.'"[82] So when it came to categorizing the expanding variety of Asian ethnic cuisines, sight had its limitations. It could be misleading and therefore undependable. What eyes could not adequately categorize, the tongue did.

As the American palate learned to decipher Thai food and other kinds of food, taste and flavors also developed into a means to discern Thai people from other kinds of people. Local food critics played a lead role in explaining the difference between Thais and other groups through sensory experiences with Thai cuisine. Colman Andrews, Rose Dosti, Lois Dwan, Jonathan Gold, Barbara Hansen, and Ruth Reichl wrote extensively on the city's Thai food scene in the 1970s and 1980s, specifically for the *Los Angeles Times*. They not only introduced Los Angeles to the "delicate" and "complex" flavors of Thai cooking, they were also among the first to publicly document the experiences of the Thai community in Los Angeles with some authority. They profiled the background and lives of Thai restaurateurs. They spotlighted the culinary perspectives of Thai chefs. They took photographs of Thais. They offered snapshots of Thai history, culture, and immigration. In short, they made Thais visible to U.S. society through restaurant food practices.

Food critics often indirectly shaped race and ethnicity by linking taste, place, and human diversity. In their view, human populations could be defined and understood using flavors, textures, and smells. They also assumed that there was, despite cultural interaction and change, a significant level of uniqueness for each of these populations. In 1981 Colman Andrews authored another piece in the *Los Angeles Times* where he charted the difference between Thai and Chinese food and, again, proclaimed that Thai food was "very much its own thing: an original, complex, remarkably well-defined cuisine." Andrews argued that contemporary Thai food in Los Angeles, a "major culinary treasure," was the result of a "distillation of thousands of years of history in the heart of what is perhaps the greatest cultural crossroads in the world." Moving swiftly through these thousands of years of Thai food history, Andrews emphasized that it was "most influenced by the food of south India and Ceylon [Sri Lanka], and possesses many similarities with that of Malaysia (which Thailand borders) and Indonesia" and noted that "the obvious Chinese touches are probably fairly recent—the work of the country's large Chinese minority." He mentioned the way cultural contact and trade, such as with South Asian Indians and the Portuguese, led to new ingredients and forms of food preparation. He also celebrated Thailand's ability to avoid European colonization and remain independent, a feat that helped "maintain the integrity and identity of Thai cooking, as surely as the kingdom's almost-encyclopedic cultural intercourse helped to develop it."[83]

Andrews's compelling historical overview of Thai cooking classified Thais racially. In a much more subtle argument, he asserted that centuries before the Chinese invented "classical Chinese cuisine" or before organized agriculture flourished in the Middle East and in Central America, indigenous peoples who inhabited Southeast Asia around 10,000 BC had already developed sophisticated cultures—including cooking styles and other advancements in food like rice cultivation. "Today's Thais," he asserted, "are descendants of those Southeast Asian groups, and—most important—a Mongolic Lao-Thai people."[84] In categorizing Thais as a "Mongolic Lao-Thai" people during the 1980s, Andrews at once grouped Thais into a discrete geographic category that separated them from Chinese and other Asians. Most importantly, he classified Thais at a time when the U.S. nation-state had no official racial or ethnic classification for "Thai."[85] As a result, he not only illustrated how Thai cooking was different from Chinese cooking but also implied that this culinary difference, captured by flavors and tastes, meant that Thais as a group were distinct from other peoples from Asia.

Some food critics even went as far as to say that Thais were biologically well suited to eat spicy food and to be cooks. Lois Dwan explicitly said that Thais had a physical capacity to handle spicy heat that white Americans did not—and most likely would not attain. "I am not crusading for the hot chili pepper. Most of us will never acquire the calluses or whatever is needed to cope," Dwan wrote as she enlightened readers about the indispensable role of spicy flavor in Thai cooking.[86] Food critics also made a series of claims about the racial and cultural fitness of Thais to cook. In their view, the large number of Thai restaurants in Los Angeles was a sign that Thais were naturally gifted, or at the very least culturally inclined, to prepare food. In a 1982 column, Dwan remembered a friend asking, "Was everyone in Thailand a chef?" and followed with "Or are they all naturally good cooks? All these restaurants . . ." Similarly, Charles Perry observed, "sometimes, to judge from the high quality of Thai restaurants in California (I'm not speaking of the "Thai-Chinese" places), it seems the Thais must be a nation of natural cooks."[87] Although lighthearted, comments like these contributed to the idea that Thais were not only racially and ethnically different but also uniquely suited for food service.

Thais played right into this discourse of racial, ethnic, and national distinction. They, too, relied on taste and flavors to set themselves apart—but also above—other groups, particularly Chinese and Southeast Asians. When food critics stereotyped Thais as having a cultural and natural ability to handle spicy food like no other, Thais responded pridefully, "Americans can't eat so hot like we do."[88] When critics described the taste of Thai cuisine as "more coherent than any other in Southeast Asia," Thais emphatically agreed.[89] For restaurateurs and chefs this coherency meant they were more creative and skillful at combining flavors than other Asians. Thai cuisine was also a way for Thais to express ethnic pride and nationalism because it embodied anti-colonial resistance.

Drawing on dominant narratives of Thai food history (that it developed from centuries of trade and exchange with the Chinese, South Asian Indians, Portuguese, and neighboring populations), Thai chefs interpreted Thai flavors as a successful borrowing, mixing, choosing, and discarding of food practices and ingredients.[90] They depicted it as a product of Thai peoples' political savvy and cleverness—characteristics that enabled Thailand to remain the only sovereign nation in Southeast Asia.[91] In her 1986 cookbook *Thai Home Cooking from Kamolmal's Kitchen* chef and restaurateur Kamolmal Pootaraksa wrote that in spite of its "outside" influences, "Thai food has a character distinct from that of the other countries in Southeast Asia. This is due in part to the rugged independence of the Thai people, but perhaps more to the fact that Thailand is the only country in Southeast Asia that was never colonized by a Western power."[92] Prakas Yenbamroong shared this view and emphasized the superiority of Thais over fellow Southeast Asians. He explained, "the history of Thai cuisine ... we developed by adopting and adapting and then defin[ing] to create our own ... what our ancestors did was a neat thing."[93] "Southeast Asian[s]," he added, "we share many of the ingredients, but the Thai came out ahead ... so balanced, so ... harmonious."[94]

Thai restaurateurs and chefs also relied on taste to highlight regional differences amongst themselves. During the 1980s, regional identities in Thailand operated as salient and celebrated points of distinction, especially between the rural northeast and the urban cosmopolitan central region where Bangkok was located.[95] This regional distinctiveness played out in Los Angeles's Thai community with a third wave of Thai immigration. By the early 1980s northeastern-style Thai cuisine, or Isaan, had become part of the city's Thai food scene.[96] Los Angeles was perhaps the only place outside of Thailand with restaurants specializing in this regional culinary style. Unlike the "palace influenced," central Bangkok-style Thai cuisine many Americans had come to know as Thai food, Isaan cuisine was simpler, spicier, bolder, and more bitter and pungent. It reflected a deep Lao influence given the close proximity of the region's provinces to the Laos border. Northeastern Thais were even considered "of Lao extraction" and closer "linguistically, culturally, and gastronomically to Lao than to their own countrymen around Bangkok."[97]

Isaan dishes were, according to food reviewer Linda Burum, "dramatically different" from Bangkok-style Thai dishes. "The familiar mee krob—stuffed, deep-fried chicken wings—or complex coconut-milk-based curries," wrote

Burum, "are far more elaborate than rustic, uncomplicated Isaan dishes." Yet the simplicity did not mean simplicity of flavors, as "Isaan cooks transformed their limited range of ingredients into glorious fusions of taste and texture: Meats are simply charcoal-grilled-or even served raw—and accompanied by fiery dipping sauces. Or they are sliced and tossed with chile and lime into fresh herb-filled salads."[98] Dishes such as *larb*—a chopped meat-based (chicken, beef, pork, or duck) dish mixed with lime juice, dry ground red chilis, and roasted ground rice powder—and *sup nor mai*—a tart spicy shredded bamboo shoot salad—exemplified the culinary tradition. Khao niao (sticky white rice) was another mainstay of an Isaan meal. Instead of steamed white rice, Isaan restaurants served dishes with khao niao, often in a *kra tip* (classic Isaan-style woven basket). Diners picked it up with their fingers and used it to sop up sauces and morsels of food.

Restaurants allowed northeastern Thais to sustain and assert their regional identities alongside their Thainess in the United States. A handful of places showcased northeastern flavors enough to gain recognition for both Isaan cuisine and people.[99] Mongkorn Kaiswai, a chef and restaurateur from northeastern Thailand, was featured twice in the *Los Angeles Times* during the 1980s for his ability to manage "a fascinating balance of tastes from ingredients traditionally used in his native northeastern Thailand."[100] As head chef of Thai Gourmet in Northridge, Kaiswai committed himself to keeping the essential character of Isaan cooking in a restaurant that served majority central-style fare (northeastern dishes listed separately under "house specialties") and catered to the American palate. While his dishes might have at times strayed "a little to the south [of Thailand] and elsewhere," Kaiswai's northeastern culinary skills gave "distinction to the familiar." His cooking earned Thai Gourmet a prestigious Gault-Millau award as the highest-rated ethnic restaurant in Los Angeles. After Kaiswai left Thai Gourmet to open his own restaurant, Rama Thai, in nearby Van Nuys, his food continued to attract fanfare. Jonathan Gold called Kaiswai "perhaps the most celebrated of local Thai chefs" and praised the "light, fresh, searingly hot" Isaan dishes at Rama Thai for giving Thai cuisine a boost beyond "the Malaysian-influenced Bangkok cooking that you might be sick of by now."[101] Despite sometimes subsuming Isaan dishes under the generic "Thai" in menus, Isaan chefs managed to shine light on Thailand's regional diversity and the complexities within Thai America through taste and flavors.

Another major development in the taste and flavors of Thai cuisine in Los Angeles in this period was the "Americanization" of Thai food.[102] Thai restaurant chefs altered flavors to appeal to the American palate. Put another way, they adapted to what white Americans considered acceptable to eat. This meant accommodating novice and less adventurous palates by reducing or eliminating spiciness, adding more sweetness, and discarding staple ingredients that might be seen as too exotic or repulsive, such as nam plah (fish sauce) or congealed pork blood.[103] In 1985 food critic Charles Perry praised Thai food as "an exotic cuisine that has retained its native qualities remarkably well transplanted to our shores," but added disappointingly, "In the last couple of years, though, it seems to me that its range of flavors is slowly being constricted in order to cater to the American sweet tooth—the apparent fate of any cuisine that ever puts sweet sauces on meat or salad."[104]

Thai chefs also catered specifically to white Americans by incorporating "Western" ingredients, flavors, and preparation techniques. No one accomplished this quite like Tommy Tang. At his Siamese Café on Melrose Avenue, Tang created a number of Thai crossover dishes, such as Thai Risotto and Duck and Arugula Salad, which struck a balance between the exotic and the familiar.[105] One exemplary dish was his crispy duck. Tang took roasted duck and gave it a Thai twist by preparing it flash deep fried to make the skin crispier and serving it deboned, sliced, and drizzled with a Thai honey ginger sauce—a mix of honey, ginger root, and plum sauce.[106] Food critic Rose Dosti praised the dish as an "example of the innovative intermixture of flavors that please the Western palate while respecting the authenticity of its Southeast Asian roots."

For Tang, who came up with the dish because he wanted to combine his love of both French duck and Chinese duck, it stayed true to his culinary philosophy. Tang's cookbook *Modern Thai Cuisine* further revealed the thinking behind his version of Thai cuisine and the dishes served at his restaurant: "I use a number of ingredients that are not indigenous to Thailand's cooking, preferring to mix the best of East and West into my own lighter, simpler, and more versatile cuisine. Such ingredients as rosemary, arugula, cream, pine nuts, and olive oil do not belong to the standard Thai repertoire, but I find that they enhance it immensely. Additions like these put my own personal stamp on the recipes, not to mention making them uniquely delicious."[107]

By altering flavors to accommodate American palates, Thai chefs like Tang were no doubt trying to broaden their consumer base and make customers happy. However, they also exhibited their culinary range as they twisted and tweaked flavors to create new versions of Thai dishes. Moreover, they challenged rigid, monolithic notions of "traditional" and "authentic" Thai cuisine. But above all, Americanized Thai food allowed Thai chefs to distance themselves from immigrant-ness. This was especially true for Tang. He had desperately wanted to shed his immigrant status, made clear by his many comments about there being "no future" for him within the Thai community (by which he meant Thai immigrants). Translating Thai cooking to American taste was his way of helping Thai cuisine cross over and integrate into the Los Angeles culinary mainstream. Yet it also facilitated his integration, as a Thai immigrant, into dominant U.S. society. Tang's dishes communicated on the plate that Thais were willing to adjust, change, and "go out and meet" white American society rather than force white Americans to change for them. He wanted to show that Thais could maintain yet adapt (rather than discard) their culture and make it palatable and therefore nonthreatening.

Cooking Americanized and "modern" Thai cuisine was directly related to the racialization of Thais. To be clear, it did not mean Thais in Los Angeles rejected Thainess or even foreignness. Rather, it embodied a collective fear of being seen as too foreign and too exotic for American society. Thai restaurants simply did not have the luxury of cooking with so-called unusual ingredients or street-style fare for white customers because Thai dishes were inextricably associated with Thai bodies. They had to be mindful of ingredients, flavors, and preparation methods lest they break the threshold of acceptable multiculturalism and, as a result, be deemed repulsive, backward, uncivilized, and "Third World."

BEHIND THE KITCHEN DOOR

Thai restaurants were more than sites for the creation and consumption of new commercial cuisines. They were also sites of Thai American labor. Behind the success of Thai chefs and the increased popularity of Thai food were Thai workers who prepared and brought food to tables. They confronted and negotiated the class and gender inequalities endemic of the restaurant industry, especially in global cities that depended on low-wage jobs and consumer services. Thai restaurants were not simply places for eating out or interactions with the exotic but also, "behind the kitchen door," places rife with exploitation, human rights violations, poor working conditions, and racism and sexism.[108]

Thai eating establishments were plagued by a number of issues that exacerbated class divisions in Los Angeles's Thai American community. Restaurant owners relied heavily on the low or unpaid labor of family and friends, especially their children. When they did compensate workers, restaurants paid low wages often well below minimum wage (and under the table) and offered little to no benefits.[109] They also took full advantage of the labor of undocumented Thais and other immigrants. During the Thai food boom, East Hollywood supplied the Thai restaurant labor force. These food-service workers were indispensable, to extend from Mike Davis, to the "Oz-like archipelago of Westside pleasure domes—a continuum of tony malls, art centers and gourmet strips" that was "reciprocally dependent upon the social imprisonment of the third-world service proletariat who live in increasingly repressive ghettoes and barrios."[110]

The racialized gendered divisions of labor and exploitation that characterized the post-1965 service sector economy were also prevalent inside Thai restaurants. Whereas Thai men worked a wide range of jobs—dishwashers, cooks, servers, busboys, and deliverymen—Thai women, including mothers and grandmothers, mostly performed the cooking duties in the "back of the house" in groups led by a *mae krua*.[111] Younger Thai women, however, also worked in the "front of the house" as waitresses and servers to fulfill a prescribed role as a physical, gendered embodiment of exotic Thai culture. The owners of Chan Dara exploited the sexuality of Thai women by hiring "waitresses on how they look, and especially on how they dress."[112]

Thai restaurant workers also endured difficult working conditions and poor treatment from employers. Kitchens were dangerous environments. They contained a number of hazards in a physically small, contained space: sharp blades, slippery floors, open fire, smoke, hot oil splashing, and hot pots and pans. Cooking and preparing food also required repetitive and intense physical labor that often resulted in muscle strains, joint pains, and other nagging injuries. Additionally, workers were often forced to skip meals and breaks during peak hours. Aside from the physical toll, the restaurant business involved a great deal of stress and pressure that also had a damaging emotional and psychological impact on Thai workers. Verbal abuse from owners was common. As employers, parents, and middle- and upper-class Thais with clout in the community, owners often used their power and authority to dominate employees into properly performing and executing tasks. Workers, in turn, had little room to fight for better treatment because of the hierarchical structure of restaurants, their low social capital in the community, and for many their citizenship status.

The grueling hours and unrelenting schedule of restaurant work left little time to spend with family or for any semblance of a social life. This was not only true for lower-level cooks and servers but also restaurant owners. The owners of Chan Dara, Bhasuwongse "Vavy" and Sukhum "Ken" Kittivech, committed 15-hour days to grow their restaurant into one of the busiest and well-known Thai eateries in Hollywood. By 1983 the couple had opened another Chan Dara in nearby Hancock Park, employed about 50 people, and served approximately 450 people a day. But their economic success came at a personal and emotional cost. *The Los Angeles Times*'s Charles Keeley poignantly captured the toll in a piece on Vavy and Ken: "'We have been a big success in business,' [Vavy] smiles, tears suddenly welling up in large black eyes. 'Our family life has not been so successful.' Ken squeezes her shoulder. Silently they look at each other for a moment before returning to work—she in Hollywood, he in Hancock Park."[113]

Wandee Pathomrit's experiences as a cook in Thai restaurants across Los Angeles highlights the typical yet unique, individual ways Thai workers persevered behind the kitchen door. Born in Thailand in 1955, Pathomrit began cooking in restaurants in the mid-1980s, right as Thai cuisine hit its stride in popularity. She learned about Thai food-service jobs while in Thailand. Her mother, who had already been working at Thai eating establishments in Hollywood for several years, recruited her. In 1985 Wandee came to Los Angeles on a tourist visa along with her husband, leaving their two small children behind in Thailand. She started working immediately under her mother as a cook and server at a cafeteria-style Thai eatery in East Hollywood catering to Thai immigrants. Over the next few years she moved around as a lower-level cook (under the *mae krua*) in a number of different restaurants before finally taking a position as *mae krua* at Arunee's House in Toluca Lake in 1989.

Pathomrit earned low wages for her labor. She worked an average of 10–12 hours a day, seven days a week, and was paid, depending on the restaurant, $150 to $200 per week. Given the number of hours worked, she made at most $2.80/hour—well under minimum wage during this period.[114] She was mostly paid under the table without overtime pay or any benefits.[115] To supplement wages Pathomrit helped Thai vendors at weekend food festivals at the Wat Thai of Los Angeles in North Hollywood. She spent most of her earnings sending money back to Thailand to support her two children, paying back her debt to family and friends who loaned her the money to make the trip to the United States, and on rent for a small apartment in East Hollywood, which she shared with several other Thai women food-service workers to save money. In 1986, she was forced to take time off without pay when she became pregnant with her third child. After giving birth to a baby girl, Wanda, she returned to work one month later.

Pathomrit spent almost all of her waking hours at work. Between the meager wages and long days, she simply did not have the money or time to spend on leisure activities or balance a social life. Plus, without sick or injury leave or health insurance she tried to work as much as possible to make ends meet. She recalled, "Going out with friends wasn't even an option. All I did was work. Didn't matter if I was sick or injured, it was only work. Even [if] injured, you have to go to work . . . I didn't have any insurance or any kind of support."[116] As a result most of her socializing took place at work with other kitchen staff, usually a small crew of Thais as well as other Asians and Latinos. During her time at Arunee's House, Pathomrit worked alongside Thais, Lao, Khmer, Chinese, and Mexicans—all of whom were working-class immigrants who "didn't have any skills [so] they came to [work] in the kitchen."[117] They worked well together and for the most part got along. She enjoyed showing them, particularly the Mexican cooks, how to prepare and develop a taste for Thai flavors. They enjoyed playing pranks on each other and laughing together, relying on gestures and facial expressions to communicate because of language barriers.

While the restaurant kitchen was a space for positive crossracial and crossethnic interactions, it also gave way to the reinforcement of ethnic stereotypes and racial ideologies. For example, Pathomrit hardened her belief of Lao as unclean and uncouth after witnessing their cooking, food handling, and communication practices: "The Lao are dirty and they are not very clean and they don't speak properly." In addition, when Arunee's House's profits started to drop she blamed it on the Mexican cooks, believing the restaurant "started going downhill when [the owner] began hiring Mexican workers."[118]

Being a cook was physically demanding and highly stressful for Pathomrit. It was, as she described it in Thai, "heavy work." As *mae krua* of Arunee's House her main responsibilities were prepping and cooking. She developed a number of lingering aches and pains from the daily repetitive tasks of cutting, chopping, slicing, and dicing meats and vegetables as well as from cooking with heavy equipment. Pathomrit specifically recalled developing long-term wrist pain from having to cook with a twenty-pound Chinese wok, which required repeated lifting to toss food for stir-fry dishes, some days for

FIGURE 3. Wandee Pathomrit working in the kitchen of Arunee's House Thai restaurant in Toluca Lake, California, ca. early 1990s. Photograph courtesy of Wandee Pathomrit.

twelve hours straight. Her wrist pain became so intense that she routinely took steroid shots. She also developed chronic nerve pain in both of her legs. Arunee's House's kitchen was also a fast-paced, pressure filled environment. It was critical for Pathomrit to make sure the kitchen was fully prepped for rush service. Lunch was the busiest and most hectic time. Lunchtime patrons had only 30–40 minutes to eat their meal before returning to work, which gave Pathomrit and her crew less than 10 minutes to prepare an entire table's dishes. A mistake sent the kitchen scrambling and the owner into a rage.

The habitual verbal abuse from the owner, "Pa Thaan," was the most punishing part of Pathomrit's experience at Arunee's House. Pa Thaan had a bad temper she frequently unleashed on workers. According to Pathomrit, when the staff made a mistake or if Pa Thaan saw "something she did not like, she would come down hard on her employees ... everything had to be clean, within codes, dishes prepared beautifully, [the food] had to taste good. If it did not taste good, if a customer complained, she would blow up on us. If customers sent their dishes back to the kitchen, she would blow up on us. It's true, [she was] very vicious. Some workers only stayed 4, 3, 2 days. I stayed a long time, thirteen years."[119]

Pa Thaan openly criticized and humiliated Pathomrit and other employees by calling them *kwai*, a common Thai insult meaning "stupid as a buffalo." Pathomrit's daughter, Wanda, despite being a young child at the time, remembered vividly the way Pa Thaan was "very verbally abusive to all her employees . . . it felt like [Pa Thaan] wasn't happy all the time . . . and she really displaced her emotions on her workers . . . and I could sense the energy of the space, it just felt really depressing, and I could see that my mom was really sad and impacted by just having to tolerate this."[120] Pathomrit tried to externalize the constant degradation at home by gossiping with other Thai coworkers about Pa Thaan. Wanda recalled overhearing a conversation in which they called their boss "bitchy" and ridiculed Pa Thaan for trying to befriend employees because "she didn't have any real friends."[121]

The power relations between Pa Thaan and her employees amplified underlying class rifts in the Thai American community. As a successful restaurateur, Pa Thaan was part of a growing number of Thai middle- and upper-class entrepreneurs in Los Angeles seeking the American dream. Pathomrit and her Thai coworkers were on the other end, part of an expanding Thai working-class stuck in low paying service jobs but also looking to achieve upward mobility. These class divisions were salient inside Arunee's House because of the restaurant's clear hierarchy of jobs but also in large part because of the family-like relationship Pa Thaan developed with many of her workers. For the employees, getting treated like a family member by Pa Thaan allowed them to get a glimpse into how the other Thais—the middle- and upper-class—in Los Angeles lived.

This was especially true for Pathomrit, who learned all about her boss's opulent lifestyle through the eyes of her daughter, Wanda. As she spent her childhood inside Arunee's House, Wanda got to know Pa Thaan and her world well. According to Wanda, Pa Thaan was nice and watched over her while Wanda's mother worked in the kitchen. Pa Thaan also had a daughter who was Wanda's age, and so she "adopted" Wanda as a child who could play with her daughter. As a result Wanda spent a significant amount of time with Pa Thaan's family. She went to sleepovers at their "grand, massive house" in the hills of Sherman Oaks with "all of these toys" and was "always riding around in a Mercedez-Benz." The stark class distinction between her mother and Pa Thaan was obvious. "I always felt weird," she reflected, "I knew there was a class difference between the employer and my mom . . . you see [these] power dynamics and you kind of don't understand it but for me it was kind of, I kind of looked down on my family because we weren't as rich. . . . I really felt that difference in class."[122]

The visible class division did not lead to any resistance (beyond quitting), critiques of Pa Thaan's labor practices, or collective mobilization for better pay and work conditions among her employees. Instead, it led to internalized classism and a desire for a middle- and upper-class lifestyle via restaurateurship. Despite years of demeaning comments and mistreatment, Pathomrit did not consider Pa Thaan to be wholly bad. Pathomrit later described her longtime employer as *kohn bahk laeng, jai dee*—a verbally abusive person with a good heart. There was a reason for this. Pa Thaan had helped her in a number of ways over their thirteen-year relationship. She recruited Pathomrit to serve as *mae krua* by promising to help her obtain a green card, which Pathomrit desperately wanted so that she could bring the children she left behind in Thailand to the United States. Even though Pa Thaan used the green card as a carrot-and-stick to maintain power over and control her labor (before Arunee's House Pathomrit walked out on several jobs over verbally abusive employers but decided to endure it from Pa Thaan so as not to risk losing her chance at a green card), she eventually delivered on the promise and sponsored Pathomrit for a green card, allowing her to reunite her family in Los Angeles. When Pathomrit was ready to move from her apartment to a larger home in suburban North Hollywood to accommodate her now reunited family, Pa Thaan cosigned the mortgage. Professionally, Pa Thaan helped Pathomrit develop her cooking preparation methods to suit full-service restaurants, taught her about city health codes and inspections, and showed her how to operate a kitchen and the "front of the house."[123] Moreover, Pa Thaan assisted Pathomrit in jumpstarting her own Thai restaurant by loaning her $5,000 dollars of startup capital and agreeing to let Pathomrit pay back the loan in $500/month payments, interest free. These acts worked to suppress resentment Pathomrit might have felt toward Pa Thaan. In fact, she felt eternally indebted to her.

At the same time the Thai restaurant industry in Los Angeles in the 1970s and 1980s produced and elevated Thai restaurateurs such as Tommy Tang into the realm of celebrity chefs, they also cornered Thai immigrants like Wandee Pathomrit into low-paying and physically demanding food service jobs. As culinary contact zones, restaurants became spaces where Thais encountered and negotiated racial, gender, and class hierarchies and struggled for dignity and pride as service-sector workers. They also emerged as central sites of Thai American racial formation through other senses besides sight. The production and consumption of Thai food in restaurants helped sustain racial thinking and practice at a moment of heightened anti-immigrant sentiment but also a blossoming cuisine-driven multiculturalism in Los Angeles. By the mid-1980s Thai food culture had spread throughout Los Angeles, taking different forms (beyond the private restaurant) in different spaces—urban and suburban. As the next chapter shows, it was not always met with celebration and enthusiasm.

FOUR

"More Than a Place of Worship"

FOOD FESTIVALS AND THAI AMERICAN SUBURBAN CULTURE

IN THE CRISP, EARLY MORNING hours of Saturday, April 17, 1982, dozens of Thais from across Southern California arrived at Wat Thai of Los Angeles in preparation for the first day of a much-anticipated weekend festival to celebrate the Thai New Year's holiday and the 200th anniversary of King Rama I's decision to move the capital of Siam to Bangkok in 1782. Chatter and laughter filled the temple as volunteers busily erected a performance stage, set up the amplifier system, and unfolded chairs on the main lawn. By early afternoon, Wat Thai was packed with hundreds of visitors enjoying live electronic music, shopping for lampshade hats and hand-crafted trinkets, and eating grilled meats on sticks and bowls of noodles. The sights, sounds, and smells were reminiscent of weekend bazaars in Bangkok, but this temple sat on the corner of a residential suburban neighborhood street in the San Fernando Valley, about one hundred yards west of the Hollywood Freeway. A local writer observed that it looked "as if it had been plucked from Bangkok and set down by accident in North Hollywood."[1]

During the 1980s thousands of Thais used Wat Thai as a transnational community space to maintain cultural practices, especially food festivals. Wat Thai food festivals brought Thai people together face-to-face to cultivate a Thai American suburban culture. Beyond simple sustenance, and a merit-making practice of offering food to monks, the cooking, selling, and eating of Thai food at the temple manifested a vibrant public suburban culture that valued an expansive, democratic, and collective use of suburban space. This Thai American suburban ideal, fueled by food culture, fostered the development of social capital, community, and a public sociability that crossed many boundaries: ethnicity, citizenship status, class, and religion.

Even so, not everyone celebrated Wat Thai food fairs. As the festivals became more popular and well attended they triggered complaints of noise, trash, traffic, and parking problems from a group of nearby residents who used zoning laws to try to turn the temple from a lively community space to a "serene meditation center."[2] The festivals constituted a visibly, audibly, and olfactorily jolting presence that offended nearby homeowners' suburban imaginary grounded in respect for private property and quietness in pristine, single-family neighborhoods with plentiful parking. Zoning laws, designed to segregate and regulate land uses, provided legal backing that privileged the homeowners' vision of suburbia as the norm.

Temple food festivals allowed Thais in Los Angeles to not only recreate "home" and articulate Thainess in a suburban space but also to claim a "right to the suburb" based on an alternative suburban ideal centered on public culture and sociability that clashed with dominant imaginings of suburban life rooted in privatism. While Wat Thai and homeownership allowed Thais to inhabit the neighborhood physically, Thai food festivals allowed them to participate fully in the suburbs. That participation was the main point of conflict. The temple's everyday religious functions conformed to the neighborhood's privatist suburban ethos. The zoning boards and nearby residents approved of Wat Thai because they believed the "contemplative, meditative nature of Thai Buddhism" would not disrupt the peace and quiet of the neighborhood.[3] Food festivals, however, became the focal point of controversy because they exposed contrasting visions about the use and meaning of suburban space. While Thais considered food festivals indispensable to Wat Thai's purpose as a community center, many of the residents viewed them as a direct violation of the permitted proper use of suburban space.

The conflict forced both supporters and opponents of Wat Thai food festivals to make sense of their issues in order to resolve them. Framed by local media as a "culture clash," the controversy was at its core inextricably intertwined with race and class. Yet, whereas a number of scholars have written that white suburbanites' reactions to Asian American suburbanization during this period were rooted in anti-Asian bigotry, often expressed with the use of coded racial rhetoric about quality of life, property values, and slow growth, the white residents who opposed temple food festivals articulated a liberal multiculturalism.[4] They encouraged Thai cultural expressions in the neighborhood but only if stayed within the bounds of what they deemed to be acceptable adherence to suburban norms.

As the debate played out, the distinction between private and public space became further racialized: the private suburban residences surrounding the temple were encoded as white; the quasipublic Wat Thai as urban, and by extension, nonwhite. The arrival of Thais to the eastern San Fernando Valley triggered a stronger turn inward among the residents as contemporary suburban realities challenged the "white spatial imaginary."[5] Despite the fact that many of the Thai festivalgoers lived nearby, some even in the same neighborhood, they were portrayed as outsiders. The debate constructed Thais as undesirable urban immigrants and therefore subjected them to exclusion. As a result, the tangible nuisances and annoyances of the food festivals—noise, trash, traffic, and parking problems—were inscribed onto Asian immigrant bodies even though a number of visitors were not Thai. At the same time, Thais defended food festivals by claiming they were necessary for practicing Thai Buddhism. In the process, Thai foodways became more tightly interwoven with other prominent features of Thai identity, namely their religious identity as Theravada Buddhists. Thai responses and actions also revealed class and ethnic tensions inside the Thai community.

THE OTHER SAN FERNANDO VALLEY

The San Fernando Valley, a 260-square-mile area northwest of downtown Los Angeles, was in many respects the archetype of post-World War II suburban whiteness. Much of "the Valley" fit the description of a quintessential suburb, especially the west valley: white, middle- to upper-class havens of conformity for Americans who lived in low-density residences and commuted in their automobiles to work in the city.[6] Valley neighborhoods consisted of uniform houses and tree-lined streets. White suburbanites in the west valley used a range of tactics, including restrictive covenants, community appeals to the Los Angeles County Board of Supervisors, picketing, and outright harassment and other extralegal means to keep their neighborhoods all-white.[7]

But the Valley was much more racially and ethnically diverse, as well as working class. Since the establishment of the Spanish mission and rancho system in the late 1700s, the northeastern section of the Valley was a multiracial and multiethnic hub within a region that was overwhelmingly white.[8] From the early 1900s through World War II, Pacoima, for instance, developed into the only Valley interracial community that was home to a small yet noticeable number of black, Japanese, Chinese, and Mexican residents.[9] After the war, thousands of African Americans migrated to Pacoima to take advantage of new tract homes built and sold on a relatively unrestricted basis.[10] By 1950, five thousand residents out of the 402,538 total Valley residents were nonwhite, and nearly all could be found concentrated on the eastside.[11] In 1960 no other section of the Valley had a nonwhite population larger than 1 percent.[12] Moreover, Pacoima was one of the poorest areas of the Valley but also of Los Angeles as a whole, with some of the lowest levels of education, income, and representation in white-collar and professional work.[13] Thus, as these nonwhite groups experienced suburbanization on their own terms and created "places of their own," they remained largely cut off from the rest of the Valley by "invisible borders" as well as freeways and streets.[14]

The 1970s and 1980s marked a significant demographic transformation as Filipinos, Koreans, Guatemalans, and Salvadorians—many of whom were immigrants—bolstered this diversity.[15] Not surprisingly, this transformation occurred most definitively on the Valley's eastside, particularly in Arleta, Sun Valley, and Pacoima.[16] This movement of Asian immigrants and Asian Americans into the Valley during this period, a result of the Immigration Act of 1965 and to a lesser extent the growth of an Asian American middle class, also altered the composition of adjacent neighborhoods, such as Panorama City and North Hollywood, that were historically predominantly white.[17] During the 1970s this area was 68.6 percent white, 1.3 percent black, 16.8 percent "Spanish Origin" (both "white" and "other"), and 10.65 percent Asian.[18] A decade later, the White population dropped to 49.8 percent while the percentage of every nonwhite population group increased: Blacks to 2.2 percent, "Hispanics" to 25.9 percent (both "white" and "nonwhite"), and Asian or Pacific Islanders to 22.5 percent.[19] Equally important, in 1980 approximately 24 percent of the residents were listed as foreign born; by 1990 the percentage increased to 38.4 percent, or a total of 1,807 people out of 4,704 in the area.[20] This foreign-born population included both naturalized citizens and noncitizens, but recent arrivals who entered the United States between 1970 and 1990 made up 85.6 percent, or 1,547.[21]

Of the Asian/Pacific Islanders in the area, Thais made up the second largest ethnic group (25.7%) as a little over two hundred lived within a several block radius of the temple.[22] At the time Los Angeles was already home to the largest Thai American community and the largest concentrated Thai population outside of Thailand. The number of Thais in Los Angeles grew from a few hundred in 1965 to an estimated 10,000 by the mid-1970s; by 1990 the number reached approximately 100,000.[23] Initially, a majority of Thais settled in the multiracial, multiethnic, and largely immigrant neighborhood of East Hollywood.[24] During the 1980s, however, Thais from both other parts of Los Angeles and Thailand migrated to Arleta, Pacoima, and North Hollywood. By 1990, more than 1,000 Thais lived in the Valley, which eclipsed East Hollywood as the largest concentration of Thais in Southern California and in the nation.[25] One main reason why Thais moved to this part of the Valley when they did was to be near the newly erected Thai Buddhist temple, Wat Thai of Los Angeles.

WAT THAI OF LOS ANGELES

In 1979 Wat Thai of Los Angeles in North Hollywood became the first official Thai Buddhist temple in the nation. In July 1968, Phramaha Singsathon Naraspo and two other Thai monks traveled across Southern California to find a suitable location for America's first Theravada Buddhist temple.[26] They wanted a plot of land large enough for a temple, lecture hall, and housing facilities for resident monks. Initially, two sites were proposed: one in Palm Springs, roughly one hundred miles east of Los Angeles; one in Antelope Valley, about forty miles north. The monks deemed both sites to be too far away to adequately serve Thai residents and put plans on hold.

In the meantime, a group of Thai college students and middle-class professionals had also been organizing to build a temple. They formed the Thai American Buddhist Association and sparked serious momentum by meeting and forging relationships with Thai abbots and the monastic elite and by tapping into social and business networks to raise funds.[27] They even received endorsements from the Thai royal family, the prime minister, and major corporations like Thai Airways International.[28] In 1969, the group wrote a letter to the Supreme Patriarch in Thailand (who was appointed by King Bhumipol as the Head of the Buddhist Order) requesting that monks be assigned to Los Angeles. The Supreme Patriarch obliged, and on July 23, 1969, he sent six monks to Los Angeles.

The monks immediately developed a relationship with the community by conducting Buddhist rituals in Thai homes and attending events. On August 2, 1969, the Thai American Buddhist Association and the monks organized a Buddhist ceremony festival at Lynwood High School to celebrate the birth of Gautama Buddha. The celebration, known as *Asalah Boucha*, was the first held on U.S. soil. It attracted over one thousand participants and observers and raised nearly $4,000 in donations for a temple. More importantly, it demonstrated to Thai monastic elite that Los Angeles had enough commitment from Thais to make a temple a reality.[29]

Thais in Los Angeles needed to fill a spiritual void. Theravada Buddhism—a dynamic, complex, multifaceted organized religion—was without a doubt a salient feature of Thai identity and was often equated with *khuam pen Thai*, or Thainess. In the mid-1970s, approximately 93.4 percent of Thais in Thailand were Buddhist. As Thailand's state religion (under the constitution the king must be a Buddhist), it influenced and permeated all aspects of Thai society and life—from politics and the arts to education and the built environment—and was integrated into Thai national ideologies and identity.[30] Before arriving in Thailand, however, Theravada Buddhism spread to all parts of Southeast Asia. It originated in the fourth century B.C.E. and provided a religious system of moral virtues, rituals, and ceremonies designed to acquire merit for better rebirths. In its everyday form, the practice of Theravada Buddhism meant trying to keep and stay true to basic moral rules, observing rituals, and participating in worship and ceremonies inside the home. One of the key practices is *thambun* (merit making), which is the primary means for Thais to accumulate positive karma by giving and performing good deeds.[31] Thai Buddhist monks constitute a "field of merit" in which Thais could offer money and alms, such as food, in exchange for "spiritual merit to provide for the well-being of merit makers in this lifetime and the next."[32] Meditation was another important ritual of Theravada, and, when practiced seriously, offered a means to achieve both Enlightenment and Nirvana. These practices, which changed over time in relation to shifting sociopolitical and cultural contexts, took place in the omnipresent temples and monasteries of Thailand. As a central aspect of everyday life in Thailand, it is no wonder that Theravada Buddhism motivated Los Angeles Thais to work passionately and tirelessly to establish a temple in order to reproduce that belief system in their new home.

While Buddhism had been in the United States since the eighteenth century, the Thai American Buddhist Association became one of the first to introduce and institutionalize Theravada Buddhism and organize a Thai temple. In 1971 another mission of Thai monks, this time led by Phra Dhammakosacharn of Wat Ratbamroong, made an official visit to the United States. During their trip to Los Angeles, they met one of the leaders of the Thai American Buddhist Association, Punsak "Paul" Sosothikul, to plan the construction of a temple.

Sosothinkul was a prominent community member and the son of affluent parents in Thailand, Boonsum and Wichai Sosothikul, who owned several plots of land in Southern California. Sosothikul offered a plot in Sepulveda City near the Van Nuys airport as a proposed temple site. To formalize the process, Sosothikul and other members of the Thai American Buddhist Association created Theravada Buddhist Center, Inc., a nonprofit organization that was responsible for all temple related matters.[33]

On June 6, 1971, the Theravada Buddhist Center, with Sosothikul as president, began offering services out of a single-family suburban home.[34] The house, however, was too small. Temple officials came up with a plan to expand the site by building a large hall in traditional Thai temple architectural style. But they ran into barriers. First, they faced resistance from nearby residents who were incensed at the arrival of Thais and the increase of traffic to the neighborhood. The residents organized numerous town hall meetings and hearings with city officials to stop the expansion. City officials denied the temple a permit to construct the main hall, claiming that the structure height of the proposed building was too tall to be next to an airport, a violation of zoning ordinance. Thus, Theravada Buddhist Center, Inc. was forced to find another location.[35]

Sosothikul again came to the rescue. He borrowed money from his parents to purchase a 2.2-acre parcel of land at 12909 Cantara Street in North Hollywood—precisely where Arleta, Pacoima, Sun Valley, and Panorama City meet—and donated it to the center.[36] The new site, previously a Japanese American family-owned plant nursery, was ideal for the construction of a legitimate temple with a main hall, monk living quarters, temple court, and separate religious buildings. Two celebrations were held to recognize the donation and the start of a new chapter for the Theravada Buddhist Center, Inc. On May 18, 1972, temple leaders organized a ceremony for the passing of the deed from the Sosothinkul family to the Thai Buddhist Center, Inc. The next morning, at 6:09 a.m., the Supreme Patriarch laid the first foundation stone at the site, and a few hours later a bulldozer arrived to break ground for the temple.[37] The temple's treasurer, Urai Ruenprom, expressed his gratitude to his friend and enthused to local media, saying "he (Sosothikul) wanted to do something good for our people. . . . Religion is the most important thing for our people, the most important things in our lives."[38] To Ruenprom, Sosothikul's generous act reflected a deep commitment to Thais everywhere and acknowledgement of the importance of Buddhism to the well being of Thais in Los Angeles.[39]

Volunteerism was integral to the functioning of the new temple. Unlike in Thailand where the clergy operate the temples, lay Thais like Sosothikul and Ruenprom directed all of the activities at the Theravada Buddhist Center. This is because the first cohort of monks was not familiar with life in the United States and had to rely heavily on Thai community members to help them navigate and adjust to their new environment. Nearly all of the lay Thai volunteers were male and members of the Thai American middle class. The temple's board of directors, for instance, consisted of mostly prominent male community members and business leaders, including those from the Thai restaurant and food industry such as Surapol Mekpongsatorn and Pramorte Tilakamonkul, who served as vice president and executive vice president, respectively. They handled all operations from paperwork and fundraising to decision making and building working relationships with local, state, and federal agencies. In addition, lay Thais also took on the day-to-day responsibility of caring for the monks, who were housed in a single-family home next to the construction site. Volunteers often worked in shifts, with some even living with the monks, to handle daily chores and provide transportation.

Theravada Buddhist Center, Inc., did not have to worry about violating zoning codes at the new location. Although the neighborhood was zoned for residential use, temple officials applied for and secured a conditional use permit from the City of Los Angeles Department of City Planning's Office of Zoning Administration that allowed them to use the property in ways typically not permissible under the official zoning ordinance for the area. Put another way, the city gave the temple permission to operate with "conditions." The conditions had to be set and agreed upon by the zoning administration and nearby residents through a public hearing. So to obtain the permit, temple officials had to convince the residents and the zoning administration that the use of the temple would be compatible with the suburban neighborhood.

Temple representatives claimed the "meditative quality of the temple will be an asset to the community" and testified that "four to six festivals each year would be held, and that the religion was more meditative in nature than congregational, people would be coming to the temple frequently during the day, but not in large numbers at any one time."[40] Zoning administrator Fabian Romano approved of the conditions and granted the permit on September 15, 1972. Romano did so with the impression that the temple would not be a nuisance to the peace and quiet of the surrounding area, and that special celebrations "were to be the exception, rather than the rule."

While the temple was erected primarily with private money on private land, developing the place felt like a communal responsibility. During early construction, the plot of land had to be cleared of weeds, rocks, and several trees. Volunteers commonly shoveled dirt, cut trees, cleared branches, or nailed wooden frames for the Wat Thai's foundation. Alongside the volunteers, temple monks sawed wood, cleared trees, tiled roofs, cemented the grounds, laid bricks, landscaped, and supervised work on every part of the temple. With donated money and labor, Thai community members, temple officials, and monks completed several buildings by 1976.

The most notable (and noticeable) structure was the main worship hall. The hall, or *sala*, was clearly visible from the adjoining suburban streets over a five-foot-tall brick wall surrounding the grounds. From concept to materials, the main hall was transnational. In terms of architectural style, it was an exact replica of those found throughout Thailand. The red brick roof with extensive gold trim predominates the temple's exterior, but the detailed hand carving and woodwork, including elaborate teak window frames and golden steeples, mark its extravagance.[41] An architect from the Department of Religious Affairs in Thailand drafted the design, which was later altered by a local Thai architect to meet Los Angeles city building codes.[42] The window frames, golden steeples, and other decorative temple pieces were made in Thailand and imported.[43] The lower level of the main hall, which included two classrooms, two restrooms, a library, a kitchen, and a dining room, was completed in 1974 for $258,000. The upper level, which contained the main altar where all religious ceremonies and rituals were to be conducted, was completed in 1979 for $534,000. The *sala* was officially completed and dedicated that same year.[44] Temple secretary Sawasdi Yingyuad best captured the sentiment of the Thai community by saying, "it is the only true Thai temple in the United States. The people are very pleased."[45]

Two important additions were made to the *sala* in the 1980s. In April 1980, the main golden Buddha statue, "Phra Buddhanorthepsada Dipyanagarasathit," was unveiled in the upper assembly hall.[46] The other addition was a pair of demon-like religious statues called *yahk*—one white, one jade—acquired from the Thai Pavilion at the 1986 World's Fair in Vancouver, which were placed on each side of the stairway entrance to the hall in 1987.[47] Their large stature, approximately twenty-five feet in height, fit their purpose, as they were to guard the *sala* from evil spirits.

Despite Wat Thai's aim to serve all Theravada Buddhists, over time the temple became a "special site for articulating Thai-ness."[48] What started as a

FIGURE 4. Aerial view of Wat Thai of Los Angeles, looking north, ca. 1988. Wat Thai was the first and largest Thai Theravada Buddhist temple in the United States when it was established in 1979. Photograph courtesy of Wat Thai of Los Angeles.

religious center for practicing Theravada Buddhists, regardless of race or ethnicity, became a uniquely Thai place. This was made explicit when the Theravada Buddhist Center officially changed its name to Wat Thai of Los Angeles on June 11, 1979.[49] In addition to the construction of an "authentic" main hall and the official name change, numerous ceremonies were held to honor the completion of the temple in 1979 that brought several of Thailand's highest-ranking monks and government officials, including a visit from the King and Queen of Thailand on December 26, 1979.[50] In a sense, the temple had successfully conflated religion and ethnicity. To borrow from historian Timothy Smith's seminal work on the dialectal relationship between religion and ethnicity in America, Wat Thai allowed Thais to redefine their ethnic identity in religious terms as they strengthened their commitment to Theravada Buddhism to deal with the experience of immigration and living a new country.[51]

Through the maintenance of "traditional" Thai Buddhist standards, architecture, and blessings from the most visible and powerful symbols of Thailand, Thais in Los Angeles turned space into place and laid the groundwork for a transnational community center. Yet Thais perhaps most effectively defined and expressed their Thainess at the temple during food festivals.

WAT THAI FOOD FESTIVALS AND THAI AMERICAN
SUBURBAN CULTURE

Although privately owned and financed, Wat Thai acted as a quasipublic space that cultivated Thai American community, identity, and suburban culture. The original articles of incorporation stated that the temple was to "operate as a nonprofit corporation for the interchange of Buddhist information and education between the UNITED STATES and THAILAND."[52] To meet this mission the temple held religious services that included chanting and meditation as well as events designed to preserve, promote, and teach Thai culture, such as free Thai language instruction, classes on Buddhism, and courses on sewing and Thai cooking and decorative food and vegetable carving techniques.[53] One of the goals of these activities was to "protect" the community, especially second-generation Thai American youth, from the "aggressive nature of American culture and youth problems."[54]

Suwattana Pinwatana visited the temple regularly during the 1970s and 1980s because it helped her maintain her Thai cultural identity and connect with other Thais. Pinwatana first arrived in Los Angeles in 1974 at the age of twenty-three; she settled in East Hollywood and found work at a sewing factory in downtown Los Angeles. She frequented the venue and was "part of the temple" because it gave her a "strong sense of home.... I was really home sick when I first came to L.A. At the temple, I get to meet other Thai people, speak Thai, and eat Thai food."[55] The experience compelled her to volunteer and help in any way she could, such as cooking and making Thai food and desserts with friends and family and then selling them at the sewing factory to raise money for the temple. She started teaching Sunday school, offering introductory Thai language courses and classes on Thai history and culture to mostly second-generation Thai American children and teenagers. Pinwatana even began a daycare school. "Parents," she remembered, "would come to the temple with their children and the parents would do their Buddhist rituals with the monks while their kids are running around playing. Kids would be everywhere . . . running inside and outside the temple, out into the parking lot. They would grab things in the temple as though it was a toy." But in addition to keeping children safe and well behaved, she also felt it was important to teach kids the Thai language and "to be proud of your Thai heritage and culture. I remind them to embrace their Thai identity and learn to speak Thai."[56]

The temple organized over a dozen festivals each year to celebrate Thai national holidays like *Songkran* (Thai New Year festival) and King Bhumipol Adulyadej's birthday. On many occasions, weekend and holiday festivals attracted tens of thousands of Thais along with Cambodians, Vietnamese, Lao, and whites. In October 1979 the "Supreme Patriarch," the Thai equivalent of the Pope, attended the temple's dedication ceremony joined by over forty thousand people from across the nation.[57] When the supreme commander of the Royal Armed Forces of Thailand, Arthit Kamlang-Ek, visited Wat Thai and planted a tree in front of a crowd of 5,000 on the morning of Sunday October 28, 1984, he explained to newspaper reporters that "this temple is the center of all social activities of the Thai community."[58] "In Bangkok," Kamlang-Ek added, "we are quite interested in what happens on these grounds."[59]

Wat Thai was, as one temple volunteer put it, "more than a place of worship."[60] The pairing of cultural activities with Buddhist ceremonies challenged traditional conceptions of a religious but also private space. Temple officials and monks believed the space belonged to the Thai community in the broadest sense and that they could use it however they wished, for religious purposes or otherwise. Its function as a community space exemplified the way increased privatization of public spaces and the erosion of public services in the United States during this period blurred the line between private property and public facilities, compelling Americans to treat commercial and private spaces—shopping malls, bookstores, coffee shops—more and more as public community centers for relaxation, socializing, and even protest.[61] Thais visited for the vibrant social, cultural, and spiritual environment, not just to meditate and pray. The temple also regularly set up polling booths for political elections. Moreover, monks commonly served as counselors and social workers, especially for working-class and recently arrived Thais who needed guidance and assistance. During her time volunteering at the temple, Pinwatana met "numerous Thais who are all alone—lonely in a new country" who "just work and send money back to their families in Thailand. They have no family here, no friends, and no support. Don't know where to go if something happens to them like getting sick, injured, or any other emergencies. [They were] scared to go to police and no money to go to hospitals, plus knowing little English."[62]

The formation and use of Wat Thai as a community center was at once a claim on suburban space and an expression of a Thai American suburban ideal. While this claim and ideal may not have been intentional or fully formed, it represented an alternative to or at the very least a redefinition of dominant suburban ideals. The temple's festivals, coupled with Thai migration into surrounding neighborhoods, provides glimpses of a nascent Thai American *suburban* ideal: a middle-class desire to purchase and live comfortably in a private home, to be sure, but above all the idea that a central meeting place open to all should serve as the heart and focal point of neighborhood life and culture—not the home itself.

The temple's weekend food festivals best illustrate how Wat Thai acted as a hub of Thai American suburban culture and life. The festivals began as a small food court in the basement of the temple's main hall. As it grew in popularity, temple officials moved the food vendors from the basement, which was only big enough to hold about six or seven booths, to the courtyard of the school building and then eventually to the northeast parking lot to accommodate more food booths and larger crowds.[63] In the early 1980s the process to become a vendor was easy and straightforward. Those interested, almost exclusively Thai women, had to put in a request with the temple to sell a specific dish and get approval. Although temple officials did not yet have a formal selection procedure in place for quality and taste of the food, they did have two main criteria: dishes had to taste good and they had to be cheaper than at a restaurant.[64] Taste and affordability were important because the temple wanted to bring in as many visitors as possible.

For Thai women, becoming a food vendor meant economic opportunity and a sense of pride. Wearing hairnets and aprons, these women were able to become sole proprietors for the first time in their lives. The majority were working class migrants who came from small rural provinces in Thailand with some experience working in Thai restaurant kitchens in Los Angeles. Cooking and selling Thai food at the temple on weekends allowed them to capitalize on the skills they had but also to supplement income from restaurant and other low-wage jobs to earn a living. They benefitted greatly from the labor of family, especially children, and temple volunteers who assisted with setting up cooking stations and booths. In addition, Thai restaurant owners did not attempt to use temple food festivals to expand their brick-and-mortar establishments, so the women did not have to compete with more established and well-known restaurateurs. As they sold food for profit, however, Wat Thai required vendors to donate a percentage of profits to the temple, which was struggling financially through much of the 1980s.

With the leadership of Thai women vendors, Wat Thai food festivals became wildly successful. They ignited social activities by bringing Thais out of their homes and into contact with friends, monks, and community leaders. During the April 1982 festival for Thai New Year and the King Rama I sesquicentennial, vendors were expecting one thousand visitors but prepared for the event the same way they did every weekend.[65] They typically arrived on Friday evening to prep food and set up portable stovetops, griddles, deep fryers, steamers, and makeshift barbeques behind counters of tented booths along the inside perimeter of the temple parking lot. Then, they would come as early as 6 a.m. the morning of the festivals to finish prepping food before 9 a.m., when crowds typically started to arrive.[66] The festivalgoers, after purchasing food with temple issued plastic tokens, ate on benches or picnic-style on the main courtyard lawn.[67]

Thai American identities played out vividly at food festivals. They offered Thais a site where they publicly marked and articulated racial, ethnic, and class differences through food culture. One of the more obvious expressions of Thainess was the authenticity of the dishes. In terms of preparation, ingredients, and taste, the food at Wat Thai was arguably the most "authentic" in the entire city and perhaps in the country. Unlike Thai restaurants, the vendors and cooks were not afraid to use ingredients that might be deemed unpalatable or unusual—like beef intestine and tripe—or to use bold flavors and hot spices. There were also many dishes sold that were not available in restaurants.[68] Moreover, Thai language signs and menus suggested that the vendors catered the food specifically to Thais.[69] The food was also cheap. For a few dollars, one could purchase grilled Thai sausage on a wooden skewer, chicken satay, *mee krob* (sweet crispy noodles), *sohm tham* (papaya salad), fish cakes, noodle soups, fried bananas, coconut desserts, and the popular mango with sticky rice.[70] Snack-portioned items, such as the meat skewers, were served on styrofoam plates or stuffed in small paper bags while larger-portioned dishes, like noodle soups, were served in foam bowls with plastic utensils.

The aroma of food announced Wat Thai as an ethnic immigrant space and, equally important, as a public space in contrast to the surrounding residential neighborhood. "A hawker's cart," described one magazine columnist, "exudes the pungent odor of keuay teiw nam—noodle soups to which diners add red peppers and sweet sauce. Atop a brazier, skewers of nue yang (barbecued beef) grill to a tempting brown."[71] The fragrance of food wafting out from the temple turned Wat Thai into an alluring sensory world of Thai cuisine, people, and architecture. The scent of grilled meats, fried bananas, and aromatic soup broths transported visitors to Bangkok's street food scene and open-air markets. Such smells made the temple's Thainess more salient and enhanced its "ethnic" and "immigrant" essence because it presented an alternative olfactory experience of suburban life. The smell of Thai food in the neighborhood air helped define Wat Thai's difference against what was largely imagined as an odor-less suburban space.[72]

Beyond sustenance for the Thai community, however, food festivals acted as a purveyor of racial and ethnic difference. The food and ambiance attracted non-Thais who went to the temple to indulge in a different culture. Tanit Karschamroon, who was one of the few Thai men to regularly help women vendors set up booths and cooking stations, recalled the festivals bringing in an "international" crowd of whites, Mexicans, African Americans, and Chinese and Vietnamese visitors.[73] Despite that fact (or maybe because of it) vendors and cooks did not try to "sanitize" or make their food more palatable; it ignited a "gustatory relish" for Thai food among non-Thai temple visitors.[74] This "carnal desire" led to positive feelings toward Thai culture and people at a time when immigrants were blamed for draining national resources, and for contributing to crime, poverty, and the breakdown of American culture. As Uma Narayan contends, ethnic food festivals are "one of the rare public events where one is visually, viscerally, and positively conscious of the range of diverse ethnicities and identities that in fact constitute us as a community."[75] While the positive feelings likely stemmed just from eating Thai dishes without any deeper knowledge of Thai culture or history, it contributed to, at the very least, a recognition and appreciation of Thais as part of the American fabric.[76]

Wat Thai food festivals served as another physical culinary contact zone in which cuisine became the gateway for a broad range of people to meet across gender, class, ethnic, and racial lines. The relationship between Thais and white Americans in particular benefitted greatly from these events. In her ethnographic study of a Wat Thai in Silicon Valley, California, anthropologist Jiemin Bao found that Thai middle-class immigrants, who are often perceived as being lower-class because of their racial identity and immigrant status, "practice" to make visible their middle-class status by forging networks with white Americans, who carry both "symbolic power of middle-classness" and Americanness.[77] This might explain why temple officials at

FIGURE 5. A typical festival crowd at Wat Thai of Los Angeles in the mid-1980s. Wat Thai's weekend food and cultural festivals, such as this one celebrating Thai New Year's, or Songkran, were wildly popular and attracted thousands of Thais from across Southern California. Photograph courtesy of Monk Phra Boonlerm and Wat Thai of Los Angeles.

Wat Thai developed important connections with white Americans, such as David Christianson, who served as one of the temple's lawyers. Or perhaps why Phra Thepsophon invited white Americans to visit the temple as his guests. Arthur Lurvey, who referred to himself proudly as a "farang," thanked Phra Thepsophon in a letter for making Wat Thai a place where "non-Thai communities could learn about Buddhism, could be introduced to Thai customs and culture, and could form friendships with Thai-Americans."[78]

It seemed as if everyone loved Wat Thai food festivals. The food was delicious and cheap. The atmosphere was lively and authentic. But Wat Thai food festivals were not wholly celebrated. Due to their location in a suburban neighborhood, the festivals overstepped the spatial boundaries of multiculturalism in this case. Thais in Los Angeles soon came to realize that gathering in public however and whenever they wanted was not readily admissible in the suburbs. A small group of nearby homeowners, whose tolerance for temple food festivals had reached its limit, started protesting the public gatherings and searched for ways to shut them down. In the process, the homeowners put forth their own ideas of what a suburban neighborhood should look and feel like. Wat Thai officials, community leaders, and temple supporters were forced to explicitly articulate and defend food festivals.

THAI FOOD FESTIVALS AND THE WHITE SPATIAL IMAGINARY

In the early 1980s, the Thai community became embroiled in a bitter conflict with a small grassroots committee of suburban homeowners. These residents, who called themselves the "Neighborhood Committee," charged Wat Thai with violating its conditional use permit. The affair began on November 17, 1982, when twenty-five-year resident David Wygand, who lived across the street from the temple, submitted a letter and petition with about two hundred signatures to Los Angeles city councilman Ernani Bernardi.[79] They appealed for the Office of Zoning Administration to curb Thai food festivals and other Wat Thai events because of parking problems, noise, and trash that threatened their quality of life and property values.[80] As chairman of the committee, Wygand requested the Zoning Administration assess the negative impact of weekend festivals to determine if they were in violation of its conditional use permit. The letters and petitions ultimately ended up in the hands of the Associate Zoning Administrator, Robert Janovici, who ordered a zoning analyst to inspect the temple.

After visits on December 8, 1982, and January 10, 1983, the analyst sided with the homeowners. He identified temple noise as a disturbance to the surrounding area. The analyst also stated visitors were illegally parked and participants at the festivals were "unneighborly, uncooperative, unconcerned, and inconsiderate and nasty to residents of the area when confronted" about these issues.[81] To stay in operation Wat Thai had to agree to a set of corrective measures established by the analyst and homeowners. They included: (1) reducing the number of outdoor festivities from one per week to one per month, (2) securing additional off-street parking, (3) maintaining a litter pick-up campaign led by Boy Scouts, (4) towing illegally parked cars using two trucks owned by Thai businessmen, (5) reducing hours of use and duration of the sound amplification system, (6) establishing communication with residents by opening a complaint line, (7) providing an English-speaking booth at all festivals, and (8) educating the congregation about their responsibility to be respectful of the surrounding neighborhood by complying with these measures.[82]

The question of by whom and how these measures would be enforced triggered a series of public hearings, city council meetings, local courtroom debates, and letter writing. Equally important, the measures provided a glimpse into the homeowners' underlying desires for a suburban ideal before any of the public debates took place. In essence they wanted fewer people, regulated use of space, quiet and clean streets with ample parking, and communication in English. The measures also inversely presented Thai American community life as replete with immigrant dirtiness, noise, disorder, and disrespect.[83]

Based on the complaints, the residents claimed they were willing to embrace Thai cultural practices in the neighborhood, but only if they were privately-based and passive. At the first public hearing on January 28, 1983, which lasted four hours, the residents declared that they did not oppose Wat Thai because it was a Buddhist temple.[84] Instead, they argued that temple food festivals moved outside the agreeable parameters for a religious center set in the conditional use permit. In a written complaint to the Department of City Planning later that year, a member of the neighborhood committee wrote, "it is this traffic and its related parking that has caused the temple to become an incompatible use. . . . This problem typically occurs on festival days. . . . The rest of the time the temple . . . is a very quiet place with very few people on the site. . . . It is the nation's largest Thai Buddhist temple. It could be a landmark for Sun Valley."[85] So while the residents described Wat Thai as a potential cultural attraction for the area, their understanding was rooted in the idea of a Buddhist temple (certainly perpetuated by Wat Thai officials) as a site for small, private ceremonies that would not intrude upon the surrounding single-family homes. Robert Janovici stated at the hearing that if he had known about the festivals and frequency of visitors prior to reviewing the conditional use permit "the request would have been <u>denied</u>."[86]

The residents did not necessarily oppose immigrant cultural centers. On the contrary, some voiced support for ethnic community centers as a bedrock of American society. Yet it was clear they only found them beneficial as long as the cultural practices were contained in urban areas and did not spill over into the suburbs. Homeowner George Carroll, for example, gave his opinion about Wat Thai food festivals to the *Los Angeles Times*, "like all immigrants to this country, all immigrant groups need and have had community cultural centers. I come from New York City, and the (North Hollywood situation) is not like a Jewish or Italian neighborhood, which encompasses five to ten blocks. . . . These are people from all over

Southern California coming to our little neighborhood, and we can't handle it."[87] Although clearly not opposed to cultural pluralism, Carroll believed the proper place for ethnic festivals was in densely populated cities. For him, temple food festivals were valuable as long as they were not in his backyard.

Surely, the homeowners were annoyed. Temple visitors tossed used chicken skewers and other food waste on their lawns. "Rock and roll music" blasted out of the Wat Thai's amplifier system in the early morning. Parking was a nightmare, so much so that the issue was brought up in nearly every meeting and in written complaints to the Zoning Administration, especially from Wygand.[88] Several residents attested to temple visitors parking in front of fire hydrants and red zones as well as in front of their homes, their driveways, and in some cases even parking on their driveways. No one enjoyed having to search for the owner of an anonymous car parked on their property. At a hearing in March 1984, nearby resident Phyllis Carroll told the zoning board, "all I want is for my children and grandchildren to be able to park in front of my house when they come to see me."[89]

While the residents' grievances may have appeared as neutral concerns over quality of life and land use, they were inseparable from race and class. The anger and frustration emanated from real and symbolic challenges to what George Lipsitz refers to as a "white spatial imaginary." The white spatial imaginary presents "the properly gendered prosperous suburban home as the privileged moral geography of the nation" and "idealizes 'pure' and homogenous spaces, controlled environments, and predictable patterns of design and behavior."[90] The residents valued middle-class norms of the sanctity of single-family homes, order, peace, and quiet—and they demonized mixed-use heterogeneity, chaos, and noise associated with urban space.

They also privileged private property values, or more specifically the rewards and material advantages that come with owning a home in the suburbs. Homeowner Viola L. Smith expressed these ideals in a letter to the zoning administration, opposing attempts by Wat Thai to rezone single-family dwellings adjacent to the temple. Smith wrote, "these units are located directly across the street from my home of thirty years. The community has always been one of single-family homes. To re-zone the area now after such a long established precedent of family living seems both unwise and unfair to the community residents. This is where I chose to live a long time ago, and re-zoning would have a significant detrimental effect on my property value."[91] Smith's letter was accompanied by a petition with 161 signatures of property owners living within six hundred feet of Wat Thai who wished to "protest any further encroachment into our residential community."

The homeowners' spatial imaginary was also a utopian one. In fighting against nonnormative use of space by nonnormative "others," they were fiercely devoted to a static, timeless ideal of a simpler 1950s suburban existence. They created and bought into the fantasy in part because they were dissatisfied with the changing world around them and wanted retreat to a time and place where their sensibilities went unchallenged. This was in line with utopian tradition. In their seminal work *Utopian Thought*, Frank E. Manuel and Fritzie P. Manuel write that for great utopian thinkers "escape from everyday conflicts and disappointments has a childlike quality. And their way back from utopia, their return to the real world they had abandoned, is often characterized by devotion to a fixed idea with which they became obsessed."[92] So when Wat Thai food festivals brought contemporary realities of traffic, parking problems, noise, and trash to the neighborhood, the residents clutched "frantically at this overvalued idea that at once explains all evil and offers the universal remedy, and they build an impregnable fortress around it."[93]

This romantic and utopian spatial imaginary fueled an allegiance to hostile privatism. The homeowners prioritized the protection of private property and private use of space above all other social goals without much regard for the consequences for public life. Privatism, in other words, was seen as the basis of the neighborhood and a solution to perceived outside threats and the evils of modern cities. More broadly, the concept illustrated the ramifications of the "privatization of everyday life." Although privatization is typically used to explain the larger economic and political processes by which private entities, primarily concerned with making a profit, take over government-operated public goods such as schools, transportation, and other basic services, the term can also be extended to describe the impact these shifts have on social relations and cultural ideologies. As Henry Giroux, Gerald Frug, and Bruce Schulman contend, privatization is at once a pervasive yet historically specific cultural logic that infiltrates the textures of everyday life.[94] It shapes suburban structures of feeling and "structures the consciousness" of a citizenry by promoting a distrust of public space and disgust with public life.[95] By encouraging individual escape, it cultivates an antidemocratic world view, which is reflected in the desire for increased regulation and policing of public crowds.[96] While privatism did not emerge as a new suburban value during this period, it intensified in Los Angeles during the 1980s with, as

Mike Davis astutely described, an all-out "destruction of public space" and amenities.[97]

The suburban ideal also impelled a commitment to defensive localism. The residents' reaction to Wat Thai food festivals revealed their deep investment in local power as another viable solution to defend their quality of life. Banding together to create an ad-hoc committee of homeowners, and relying on neighborhood-level political mechanisms such as zoning law provided a sense of control over decision making, while simultaneously allowing disassociation from city, state, and federal politics. The ideal also mirrored other acts of defensive localism that took place throughout Los Angeles and the nation. By the 1980s, localism had emerged as a hallmark of suburban political culture, as white suburban homeowners turned to zoning, municipal ordinances, taxation, and homeowners' associations to keep the structured advantages of whiteness that included better schools, amenities, services, and higher property values.[98] Using color-blind rhetoric grounded in localism—from "slow growth" and "not in my backyard (NIMBY)" to "tax revolt" and "property rights"—suburbanites organized to enact policies that worked to exclude racial minorities, immigrants, and the urban poor from disrupting the white spatial imaginary. The San Fernando Valley, in fact, gave birth to some of the more powerful movements that mobilized such discourses and policies, namely slow-growth movements spurred by homeowners associations.[99]

Class pressures, too, played a role in the exclusionary zoning stance of the homeowners who, similar to Becky Nicolaides's South Gate residents in the early 1960s, grasped "willfully for a middle-class life" in a suburban neighborhood with "working-class roots."[100] The temple's neighborhood, sitting in the multiracial and working-class east San Fernando Valley, did not have high-priced homes that automatically excluded nonwhites. The white residents near the temple were most likely part of the working to lower-middle class. Just to the east was the highly industrial area of Sun Valley. To the south were the more exclusive and wealthier neighborhoods of Sherman Oaks and Studio City as well as the higher-priced parts of North Hollywood, from which the area's residents were priced out. Though it may not have been a product of individual racism, the homeowners' precarious class and racial position in the neighborhood compelled them to turn to zoning to achieve their exclusive privatized suburban ideal.

In the context of the Wat Thai conflict, zoning law defended the homeowners' suburban ideal. Zoning helped reinforce hostile privatism and defensive localism and thus extend the white spatial imaginary of the neighborhood. Zoning, which developed in the United States at the turn of the twentieth century as a means of organizing urban land use, gave community builders and planners the legal power to regulate, or "protect," the character of suburban residential neighborhoods through seemingly neutral criteria like "residential occupancy," "density," and "minimum standards for housing development."[101] But zoning is hardly neutral. The core logic of suburban zoning is to use the state to alter market outcomes, promote certain social objectives, and to defend against outside threats to private property values and the quality of neighborhoods. The process of conceptualizing and defining which characteristics are desirable versus which are "incompatible" is not an objective one. Class and racial biases have informed them from the beginning.[102] When the racial and class objectives of suburban zoning are backed by state power (state law empowers suburbs to engage in exclusionary zoning), hostile privatism and defensive localism appear as commonsense and therefore neutral even though they structure feelings, institutions, and ideas of the suburban "good life."[103]

These types of seemingly race-neutral "quality of life" debates were one of the most significant political issues for communities of color in the suburbs, especially for Asian Americans.[104] Asian religious spaces, including Thai Buddhist temples, have often been at the center of such battles.[105] In addition to the original Theravada Buddhist Center conflict, Thai temples faced enormous resistance in other suburban neighborhoods outside Los Angeles. In 1983, after moving from a rental house to a permanent home, the Wat Thai in Silicon Valley dealt with intense opposition from local residents. The neighbors harassed monks and the laity and tried to prevent further construction of the temple by petitioning the city over traffic, illegal parking, and violation of single-family use.[106] According to Jiemin Bao, Thais were not welcomed because they were "misrecognized as poor immigrants or 'boat people,' although they were predominately urban, affluent, well-educated professionals." The residents feared that the newcomers would "ruin the neighborhood" and that "Thai cooking smells would be offensive," especially pepper and curry smells. Some even expressed concerns about having a Buddhist "cult" in their midst. The residents raised these concerns at public hearings where the Wat Thai Silicon Valley board begged for permission to build a prayer hall. Temple officials believed the neighbors were prejudiced and were convinced that these prejudices were "being hidden behind some legitimate claims."[107]

While the negative reactions of white suburbanites toward Asian spaces were often driven by anti-Asian sentiment, the conflict over Wat Thai of Los

Angeles was much more complex and cannot be adequately understood as being motivated by anti-Asian racism alone.[108] It also stemmed from a wide range of issues and concerns over land use, public culture, quality of life, the infiltration of urban ills to the suburbs, concerns about potentially declining property values, and everyday annoyances such as trash, traffic, noise, and parking. Yet surprisingly but even more importantly, the homeowners' responses were also informed by a liberal multiculturalism. They genuinely believed that not only were they not racist but that they were also tolerant, respectful, and welcoming of cultural differences. When given the opportunity, many of them spoke fondly about Wat Thai. The problem was the food festivals. They presented a jarringly different version of Thai Buddhism that collided with the residents' interpretation of a Buddhist temple. The conflict erupted because the large crowds, noise, and smells presented an excess of Thai culture that tested the residents' attempt to maintain a "carefully calibrated balance of acceptable multiculturalism."[109]

The residents were not entirely hostile. They held complex feelings and opinions. Some worried about the implications of trying to shut down the food festivals and curb temple activities and feared being labeled as "racist." For example, George Carroll expressed his tolerance and sympathy for Thais but also his concern about how the conflict might make him and his fellow suburbanites look. Carroll told the *Los Angeles Times* that "a number of us feel a sense of regret. We're not against the temple or the Thais. We even have inhibitions complaining about this, because it is a religious thing, it is a racial thing."[110] Others, like the more outspoken leader David Wygand, believed cultural differences and Thais' refusal to assimilate to U.S. society led to the conflict. He saw suburban zoning as an opportunity to teach Thais about American rule of law. "They've [Wat Thai visitors] been misunderstanding," he said to a reporter, "and we're trying to set them on the right track. A lot of it is lack of knowledge of the laws of our country."[111]

There is no concrete evidence to suggest the homeowners held personal racial animosity toward Thais. While they did not make openly racist comments, overt expressions of racial bigotry are also not reliable indicators of how racism functioned in the 1980s mainly because publicly expressing racist attitudes in a post-civil rights "color blind" society was socially undesirable.[112] Instead, the residents and zoning officials relied on the racialized concepts of "property value" and "quality of life."[113] Though it was certainly possible that these concepts were used to mask racist attitudes, the Wat Thai controversy was about race not because the homeowners were inherently racist and therefore used zoning to exclude Thais. Rather, the controversy was racialized because, as Lipsitz contends, "land-use policies produce a certain kind of whiteness that offers extraordinary inducements and incentives for a system of privatization that has drastic racial consequences."[114]

The residents' use of zoning law to try to shut down Thai food festivals and curb the temple's community-based activities served to defend a white spatial imaginary and consequently the material and affective advantages of whiteness. For some of them, this understanding was separate from their feelings and attitudes toward Thais and Thai culture. Despite the fact that overt expressions of racism were largely absent from public debate, the rhetoric of property values and quality of life influenced all members of the neighborhood committee to advocate for exclusion of weekend food festivals. The combination of words, actions, and institutionalized policies presented a formidable barrier for Thais to become full participants in suburban life, even if many were able to purchase homes in the area and enjoy the economic and social benefits of homeownership.[115]

A "RIGHT TO THE SUBURB"

The Thai community's responses to the zoning grievances centered on proving that Wat Thai was compatible with the neighborhood. Thais agreed to work rapidly to resolve the issues to ease tension and threats from both the residents and the zoning administration. In the meantime, temple officials devised another clever solution: purchase several single-family homes adjacent to temple property. If Wat Thai purchased the homes, temple leaders reasoned, they could eliminate complaints by replacing opponents of the temple with monks and distinguished visitors. This strategy, which was legal, only increased suspicion about temple activities and exacerbated complaints. Members of the neighborhood committee, for example, feared that temple's attempt to rezone the neighborhood would negatively impact their property values.[116] In another report to the zoning administration, Wygand demanded David Christianson, the temple's lawyer, answer the following question: "How many monks or visitors are actually residing in these four private residences on Van Noord Ave.?"[117] Implicit in the rhetorical question is fear that Thais would convert private single-family homes into multi-use facilities with overcrowded living conditions. In spite of the reaction, Wat Thai purchased at least four homes on Van Noord Ave along the temple's western boundary.[118]

The conflict was widely interpreted by Thais as a product of cultural differences between Thailand and United States. At the first public hearing, temple representatives and other supporters claimed that the main problem was that visitors to the temple were not "familiar with Western culture/ways of conduct."[119] Over time, they insisted, "these cultural differences could be at least satisfactorily resolved" through active educational programs.[120] Wat Thai secretary and monk Phra Sombat Seelasara believed, "I think it's our fault, not their (neighbors') fault. If we understood them and they understood us, this wouldn't have happened. They want to teach us how to be good. I think that is good."[121] At several points during the conflict, temple officials led efforts to foster cultural understanding with the homeowners. In a letter to Wygand in August 1984, Phra Thepsophon wrote, "we certainly appreciate your helping the Temple to correct the problems of the past and look forward to your advising us on matters concerning future activities. . . . We know that in this way we will better be able to strengthen the relationship between our neighborhood friends and the Temple and people of Thailand."[122]

Concern over the behavior of Wat Thai's congregation was informed by growing class divisions happening inside the Thai community. A majority of temple officials and Thai American community leaders were middle-class Thai businessmen with formal education.[123] Part of the first wave of Thai immigrants, they owned homes, restaurants, grocery stores, and other small businesses. By the 1980s, however, there was a growing number of younger, working class Thais who recently arrived from Thailand with few English skills. They worked low-wage jobs as cooks, busboys, janitors, garment workers, and hotel maids. They were the ones who attended Wat Thai festivals in search of community and collective identity in one of the only leisure spaces open to them.

Anxieties about the presence of these visible working-class Thais at festivals, rooted in the class rifts occurring within Thai Los Angeles, may have led temple officials to agree with the homeowners' middle-class idea of respectable behavior in the suburbs, like parking a car properly. This could also explain why some Thais wanted to conform to those ideas by "educating" fellow temple visitors. Lao, Khmer, and Vietnamese visitors were often singled out because Thais mainly perceived them as low-class refugees. One temple volunteer, Jintana Noochia-or, asserted that Thais should not be blamed for the residents' woes because Southeast Asian refugees were causing the problems due to their ignorance of American ways. "Lots of refugees came over from Cambodia, Laos, and Vietnam (and) they have no home," she told the *Los Angeles Times*. "They came to the Thai temple because they feel that it's their home." Noochia-or added, as if a member of the neighborhood committee herself, "They didn't know how to behave. We try to say, 'Be careful when you park.' We have to be strict [with] them."[124] The scapegoating of other Southeast Asians reflects class divisions being expressed as ethnic and national differences.[125]

In spite of circulating claims that the neighborhood committee and the zoning administration were racist and trying to restrict freedom of religion, Wat Thai leaders decided not to pursue a case for racial or religious discrimination. Thai newspapers in the United States and in Thailand pointed to the hypocrisy of Americans who preached freedom of religion while attacking Thai Buddhism. At a March 1984 hearing, Rabbi Alfred Wolf told the zoning board that the restriction on Wat Thai's festivals "leaves the impression . . . that this group is being dealt with restrictively simply because they are 'foreigners."[126] Yet when asked by media reporters to call attention to racism from homeowners, temple lawyer David Christianson declined. Christianson, a white American, advised Thais that bringing up race would be "counterproductive" because "there's always a little bit of racism."[127] His fear that race was divisive and racism incurable reflected an understanding of racism as a problem of personal prejudice and intolerance rather than a matter of power that produces structured advantages and disadvantages. Given that homeowners denied holding any prejudices against Thais, and that the zoning administration believed race had nothing to do with law and public policy, Christianson probably knew that Wat Thai had little choice but to leave racism out of the equation.

Wat Thai officials and Christianson turned their attention instead to presenting a more holistic view of Thai food culture to the zoning administration. The goal was to convince the zoning board that food festivals were a part of Thai Buddhism, and that the homeowners and zoning officials, with this new knowledge, would be inclined to allow them. One line of reasoning rested on economics, in which leaders argued that selling Thai food was a vital fundraising activity to maintain temple grounds and support the monks. Another argument linked commercial Thai food and Buddhist practices. Members and advocates of the Thai community explained to judges that Thai food was part of the long duration of Thai Buddhist rituals at temples. They claimed that unlike other religions in which "you listen to the minister and you go home," when Thai Buddhists visit temples they may stay for the entire day to talk to monks, and food prevents them from going hungry.[128] As Christianson recalled, "our argument about the food is that the whole family comes and it's an all day long kind of thing... and so our pitch was that it all ties in together ... so we can't change any one part of it otherwise it will undermine the religious values and the religious experiences they have."[129]

By presenting Thai Buddhism as a community affair and not as individualized prayer or consumption, Wat Thai officials tried to carve some room for public space and culture in the suburbs. On January 19, 1984, the zoning administration ruled not to revoke Wat Thai's conditional use permit. Most importantly, Associate Zoning Administrator Robert Janovici explained to all parties that Wat Thai could continue to hold cultural festivals so long as they meet a total of twenty-three conditions. The most notable condition, or restriction, was "no more than four special events shall take place on the site during any calendar year... special events shall be defined as any occasion at which more than 160 persons are on the site at any one time over the course of a weekend."[130]

Initially, David Wygand and the neighborhood committee accepted Janovici's ruling. However, when Wat Thai officials announced plans a few months later to expand the temple by erecting a two-story, 38,000 square foot Sunday school, the homeowners' relationship with the zoning administration soured.[131] In December 1984, Wygand responded by sending a preemptive letter to James Crisp, a sympathetic analyst, painting temple officials as cunning and immoral. "The Temple authorities have become scofflaws," Wygand wrote, "which must not be tolerated by an organization which by character of being a religious organization, should be completely moralistic! We would shudder to think a permit would be granted to construct a two-story building."[132] The homeowners won the first round against temple expansion at a hearing in February 1985. But only four months later on June 5, 1985, after listening to passionate testimonials by the Thai community, including one from Phra Thepsophon, at a packed city council meeting in downtown Los Angeles, the board of zoning appeals voted 4:1 to grant Wat Thai's request to build the school.[133] After the hearing a *Los Angeles Times* reporter asked Wygand if he intended to challenge the ruling, to which he replied: "We are tired of being painted as villains.... We have rights, too." But he was much more direct with Christianson, whom he approached, threw up his hands and said, "I'm not [going] to fight you people anymore, you'll never hear from me again!"[134] They never did. The school and cultural center was completed on the south end of temple grounds in 1988 with approximately $700,000 in donations.

To a degree, the victory to keep Wat Thai open and to build a school can be attributed to larger transformations in the Los Angeles political economy, particularly the power of "growth" coalitions and ethnic minority politics. Tom Bradley, the city's first African American mayor from 1973 to 1993, embodied both the increasing legitimacy of a moderate multicultural politics in the region and a growth coalition politics.[135] Between 1975 and 1985, Bradley built a strong coalition that was able to secure both federal funds and foreign capital investment to help turn Los Angeles into a multicultural "global city."[136] Bradley did not funnel money for Wat Thai projects but, as a frequent guest at Wat Thai festivals and events, he did offer his political clout and influence. Christianson recalled an interaction with Bradley during the Bangkok Market's grand reopening in 1985: "I was sitting next to him and Tom leans over and he says, 'I understand the Thai temple is having some difficulty.' And I said 'Yeah, I'm going to these hearings and they're trying to cancel our conditions permit. . . . I think the temple should be there it's a beautiful facility, we're trying to work with the community.' [Bradley] says, 'Dave, you've been out to the temple, so why don't you prepare a little proposal and I'll go ahead and get it signed and we'll send it on in.'"[137]

In addition to Bradley's support, Wat Thai and the Thai community had also garnered support from a range of politicians and civic leaders. The Protestant National Council of Churches, the Catholic Diocese, and other major Jewish and Buddhist temples and organizations also backed the temple's efforts.[138] What is more, the temple managed to win over a critical mass of neighborhood residents, many of whom testified on behalf of Wat Thai at court hearings. Finally, Phra Thepsophon's leadership and charisma also played a fundamental role in Wat Thai's victory.

The victory is testament not just to the way the 1980s suburbs nurtured ethnic politics but also illustrates that the role of food culture and public space in the struggle for a right to the suburb are critical and cannot be ignored. In other words, the lesson is not about having a strong leader or powerful friends in high places—it is about the importance of everyday cultural practices in public space to building effective movements. Wat Thai food festivals made possible Thais' forging of meaningful relationships within and across communities. They cultivated community. At the same time, they fostered a public sociability that went against dominant ideas and legal definitions of suburbia. Thais recognized problems with the way suburban zoning was designed to work against public life and the negative effect it could potentially have on Wat Thai's ability to nurture community building.

While they could not determine the kind of rules to support the kind of suburb they wanted, Thais mobilized enough support to influence zoning officials to make exceptions to the law. Wat Thai food festivals did not become a suburban ideal, but they were allowed to exist for the time being.

Elucidating the history of Wat Thai food festivals offers insight into the ramifications of the production, consumption, and maintenance of multiculturalism in 1980s suburban Los Angeles. It also helps us understand the way disputes over race, immigration, and assimilation in the United States played out increasingly on the suburban stage, particularly in seemingly race-neutral public policy debates. Moreover, these food festivals allow us to see the way immigrants and people of color engaged in spatial practices that built community and social networks to become full-fledged participants in suburban life—at precisely the moment many observers were convinced that "American" community was in decline.

Yet the fact that Wat Thai food festivals, for all their popularity, generated organized opposition from a group of neighborhood residents also revealed that selling and eating Thai food alone was not going to lead to cultural understanding and acceptance from non-Thais. Thais faced critical political and social issues that Thai food simply was not going to solve. Nevertheless, Thai community activists would turn increasingly to food in campaigns for social and economic justice, relying on American consumers' multicultural sensibilities and desire for the exotic to gain political visibility. This strategy was most evident in the development of Los Angeles' "Thai Town."

FIVE

Thailand's "77th Province"

CULINARY TOURISM IN THAI TOWN

THAIS IN LOS ANGELES CONTINUED TO confront a range of social, economic, and political problems into the 1990s. In the face of global economic restructuring, increased privatization, and slashes in social spending as part of the eradication of the "welfare state," Thai American leaders developed official organizations to try and gain access to social services, housing, jobs, and health care for the Thai community. However, Thai American activists struggled with the marginalization of Thais in civic affairs and their political invisibility as a community.

The popularity of Thai cuisine represented a way to increase political visibility and viability, a view that got full expression in East Hollywood's "Thai Town." In 1999 the city of Los Angeles, in conjunction with the Thai Community Development Center (Thai CDC), officially designated a six-block stretch of Hollywood Boulevard between Western Avenue and Normandie Avenue in East Hollywood as Thai Town.[1] Nicknamed by Thais as Thailand's 77th Province, the area was established to promote "neighborhood pride, economic development, cultural exchange and tourism."

By this time a majority of Thais in Los Angeles did not live in the area but resided in the suburbs of the San Fernando Valley, the San Gabriel Valley, and Orange County. Moreover, East Hollywood was a multiethnic and multiracial neighborhood that served as a crossroads for Latino, Asian, and Armenian immigrants. The 2000 U.S. census counted 81,848 residents in the East Hollywood area.[2] Thais made up only 2.2 percent of this population, while Latinos made up 44 percent and whites 36 percent.[3] At the time of its designation, therefore, Thai Town was not an ethnic enclave. It was a tourist attraction highlighted by Thai restaurants rather than Thai residents.

This chapter focuses on the formation of Thai Town to examine the relationship between culinary tourism, civic engagement, and urban development, in the late twentieth-century United States. It traces the way Thai community leaders and everyday Thais used foodways to script Thai Town as a culinary tourist destination and gateway to Thailand. From the Thai American perspective, food offered one of the best ways to experience Thai culture and the multicultural diversity and global urban culture of Los Angeles. Thai community leaders and activists made clear that the way local residents and visitors *tasted* the city was important to Los Angeles's identity and sense of self in the late twentieth century.

By playing into cuisine driven multiculturalism, Thais were able use food to anchor Thai American identity and community in a physical place in a way that demonstrated their role in making Los Angeles a multicultural city. Yet as they used cuisine to make a claim for a right to the global city, heritage commodification in Thai Town did not challenge power because it was geared toward a neoliberal vision of multiculturalism that sought to position Los Angeles more firmly in the global capitalist economy. The attempts to showcase Thai cuisine to increase political visibility and enhance efforts for social justice only masked problems and long-standing fissures within the Thai American community. Leaders purposefully projected a positive image of Thai people and Thailand outward to American society that whitewashed the realities of Thai America.

Culinary tourism in Thai Town produced barriers to collective mobilization for Thai American activists as they struggled for political representation and decent housing, wages, health care, and, most of all, human rights. While Thai food appeared to offer some political clout, community leaders' decision to turn Thai Town into a tourist attraction meant that Thais wrestled with catering to the needs of non-Thai consumers at the expense of their own. The redevelopment of the multiracial, multiethnic, and working-poor immigrant neighborhood of East Hollywood into Thai Town demonstrates the benefits and limitations of marketing and selling food cultures to revive local urban economies.

THE THAI COMMUNITY DEVELOPMENT CENTER

Two events in the early 1990s catalyzed the rise of Thai American nonprofit organization-based activism in Los Angeles: the 1992 Los Angeles riots and

Proposition 187 (1994). Together, these events contributed to and exposed what some activists called the Thai American "invisibility factor" in U.S. society. On one hand, economic exploitation, difficulties with cultural adjustment to a new country, lack of access to social services, and other quality of life issues could not be adequately addressed because Thais were ignored or neglected by mainstream media. Their numbers were small compared to other groups, and thus, they became buried under the larger Japanese, Chinese, and Filipino American populations. On top of that, Thai immigrants, no matter how difficult their individual situations, could not gain access to government assistance because they were not legally recognized as "political refugees" like many of their Southeast Asian counterparts. The assumption made by Thai American activists was that only when U.S. politicians and society at large became aware of the Thai community's needs could Thai Americans begin to improve their life chances.

Los Angeles was experiencing its own social and political turmoil. This culminated on April 29, 1992, when a predominantly white jury acquitted four white Los Angeles Police Department officers caught on video for brutally beating Rodney King, a black motorist who was pulled over by the officers after a high-speed pursuit a year earlier. When the verdict was announced through the media at around 3:15 p.m., outrage at the acquittal, viewed as representing yet another act of racism and police abuse turned into rioting, looting, arson, and physical violence across urban Los Angeles that was mostly contained to south central Los Angeles. The rioting and looting intensified over the next few days, with Korean merchants and their stores becoming the primary targets due to their omnipresence in black neighborhoods and their racially marked foreignness. California Republican governor Pete Wilson called on the federal government to send the National Guard as well as U.S. soldiers and Marines to help quell the unrest. In the end, the uprising contributed to fifty-three deaths, thousands of injuries, and over $1 billion worth of property damage.

While Korean Americans dealt with the destruction of over two thousand stores and $350 million in property loss, several Thai-owned businesses were destroyed and looted as well. But the plight of Thai American store owners went unnoticed because of the overwhelming media attention given to Korean Americans and racial tension between blacks and Koreans. In the immediate aftermath, the Thai consulate general in Los Angeles spearheaded efforts to investigate damages and locate money to help Thai store owners recover. During a press conference on May 4, 1992, the consul general announced that the Royal Thai Consulate in Los Angeles, the Royal Thai Embassy in Washington, D.C., and the Ministry of Foreign Affairs were working to secure loans to assist Thai business owners in their recovery efforts. The consulate also held a fundraiser with the Thai Mass Media Association at Wat Thai. Moreover, the Thai Association of Southern California encouraged Thai storeowners to seek funding by reporting losses to community redevelopment agencies.

For Thais, the 1992 Los Angeles riots exposed their social and political marginality, pushing them toward formal political participation. Thai Americans thought deeply about the causes and meanings of the uprising. A few expressed their views about the rioters, racism, and American culture in editorials and opinion pieces printed in Thai-language newspapers. They abhorred the "disgusting behavior" of rioters and looters and chastised them as "uncivilized" people who took advantage of the Rodney King verdict and used it as an excuse to be destructive.[4] While some urged Thais to stick together, to have faith in the U.S. legal system, and not to retaliate or call attention to themselves, others encouraged Thais to look toward strengthening their political power by supporting local politicians who could represent their interests. The uprising raised the question of whether Thais should fight for resources and visibility or maintain a low profile and avoid confrontation. And if so, what kind of politics would the Thai American community adopt after experiencing what many believed to be a mockery of law and order?

A growing anti-immigrant sentiment across the nation during this period also spurred Thai American community mobilization. An editorial that appeared on April 15, 1993 in *Khao Sod,* a Thai-language newspaper, described Los Angeles as a "city of fear" that not only consisted of racial tension between blacks and police officers and blacks and whites but also between blacks and "Orientals."[5] The writer warned Thais to be more cautious of their personal safety (from black perpetrators) because when it comes to "Orientals," most people could not differentiate one nationality from another. The fear among Thais in Los Angeles that they could be physically assaulted was not simply paranoia. Historian George Sanchez has argued that despite the media's fixation on black-white conflicts, many of the physical attacks during the 1992 riots occurred in multiracial and multiethnic contexts as African Americans also assaulted perceived Latino and Asian foreigners in an act of anti-immigrant hostility that represented the rise of a "new racial nativism" in American society.[6] In 1994 the potency of racial nativism came to full expression with California's Proposition 187, the "save our state" ballot initiative designed to prohibit education, health, and social services for "illegal immigrants."[7] Some Asian American voters supported the measure along with such organizations as Asian Americans for Border Control, a ten-member group working under the direction of the Orange County-based California Coalition for Immigration Reform.

Under these conditions the nonprofit Thai Community Development Center (Thai CDC) was established in April 1994. Spearheaded by twenty-six-year-old Thai American community activist Chanchanit "Chancee" Hirunpidok, the Thai CDC followed the lead of other Asian American organizations in Los Angeles to turn attacks against undocumented immigrants into opportunities to increase Asian American political clout through pan-Asian coalition building. They received a great deal of support. Several groups, including the Asian American Drug Abuse Program and the Little Tokyo Service Center, provided mentorship, and the Korean Immigrant Workers Advocates (KIWA) even shared their office space on 2430 W. 3rd St in Westlake, California, with the Thai CDC. One of Thai CDC's first battles involved joining over sixty other Asian American organizations across California to form Asian Pacific Islanders against Proposition 187. So from the beginning the Thai CDC made protecting immigrant rights a central part of their overall mission to help Thais, regardless of citizenship status, gain access to resources. The Thai CDC's mission statement captured their broader goals as well:

> To advance the social and economic well-being of low and moderate income Thais and other ethnic communities in the greater Los Angeles area through a comprehensive community development strategy including human rights advocacy, affordable housing, access to healthcare, promotion of small businesses, neighborhood empowerment, and social enterprises.

For the first few years, the Thai CDC taught Thai immigrants about standard labor rights and available resources and benefits at a class offered at Wat Thai, and sent Thai youth to summer camp. Chancee collected enough public and private money to pay herself an annual salary of $13,000 and hire two part-time staff members. The center depended mainly on volunteers.[8]

The Thai CDC projected Hirunpidok's political views and agenda. Born on April 12, 1968, in Bangkok, Thailand to Somnuck Hirunpidok and Somchua Rachatawan, Chancee first arrived in Los Angeles with her parents in 1972 at the age of four. The Hirunpidoks settled in the Asian and Latino immigrant neighborhood of Pico-Union, adjacent to downtown Los Angeles and directly across from MacArthur Park. Growing up as an Asian immigrant youth from inner city Los Angeles shaped her understanding of the world and her place in it. In high school, she was bused to Chatsworth High School in the west San Fernando Valley. It was a "culture shock," she remembered, "because I went from an inner city environment to an almost exclusively white environment, an affluent environment, with kids who drove to schools in Mercedes, and Beamers, what have you . . . that whole experience was totally alienating."[9] Coming from Pico-Union, she was convinced that her classmates were unaware of the kind of struggles her family and the people in her neighborhood faced on a daily basis. Hirunpidok's high school experiences galvanized her into activism. She became interested in fighting poverty and inequality. She also became committed to civic engagement and ethnic politics, participating in a range of activities, such as the Youth Advisory Council in Los Angeles, where she "literally lived and breathed City Hall." She remained active as an undergraduate at the University of California, Los Angeles, in the late 1980s. Upon graduating with a degree in political science, she took up employment and several internships with local and state politicians, including mayor Tom Bradley and councilman Michael Woo. She went on to earn a graduate degree in urban regional/third world development at UCLA's School of Urban Planning.[10]

Before establishing Thai CDC, Hirunpidok fought mightily to educate fellow Thais and the general public about the historical struggles of Thai Americans to combat the invisibility factor. Shortly after the 1992 Los Angeles Riots she organized and trained a group of Thai American college students to conduct the first-ever needs assessment survey for the Thai community in Los Angeles. The survey identified and documented community demographics, social and economic characteristics, and human and welfare needs. It was completed to demonstrate a need for resources in the community in the wake of the riots, as Thai businesses were destroyed but did not receive any rebuilding funds. Hirunpidok used the survey's findings as a tool to demand representation and resources that led to the creation of Thai CDC and its programs.

Right around the same time, Hirunpidok began teaching the first-ever college course on the Thai American experience at UCLA. She decided to launch the course in 1992 after being approached by Professor Glen Omatsu of the Asian American Studies Department. Working with a dearth of materials, she focused on Thai history and culture, immigration, identity formation, gender

FIGURE 6. Chanchanit "Chancee" Martorell (Hirunpidok), pictured here front row, second from right, with Thai American UCLA students, a member of Thai Chamber of Commerce, and Los Angeles mayor Tom Bradley in 1992. Martorell organized and trained the students in survey methods and data analysis to conduct the first needs based assessment survey for the Thai community in Los Angeles, which ultimately led to the creation of Thai Town in East Hollywood, California. Photograph courtesy of Chancee Martorell and the Thai Community Development Center.

and social systems, and Buddhism, and brought in Thai American community activists and leaders to speak throughout the course.[11] Hirunpidok's mission of increasing Thai American visibility was explicit in the course syllabus: "the latter part of the course will pay particular attention to the overall marginalization of Thais as an ethnic group and their invisibility as a community." One of the central course objectives was to help Thai Americans "overcome the invisibility factor" and in the final week of the course, students focused on "breaking through the invisibility factor" by discussing topics like community empowerment, coalition building, leadership infrastructure, and institution building.[12] In an interview about the course with *AsianWeek*, Hirunpidok informed the magazine about the plight of Thai Americans and the neglect they faced. "It's not that the Thai community is special," Hirunpidok said, "but we lack any kind of visibility ... unless that is addressed, we will not get the much-needed assistance from either the public or the private sector.... The Census Bureau also reports an undercounted figure of Thais, so that in itself is something we have to deal with."[13]

After Thai CDC was up and running, Hirunpidok had to deal with a lack of political engagement and community involvement among Thais in Los Angeles. She attributed this to Thais themselves and identified several causes. First, she believed that there was a lack of interest in U.S. affairs. To her, Thai immigrants had bought into the "sojourner myth" and, as a result, remained more interested in the political issues of Thailand, their past and future home, instead of working to build a life in the United States. Outright antagonism among Thais toward any kind of community participation, let alone political participation, represented another barrier. On one level, Hirunpidok interpreted this antagonism as endemic to Thai social structure, claiming that there is "no history of activism or organizing" because "many Thais don't understand the value of community work. . . . Thailand is still at a stage of development in which people aren't used to thinking institutionally."[14] On another level, Thais who wanted to assimilate to American society refused community engagement in order to disassociate themselves from other Thais. Third, she felt that Thai immigrants behaved in ways that prevented the forging of community bonds, affinity, and social capital. Hirunpidok believed Thai immigrants were too consumed with trying to be more successful than their fellow countrymen and improving their class status at the cost of working together.

Thai cuisine was one of the most challenging barriers to collective mobilization. Hirunpidok knew that Thai food was a powerful, edible introduction to Thai American life. She acknowledged that "Thai food certainly . . . had a lot to do with, you know, people knowing more about Thai culture and Thailand . . . so the food, I think also, was a way for people to become more intimately familiar with Thai culture and Thailand."[15] The problem, according to Hirunpidok, was that "the popularity of Thai restaurants is a source of pride and income for many Thai Americans, but food is just one aspect of Thai life and culture; receiving exposure in the mainstream media for food alone is not balanced coverage." The popularity of Thai food also distracted from addressing more pressing needs and problems in the Thai community. "We need to start organizing around real issues," she asserted, "not just cultural events and food festivals."[16]

The reason Thais in Los Angeles cared more about food than formal political activism, though, had more to do with a growing culture of privatization and less with Thai people or a culture of fatalism. The intensification of global capitalism, commercial culture, and sustained attacks on the public sphere in the 1990s contributed to the decay of public culture. As a result,

Americans turned increasingly inward to their private lives and became more invested in their power as consumers than as citizens.[17] Thus, the lack of political engagement and declining sense of community among Thais reflected a larger trend in American culture and life.[18] Apathy and cynicism toward formal politics were not a Thai or even immigrant problem; they were an American problem. Thais turned their attention to Thai food because it represented a site of political possibility in a consumer-based multicultural society. Cooking and selling Thai food held more promise of social integration, economic mobility, cultural understanding, and community building than did a ballot or nonprofit organization. In short, a growing privatization of society influenced both the lack of Thai American political activism and the commitment to Thai food culture as a means of creating change.

"BETWEEN A ROCK AND A HARD PLACE": THE 1995 EL MONTE SLAVE LABOR CASE

On November 4, 2000, Sokanay Sutthiprapha and her boyfriend, Win Chuai Ngan, opened Win's Thai Cuisine in North Hollywood, California. The couple purchased the restaurant for $10,000 and spent another $10,000 on food, equipment, and other requirements.[19] Sutthiprapha and Chuai Ngan said they got the idea to open a Thai restaurant during a visit to Thailand. While the couple was enjoying a meal with friends, someone recognized "this kind of food foreigners like," planting the thought in their heads. Upon returning to Los Angeles, Sutthiprapha, who was in her late thirties, trained as an assistant cook for five months at a Thai restaurant in Eagle Rock, California before she and Chuai Ngan decided they were ready to operate their own restaurant. On opening day, the small, narrow establishment on the southeast corner of Magnolia Boulevard and Colfax Avenue managed to make only $150, in large part because the majority of the "customers" were family and friends. Business soon improved, however, as white, Latino, and Thai customers from nearby offices frequented Win's to try Sutthiprapha's *tom kha gai*—hot, spicy, and sour coconut-based soup—and *yum woon sen*—glass noodles tossed with onion and shrimp. A year later, Win's Thai restaurant was earning several times the profit they made on the first day. The Asian Pacific Islander Small Business Program also honored Win's Thai Cuisine with its "small business of the year" award.

Local media, business leaders, and community activists considered Sutthiprapha and Chuai Ngan's success story a product of personal but also collective efforts. Just a few years prior to opening their restaurant, both had been working under slave-like conditions in the Los Angeles garment industry. H. Cooke Sunoo, director of the Asian Pacific Islander Small Business Program, underlined the "fact that they moved from virtual imprisonment to entrepreneurship is the embodiment of the ideal of entrepreneurship," and that "they overcame remarkable odds, coming out of a difficult situation to accomplish something significant."[20] The two toiled for years at S. K. Fashion Factory in El Monte, California, roughly thirteen miles east of downtown Los Angeles (and fifteen miles southeast of Thai Town) in the San Gabriel Valley. In 1992 Chuai Ngan managed to climb over the factory's perimeter wall and escape into the night with $300 in his pocket. Sutthiprapha was later freed during a headline-making raid in 1995. She met Chuai Ngan shortly after her release and a romantic relationship developed. Although the couple at first returned to work in the garment industry, Chuai Ngan received financial support from his younger brother (also an escapee) as well as assistance with navigating municipal permitting, leases, and other tips for operating a small business from various Thai organizations including the Thai CDC. The Thai CDC, in fact, had helped Sutthiprapha adjust to life in the city following the raid. Chuai Ngan reflected on his journey from sweatshop laborer to restaurant owner, telling the Los Angeles Times in 2001, "the old work [was] harder, you have to concentrate a lot so you can finish everything. . . . You have to push, push." Then, the couple explained together, "in here, we can stop and rest any time we want . . . we can go anywhere we want."[21]

August 2, 1995, was a watershed moment in Thai American political activism and visibility. In the early morning hours of that Wednesday, a multiagency task force that included U.S. federal and state marshals, the California Labor Commission, the U.S. Department of Labor, the California Employment Development Department, the California Occupational Safety and Health Administration, and El Monte and Los Angeles police officers raided the El Monte sweatshop complex to release Suttiprapha and seventy-one other Thai nationals from "indentured servitude."[22] It was regarded as the first official case of modern-day slavery in the United States since slavery was legally abolished with the passage of the 13th Amendment in 1865. The city, nation, and world quickly learned of the horrific conditions these workers endured while sewing named-brand clothing for American companies such as Anchor Blue, High Sierra, and B.U.M Equipment that sold at May Department Stores, Nordstrom's, Mervyn's, and Target.[23] The compound was a two-story, eight-unit apartment building converted into a sweatshop. The perimeter was barricaded by barbed razor wire and five-foot-tall spiked fences, and was patrolled by armed guards hired to prevent workers from escaping the premises and to intimidate through the surveillance of phone calls, letters, and daily activities.

An overwhelming number of the seventy-two Thai laborers at the complex were women, sixty-seven in total, and they were trained seamstresses. Out of the five men, several were sewing machine technicians.[24] All were undocumented. They were turn-of-the-twenty-first-century "guest workers." The ten Thai nationals in charge of the El Monte complex, family members who worked under the direction of their mother, recruited the workers from rural Thailand by luring them with promises of wages between $1,200 to $2,400 a month—fifty times what they could earn in Thailand—good hours, and freedom. If they agreed, the recruiter proceeded to give them false documents to enter the United States. As one worker later said, "we understood we were going to the City of Angels."[25] As soon as the Thai workers arrived at Los Angeles International Airport however, they were immediately packed into a bus and transported across the city to the compound. The factory bosses then told the workers they were responsible to pay back the $5,000 debt they accrued for their passports, visas, and other passage fees to the United States by working up to twenty hours a day for $1.60 an hour.[26] Confined in the sweatshop under threat of violence and deportation or both, the workers labored for the next several years in debt peonage.[27] The raid resulted in the arrest of the ten Thais who participated in running the compound, eight of whom were charged by a federal court for harboring "illegal immigrants" and transporting them in connection with the operation.[28]

The aftermath of the El Monte raid exposed the reluctance of U.S. government agents, labor officials, and law enforcement officials to serve and protect workers from exploitation and human rights violations in favor of securing national borders. Upon being rescued from the El Monte compound, the Thai workers did not find freedom. Instead, they found more fear and uncertainty as Immigration and Naturalization Service agents detained them, loaded them onto government busses, and sent them to a downtown Los Angeles detention center for working in the United States illegally. Interestingly, INS officials had received a tip about the sweatshop three years earlier, but they refused to take action until state labor officials issued a warrant six weeks before the August raid. Julie Su, an attorney with the Asian American Legal Center, warned of the consequences of such an approach by law enforcement agencies, claiming, "it sends the wrong message, that if you're exploited and you assert your rights, we'll lock you up."[29] Chancee (now with the last name Martorell) also explained that the Thai workers were "doubly victimized" because of their citizenship status and that they basically went from "one prison to another." Over the next nine days the Thai workers were transported, in shackles, back and forth between the downtown detention center and Terminal Island federal prison to be questioned as material witnesses while they faced immigration hearings and possible deportation.

Community organizations, including the Thai CDC, fought for the release of the workers and, on their behalf, organized legal action against the Los Angeles garment industry. As soon as the Thai workers arrived at the detention center, Martorell and Su developed an organization called "Sweatshop Watch" to monitor INS treatment of the workers. They created a makeshift office in the detention center's waiting room. Within a few days, they managed to get the workers released on bail, with the support of several Thai community members. The U.S. Department of Justice also indicted nine of the individuals who were in charge of the El Monte compound. "I'm really proud of them," Su said in response to the indictment, and in what was ventriloquism of American exceptionalism to gain the public's support, continued, "but I'm also proud of America because this nation opened its arms to them and showed its best ideals of freedom and human rights."[30] A month later, they pursued legal redress by filing a lawsuit against those responsible for the El Monte sweatshop and the major retailers who hired them as contractors. In 1998, they won the case and received back wages worth $2 million.[31] The various community groups that supported the workers believed they provided access to the legal system and thus the tools for the workers to, at the very least, successfully win monetary compensation for their labor and a sense of justice.

In addition, the Thai CDC and other agencies helped the Thai workers adjust to life in Los Angeles, which remained a difficult challenge after their "liberation." Initially many of the workers wanted to return to Thailand but feared retribution. During their time in the compound, the bosses and supervisors threatened to kill their family members if they ever tried to go to the police. Therefore, they kept a low profile. Some decided to return to domestic work. The Thai CDC helped the workers find jobs that paid at least minimum wage with good labor conditions, especially for those who returned to the garment industry. The Wat Thai of Los Angeles held several events for the workers to help them heal and regain their confidence in life. Volunteers at the Thai CDC taught the workers how to perform basic daily American tasks such as using a pay telephone or going to a 7-Eleven convenience store.[32] The workers, however, also developed their own support network, meeting every two weeks at the Thai CDC and the Wat Thai. During their meetings they focused on sharing and helping each other adjust. At one meeting, they practiced how to order pizzas as part of an English-language lesson.[33] The workers also revealed to newspaper reporters that they enjoyed picnicking in Griffith Park, visiting Universal Studios, and looked forward to going to Disneyland.[34] Participating in these activities, in a small way, helped the workers move on and reframe their perception of American society.

For Martorell and the Thai CDC specifically, the El Monte case pushed them to become more international in scope as the Los Angeles Thai community went from being invisible to visible overnight. The global issue of human trafficking, especially the smuggling of Thai women, became a top priority for Martorell and her volunteer staff. Although El Monte was the first and most extreme case, the Thai CDC worked on more than six human trafficking cases, including sex trafficking, over the next several years involving over six hundred Thai victims.[35] They also strengthened their commitment to Thai labor rights in Los Angeles, but they now saw labor rights as part of a larger struggle for human rights. Instead of just a set of grievances within the legal ramifications under U.S. law, the garment industry, as a transnational enterprise, needed to be challenged not only by U.S. law but also by international law. Finally, they continued to nurture the politicization of the sweatshop workers. Martorell considered the workers "change agents" and trained them to fight against other injustices in the garment industry based on their own experiences from the compound and the courtroom.

The Thai CDC also made clear that the El Monte case, though certainly exceptional in terms of the media attention and severity of the violations, was but a symptom of the larger problem of global capitalist exploitation that produced racial and gender subordination in the United States that was not being addressed or fought. Christopher Scheer, a *Los Angeles Times* reporter, underscored the gendered dimension of the case and the potential for Thai women's activism. He wrote that "unless [the workers] are transformed, unless they begin to claim their rights for themselves, their victories will be fleeting—just handouts, really . . . because this world is run by the rich and by men and by bureaucracies. It is not run by 85-pound Thai women who were harvesting rice at age 7 and sewing dresses at 13. They don't run anything; they are the run."[36]

The visibility of Thais caused by the El Monte case and the continued efforts to fight human trafficking by the Thai CDC generated strong responses from Thais in both the United States and Thailand. The opinions, which ranged from disgust and disbelief to outrage and blame, widened divisions and fractured the already fragile community bonds. When the Thai consul general, Suphot Dhirakaosal, heard the news he immediately went into damage control mode and decided not to help the victims in hopes of sweeping the event under the rug. A Thai volunteer said: "The consulate, the Thai government has no interest in helping these people. All they care about is saving their face . . . the consulate is telling them: 'You're costing the U.S. government money. It's embarrassing. You should go back."[37] Scheer also claimed that the consul general wanted the workers to accept money and fly immediately back to Thailand. But the consul general denied the allegations, replying "our duty is to protect the interests of these people . . . they are scared. If they would like to go back, they should go home . . . the Thai government will pay their way if they decide to go home."[38]

Moreover, other community activists criticized Martorell for trying to steal the credit for the raid to boost her own political career. One elderly Thai woman activist, Rusmee Jongjarearn, director of the Thai American Citizen's Alliance, claimed that other Thais "would like to help them, but [Martorell] is doing this all by herself without consulting us. . . . I think it's a one-person show where she can earn all the credit for herself and her organization."[39] She wants to be the hero, they claimed, and to deny access to those who wanted to assist the workers. Martorell responded to these allegations by suggesting that the critics were "considered elders in the community, and they feel we haven't included them on this . . . we feel we're better in touch with the system."[40]

Above all, Thais in Los Angeles were more concerned that the increased attention given to Thai immigrant exploitation tarnished the image of Thailand in front of the entire world. Whether producing perpetrators or victims, the events made Thailand, its people, and its culture look bad as they stained "the image of modern Siam, slavery not fitting in with the Edenesque advertising of beaches, food, and sex."[41] The problem worsened when the community discovered in January 1998 that a wealthy Thai socialite forced two Thai immigrant women to work as servants in her home and restaurant in Woodland Hills in the west San Fernando Valley.[42] The discovery led some members of the Thai community to explain that servitude, especially for Thai women, was common practice in Thai culture because that was the lot in life for "lower-class" Thais. But the attention still centered on how issues such as these would shape perceptions of Thais and Thailand in the United States. Somchet Phayakarit, an editor for a Thai-language newspaper revealed that people in the "Thai community know that things like this happen . . . when El Monte happened the reaction was the same. The Thai community is really upset. They know stories like this are not good for the Thai community's image."[43]

When placed within the context of Thai American civic engagement in Los Angeles, the 1995 El Monte sweatshop case was a "success." Thais in the United States were no longer invisible in formal politics after winning a landmark case against several leading retail corporations. Overall, the case accomplished several things in addition to overcoming the invisibility factor. First, Thai immigrants now had their "bitter" confrontation with American society—a harsh story of migration infused with racial and gender exploitation as well as a battle with immigration policy. They were just like any other Asian or racialized immigrant group. It was a narrative that allowed community organizers to link the experiences of Thai workers to other low-wage, immigrant workers in the burgeoning U.S. service economy. Second, the case put the issues faced by Thai immigrants in the United States on display to a global audience. This demanded that not only local and national U.S. authorities, but also the Thai government, address the problem of modern day slavery. Third, it spurred tensions and divisions between Thais in Los Angeles over the issue of community representation and image. The conflict was a sign of community engagement rather than retreat.

For once, it seemed to Thai American activists, U.S. society had to think about and discuss Thais in a context other than Thai food. Yet as we see with the story of Win Chuai Ngan and Sokanay Sutthiprapha, Thai food continued to be an enticing possibility for achieving the "American dream," service-sector style. Conversely, the couple's feel-good story also allowed Los Angeles to reconcile the gap between rhetoric and reality by implying that racialized immigrants, no matter how devastating their experiences, could still achieve incredible success because of Americans' openess to cultural traditions such as Thai food.

As early as 1992, Thais expressed strong interest in establishing a Thai Town, if it promised to provide a place to help express, maintain, and potentially sell their ethnic identity. In that year, the Thai Chamber of Commerce sponsored Blue Rangsuebsin, Burt Charuwon, and Tim Nokham of the Thai Smakom of UCLA to intern at the office of Los Angeles city council-man Michael Woo.[44] This is the group Martorell trained to conduct the "community needs assessment" survey to determine if Thais in Southern California needed a Thai Town and what, exactly, such neighborhood would include. The survey yielded a total of 371 completed questionnaires, mostly from Thai males between the ages of 30 and 50, those who resided in the United States for less than fifteen years, earned less than $25,000 a year, and were either permanent residents or students (25 percent listed their residency status as "other").[45] Based on the responses, an overwhelming majority of Thais in Los Angeles wanted a Thai Town—and they wanted it to be a tourist attraction. Moreover, the survey was the first to list the goals for Thai Town, which mirrored concerns about the lack of Thai American cohesion. "The purpose of a 'Thai Town,'" it laid out for participants, "is to promote a favorable atmosphere for Thai business/culture, to create a community center, and to promote Thai unity."[46]

But several years would pass before any concrete steps were taken to develop a Thai Town, mainly because the El Monte case diverted community leaders' attention and energy away from the project. On May 28, 1998, Martorell and the Thai CDC held an afternoon meeting with Los Angeles City council member Jackie Goldberg, council member John Ferraro, and the Hollywood Chamber of Commerce to jump start the Thai Town desig-nation project.[47]

The open forum meeting focused on how the development of a Thai Town might help showcase Los Angeles' multiculturalism as quintessentially American. While there was concern about funding, the council members (neither Goldberg nor Ferraro were present, but each sent representatives) and the Chamber of Commerce fully supported the Thai Town designation project. After an introduction of the project by Martorell and a presentation on the results of the 1992 survey and a recent canvassing effort by the Thai CDC, Goldberg's idea for Thai Town was discussed. Goldberg, her repre-sentative explained, was interested in making the East Hollywood area an "All-American City" by splitting up the blocks on Hollywood Boulevard to create distinct Thai, Latino, and Armenian "ethnic blocks" that, combined, would celebrate the cultural diversity of the United States. One person at the meeting disagreed with the proposal, claiming that it would be extremely difficult to split up the Thai restaurants lined along Hollywood Boulevard. Another person said that creating an "All-American City" was not going to improve Thai political clout in the city. The establishment of Little Tokyo, Chinatown, Koreatown, and Little Saigon, they reasoned, "means that there desperately needs to be a Thai Town!"[48]

More importantly, Thai Town would shift decision-making power to Thais so that they could address their own issues, set their own agendas, control resources, and determine their collective future. At the second meeting, held on July 11, 1998, the Thai CDC established an official "Thai Town Formation Committee" that presented, for the first time, a cohesive vision for Thai Town. Led by project director Ernesto Vigoreaux, a UCLA Urban Planning master's degree student, the committee promoted Thai Town as a way to allow the Thai community in Los Angeles to "unite around common goals and aspirations."[49] These goals included diversifying Thai businesses beyond the common restaurants, acting as an economic base for newly arrived Thai migrants, improving housing for low-income families, creating infrastructure and institutions to support future community projects, and "promot[ing] democratic decision-making in the Thai community by allowing Thais to be actively involved in the future of *Thai Town*."[50] It was to be a place that had the capacity to "empower the Thai community with knowledge, instill pride, confidence, and deliver a voice of representation in the diverse city of Los Angeles." Thus, the main purpose of Thai Town as articulated by the Thai CDC was to establish a political hub for Thais in greater Los Angeles that could spark Thai American civic engagement.

The committee also appealed to Los Angeles city leaders' goals of cultural diversity and multiculturalism to solicit support for the designation. The committee understood that Thai Town had to meet the needs and desires of those "outside" of the community to receive designation. It was simply not enough to focus on Thai community development and empowerment. They had to consider the broader significance of Thai Town. The slogan "Thai Town—ENRICHING CULTURAL DIVERSITY IN LOS ANGELES!" appeared in the committee members' manual and repeatedly in letters of support and petitions from city officials and broad-based community organizations.[51] In promoting "awareness of Thai culture in the City of Los Angeles," they emphasized that the preservation of Thai culture and heritage was neither parochial nor an outright refusal to be Americans but, on the contrary, part of a larger process of economic and social integration into U.S. society. In September 1998, Vigoreaux presented more evidence of the overwhelming support for Thai Town from non-Thai businesses and residents in east Hollywood based on the committee's canvassing efforts. Out of the eighty-seven total businesses in the area, 77 percent (67 total) signed a petition in support of Thai Town while the remaining 23 percent (20 businesses) did not reply or were closed during canvassing. Most importantly, Vigoreaux underlined, there was "no opposition" to Thai Town.[52] Highlighting the rhetoric of multiculturalism in their campaign proved to be a successful tactic.

Nearly a decade after the Thai Town plan's inception, on October 27, 1999, the City Council of Los Angeles unanimously approved a motion introduced by councilwoman Goldberg to designate Thai Town, which joined Little Tokyo, Chinatown, Koreatown, and Olvera Street as part of the multicultural fabric of Los Angeles.[53] The Thai CDC celebrated the designation at a ribbon-cutting ceremony in front of Thailand Plaza in the heart of East Hollywood. They unveiled signs that were to be placed at the Thai Town entrances on Hollywood Boulevard—Western Avenue to the west and Normandie Avenue to the east—and at the southbound and northbound exits on the Hollywood freeway. In addition to Hirunpidok and Vigoreaux, a diverse group of supporters and political leaders attended the event, including Goldberg and Thai consul general Suphot Dhirakaosal.[54] The designation of Thai Town was the first in the United States.

The Thai Town designation marked a critical first step for "revitalization" or bringing what the Thai CDC termed "Community Economic Development" (CED) to the entire East Hollywood neighborhood. It sparked immediate hopefulness among Thai business leaders, particularly restaurant owners, who believed the designation was going to help "clean up" the East Hollywood neighborhood and thereby attract more customers. The owner of Palms Thai restaurant, Somchai Vongparansuksa, believed Thai Town was "good for Thai people" because "we have been here a long time. It will get more business for us, be fixed up, and look better."[55] Vongparansuksa also noted that the police officers had already begun to chase away drug dealers, prostitutes, and the homeless.

A Thai Merchant's Association was created to address issues of crime, graffiti, parking, and beautification. Although the designation did not make Thai Town eligible for federal funds aimed at redevelopment, the Thai CDC was able to secure sets of matching funds, including one for $5,000, for city-sponsored beautification projects such as a lotus and orchid garden as well as a park with a fountain. A grant from the Department of Public Works Neighborhood Matching Fund allowed the Thai CDC to transport two six-foot-tall Thai "Apsonsi" (protective mythical creature) statues from Thailand to be placed at each Thai Town gateway entrance.[56] In addition, plans were also developed to build a Thai cultural community center and a Thai American museum. The designation created a mood of anticipation among Thai business owners, which led a manager of a Thai supermarket at Thailand Plaza to say, "people will know this is Thai Town and will be looking for something here from Thai culture."[57]

As the Thai CDC gained more momentum in the struggle for Thai community control over East Hollywood, they also tried to work collaboratively to include the ideas of Armenian merchants and local businesses. Together, Thai and Armenian small business owners, as well as larger corporations such as Starbucks, shared a desire for improved safety, cleanliness, better roads, and more parking while they also expressed concern for rising rents, property values, and business taxes. They all agreed that turning East Hollywood into a tourist attraction by highlighting Thai Town and Little Armenia was the best approach to economic viability and community building. Some suggested that an organization or "committee on tourism" be developed to spearhead a marketing strategy for Thai Town and East Hollywood.[58] The area, the business owners asserted, should capitalize on location and promote the area as part of Hollywood. The Thai merchants wanted to create an architectural attraction, such as a Thai cultural center with Thai boxing, art, music, and dance demonstrations, to make the cultural differences in the neighborhood visible and distinct.[59]

The Thai CDC envisioned more enterprises along the lines of the Thai Town community shop. The cooperative gift shop, which sat on the corner of Hollywood and N. Harvard Boulevards and sold handcrafts, clothes, jewelry, and silk fabrics imported from Thailand or created by the owners, opened in 2002 to boost Thai immigrant entrepreneurship by turning Thai Town into a "mecca for those seeking traditional Thai culture."[60] Twenty-four Thai women and one Thai man—garment workers, restaurant cooks, single mothers, and elderly women—put forth $1,000 each and pooled it together to create a shop they might not have been able to open alone.

Under the leadership of forty-nine-year-old Chutima Vucharatavintara, who worked at the Thai CDC and had a history of helping working-class

Thais and recent Thai immigrants settle in Los Angeles, the shop was established to allow Thais to become economically self-sufficient. For Prakorb Amornkul, who owned a pharmacy before coming to the United States to work a variety of service jobs for twenty-five years, the cooperative shop offered a chance to move away from low-wage work and be his own boss. The two-story shop, which also sold rugs, lamps, candles, and shawls upstairs and set up a Buddhist shrine used for meditating and praying, also functioned as a makeshift community center for the owners and other Thais who sought support. Still, the shop's main purpose was to attract tourists. "It's important for Americans to see our special crafts and that we are proud of our products," said Penny Bhusiririt, a Thai resident of Los Angeles since 1979, who also explained to a local newspaper reporter that "it makes sense to me that we have a shop like this that sells products direct from Thailand and allows us to show our culture to other people." The *Los Angeles Times* reported that the crafts and food sold at the cooperative shop had already attracted "locals as well as tourists from around the world."[61]

The Thai CDC followed through on their commitment to urban redevelopment and revitalization in East Hollywood by setting in motion plans to build a "Thai Town Bazaar and Food Court" to reflect the ethnic and racial diversity in the neighborhood. As part of a joint community outreach effort between the Thai CDC and UCLA's Department of Urban Planning, the public market was considered a more effective approach to urban policy in poor neighborhoods, a turn away from the "urban renewal" that has historically had devastating effects on racialized groups from gentrification to outright urban *removal*.[62] The overall goal was to create the first commercial "business incubator" in Thai Town and encourage interaction between different racial and ethnic groups by "striking a balance" between redevelopment and preserving the area's diverse ethnic communities and cultures.[63] In search of an existing model, staff project assistants researched other public market spaces around the country, including Mercado La Paloma in Los Angeles, Grand Central Market in Oakland, and Essex Street Market in New York City.[64] The permanent indoor market was to feature ethnic foods, crafts, and other products that represented Thai, Latino, and Armenian culture, and would consist of 18 start-up businesses and generate 38 jobs for salespeople, cooks, cashiers, accountants, managers, maintenance workers, and security officers.[65]

What the Thai CDC really had in mind was to give tourists a taste of the famous and popular public markets found throughout Thailand. Martorell was quick to advertise the potential commercial space, telling local newspaper reporters, "I'll be very proud to see that we've produced yet another tourist destination for the city of L.A., another gem for the city to flock to, that will put not just the Thai community on the map, but also the Armenian community and the Latino community. It's saying we exist, we have a presence, we want to drive our local economy and this is how we're going to do it."[66] While the Thai Town Bazaar and Food Court project was years away in the making, it moved one step closer to fruition when the Thai CDC was awarded a $468,821 federal grant in October 2006 to develop the market by 2011.[67]

CULINARY TOURISM IN THAI TOWN

Cultural tourism in Thai Town could be more adequately and accurately called culinary tourism, as it was the gustatory consumption of Thai cuisine that brought visitors to Thai Town. Culinary tourism did not take place solely in Thai Town's thirteen Thai restaurants.[68] There was also a concerted effort by the Thai CDC and several community-based organizations along with the Royal Thai Consulate Los Angeles to continue to hold but also create new Thai cultural events and food fairs in Thai Town "dedicated to Thai culture, tradition, food and entertainment." Under the sponsorship of the Consulate, which wanted to consolidate the numerous Thai culture and food-based events organized by various Thai community organizations into one extravagant yearly affair, the Songkran Festival celebrated the Thai New Year in April and first appeared in 2003 on Hollywood Boulevard. It was subsequently held on the first Sunday of every April. In 2004, the Thai New Year Songkran Festival Committee was formed to organize the event. Over the years, the festival has consistently included food and craft booths, religious ceremonies, cultural performances, folk dances, beauty pageants, and a parade down the closed Hollywood Boulevard as well as Muay Thai kickboxing tournaments. A number of Thai community-based organizations, businesses, and other clubs participated in the Songkran festival, demonstrating the widespread Thai community support for the event. The groups that participated in the 2004 parade, for example, ranged from the Northern Thai Culture and Thai Thaksin Association of Southern California to the Chiangmai University Alumni Association and a Thai Christian Church.[69]

The abundance of Thai food and culinary attractions brought large numbers of visitors. Thai food allowed the Songkran Festival committee to achieve its mission to "increase the spotlight on 'Thai Town'" and foster greater cultural appreciation for Thai culture while boosting the local economy.[70] As at Wat Thai food festivals, the food vendors at the Songkran Festival sold nearly every Thai food item, from the wildly popular pad thai and papaya salad to coconut-based desserts and Thai iced tea. Long lines at food booths were the norm at the all-day event, which usually began at 8 a.m. and lasted until dusk. In addition, restaurants in Thai Town stayed open just in case visitors preferred to sit and dine. Cooking demonstrations by Thai chefs, including Jet Tilakamonkul, also drew large crowds.[71] Food was so central to the event that organizers decided in 2008 to hold the first Los Angeles Curry Festival to coincide with the Songkran Festival, which featured not only Thai but also Japanese and Indian curries. In that year, the number of visitors to the festival swelled to over forty thousand people with estimates that it reached as high as 100,000—making it the largest Thai festival outside of Thailand.[72]

The popularity of Thai food at the Songkran Festival also attracted rather unwanted visitors: the County of Los Angeles Department of Public Health. The Thai food vendors had to navigate the demands issued by health officers, who told the organizers of the event and the vendors that they wanted to ensure the safety of the general public but also to protect the vendors from the possibility of being sued by a consumer. In addition to the cost of renting a 10' x 10' food booth for $450 to $500 depending on the location, vendors also had to pay up to $166 for a "temporary event" permit from the Department of Public Health to handle and sell food.[73] Most of the policies were standard: wear caps, aprons, and gloves, as well as provide sanitizer and napkins at all times.[74] What frustrated food vendors most was the food-handling codes. If the vendors did not keep food contained in a proper manner or at a certain temperature by the start of the festival, they were forced by public health officials to throw hundreds of dollars' worth of food away.[75]

One of the main sources of conflict among Thais over the Thai New Year Festival was how to fund the event without losing decision-making power to outside corporate interests. The Thai CDC claimed that the festival, which has cost anywhere between $20,000 and $100,000, received funding from "private and public partnerships" with Singha Beer, the Thai Tourism Authority, the Royal Thai Consulate, the City of Los Angeles, the Los Angeles Metropolitan Authority, Thai Airways, and the Rotary Club of Thai

Town. Yet, according to former lead organizer Surasak Wongskhaluang the reality was that these organizations and companies did not contribute every year, and the support was unevenly based on private monies.

The decision to accept large donations from private companies led to some criticism. For instance, when committee organizers secured a $50,000 donation from Singha Beer Company of Thailand in 2008, Thai newspapers complained that the festival was now under the control and driven by the needs of Singha Beer.[76] Wongskhaluang felt the festival organizers had little choice but to take the money because there was no other financial support. While the Thai general consul was given $20,000 by the Thai government to fund the first annual Songkran Festival, as the festival grew in popularity and size, funding from the Thai government diminished and the Royal Thai Consulate told organizers that they no longer had a budget for the event.[77] In addition, whereas the City of Los Angeles paid the cost of shutting down Hollywood Boulevard with barricades and provided onsite police officers for the first three festivals, the committee had to pay 50 percent of the cost for these necessities from then on due to state budget cuts. On top of that, Thai community members who supported the event in spirit could not put up the money to fund it. When Wongskhaluang asked for donations from the community in 2008, he received only $100. At times, volunteers had to pay out of their own pocket and request reimbursement.

The concerns over funding for the Thai New Year Songkran Festival was fundamentally about the loss of community decision-making power that, ironically, tourist-based events like the festival were supposed to strengthen. From the perspective of Thai Americans, the Songkran Festival was meant to build social capital among Thais in the United States through cultural practices while also providing economic opportunity for the community.[78] Although the festival lost money during its first three years, it made a minor profit of about $5,000 in 2007 and 2008, $4,000 of which organizers donated to the nonprofit Thai Health and Information Services, Inc. (THAIS, Inc.).[79]

Exploiting tourists for their money was not the main motivation for the festival. Wat Thai officials used a similar strategy when they organized food festivals and events. Yet, the Songkran Festival was different in that, unlike Wat Thai festivals, it was also a strategy for economic and political integration into Los Angeles that required organizers to appeal to the desires of non-Thai visitors. This was a conscious effort among Thai community leaders to prove to the city of Los Angeles and the rest of the nation that Thais had arrived politically and had something to offer culturally and economically. Wongskhaluang estimated that by the festival's fourth year, over 70 percent of the visitors were non-Thais. This was intentional. Organizers even turned one of Thai Town's major parking lots into a Singha "beer garden" with hundreds of kegs of beer that attracted large crowds of non-Thai visitors, especially Mexicans because "they can drink beer."[80] Wongkhaluang did not see a problem with catering to non-Thai tourists. Instead, he believed that the only true beneficiaries of the Thai New Year Songkran Festival was the Tourism Authority of Thailand and the Thai government because they were able to use the festival as free advertisement for tourism to Thailand. While the Tourism Authority of Thailand and the Thai government refused to donate money for the festival, they stood to make potential profits from Thai Town tourists.

The commitment to culinary tourism scripted the space of East Hollywood.[81] As Anthony Stanonis suggests about the U.S. South, "tourism, foodways, consumerism, and memory are tightly interwoven—indeed, oftentimes inseparable."[82] Thai American community leaders, developers, local city officials, and Thai business owners crafted and invested in a narrative about the history of Thai Town centered on the flavors and aromas of Thai food. They recast the history of East Hollywood for the purposes of culinary tourism and presented it as the place where Thai food in Los Angeles originated with the arrival of Thai immigrants. Thus, Thai Town became home to the most authentic tastes and flavors of Thai cuisine in the United States. In fact, it was Thailand in the United States.

In creating Thai Town's script, Thai leaders prioritized the desires and expectations of tourists to make sure that when tourists visited they would experience "real" Thai food and thus, "real" Thai culture. As a result, the already neglected stories of Latinos in the neighborhood were pushed even further to the margins. To sell Thai food, Thai culture itself needed to be packaged and ready-made for consumption, and the script enabled leaders and outside interests to neatly package Thai food *as* exotic Thai culture to be marketed and sold. For instance, the Thai CDC and restaurant owners perpetuated the story of Thai Town to bring economic growth to and political visibility for the Thai community, while city leaders and developers used Thai Town to showcase their commitment to the multicultural diversity. But most important, this had profound social and cultural effects. Thais in Los Angeles had to function within Thai Town's narrative as a culinary tourist destination. However incomplete this process may have been, Thai chefs and vendors had to quickly consider outside perceptions of what visitors wanted and recreate themselves in order to meet those needs.[83] Herein lies one of the major dilemmas of tourism. It sets rigid boundaries, creates narratives, tells a story, and sells an experience mainly for the benefit of the visitor that carries unseen consequences for the visited. Local populations, like the multiracial residents of Thai Town, lost decision-making power to outside interests in a postindustrial, postmodern service-based economy.

Los Angeles received local and national attention from culinary tourists and food connoisseurs as an epicenter of Thai cuisine in the United States, in large part because of Thai Town. Since its designation, Thai Town restaurants and chefs have offered Thai cooking courses as well as tasting and culinary tours. The Thai CDC led informal tours to restaurants such as Ban Kanom Thai, a Thai dessert shop, so that tourists could watch how sweet and salty snacks are made and then enjoy them.[84] In 2007, Thai Town's restaurants and culinary culture caught the attention of celebrity chef Anthony Bourdain, who featured Thai Town in a segment of an episode from his reality-based, culinary tourism cable television show *No Reservations*.[85] "You think ethnic L.A. you likely think Salvadorian, Korean, Mexican," starts Bourdain, "but one of the best and most sophisticated cuisines of Asia is best represented too . . . much like the Mexicans here the Thais have forged a place in this town that have made a colossal imprint on its makeup and on its daily diet." Chef Jet Tilakamonkul (whom Bourdain introduced to audiences as the unofficial mayor of Thai Town) gave Bourdain a tour through Thai Town's streets, his family's Bangkok Market, and Ban Kanom Thai, revealing to viewers that Thai Town exists because "Thai food came first." Finally, after consuming a bowl of spicy boat noodles at Sapp Noodle Coffee Shop with a blogger called the "Noodle Whore," Bourdain reflects on the restaurant and Thai Town as a whole:

> A spare, bare bones joint in a strip mall with a "C" rating from the health Taliban on the window and yet, I feel like I've been to Thailand and back . . . fast, cheap, and though barely a mile from the Sunset Strip, they may as well be thousands of miles away in a country not my own, but somehow more welcoming and familiar than the Hollywood freak show a few blocks over.[86]

Bourdain's culinary experiences in Thai Town certainly fit the narrative created by community and civic leaders that Thai cuisine in Los Angeles was at once exotic yet part of the Los Angeles fabric. More important than his observations though, was that he presented to a national audience the carefully crafted narrative that Thai food was a gateway to the Thai community in Los Angeles.

The marketing and selling of Thai cuisine as an economic and political strategy in Thai Town reverberated globally. Despite refusing to lend financial support for Thai food festivals, the Thai government kept a close watch on the popular Thai cuisine scene in Los Angeles before developing a campaign for national economic development centered on establishing more Thai restaurants and exporting Thai cooks to other countries. In 2001, Thailand Prime Minister Thaksin Shinawatra established the "Thai Kitchen of the World" campaign to expand Thai food and restaurants globally after recognizing the booming global popularity of Thai cuisine.[87] The main goals of the campaign were to (1) establish Thailand as one of the top five world food exporters within two or three years (ranked 14th in 2001), "with the highest credibility in safety, health, and sanitation" (2) promote more export of ingredients and materials used in Thai recipes; (3) encourage Thai restaurants abroad to act as tourist information centers for Thailand; and (4) support the increase of Thai restaurants abroad to twenty thousand by 2008 and standardize a "real," authentic Thai taste.[88] In short, the Thai government wanted Thailand to be the food industry's global leader. Therefore, the campaign was at once a national economic development strategy for Thailand and an attempt to encourage tourism and deepen foreign relations with other countries at the everyday level through foodways. Thai cuisine *as* policy.

Los Angeles' Thai restaurants and food festivals may have provided the Thai government with intuitive and anecdotal evidence of the potential for Thai cuisine to succeed globally. Still, the city continued to serve as a test site for Thai Kitchen to the World's goal of authenticating and standardizing Thai flavors and tastes. In March 2005 the Royal Thai Consul General in Los Angeles, with the observation that Thai food had become increasingly popular in California and the West, collaborated with two well-respected culinary schools in Thailand to decide the best way to introduce even more Californians to "delightful and authentic Thai cuisine."[89] The Royal Consulate General's main focus was to improve the quality of Thai food in the region and define what constitutes "authentic" Thai. They wished to put the Thai Kitchen to the World campaign into action by promoting the procurement, production, and consumption of "genuine" Thai food, which required talent and culinary professionalism but also a "profound understanding of this delicate Thai way of life."[90] The project came to fruition in Pasadena, California, at the California School of Culinary Arts (CSCA) in

August 2005, where Thai chef Sirichalerm Svast, or "McDang," taught a one-week course on Thai food for students and instructors before teaching the same course at the Culinary Institute of America (CIA) in Napa Valley, California.

Culinary tourism demands workers. Opening hundreds of Thai restaurants around the world required cooks to make and serve Thai food and to make and serve an "authentic" Thai experience. In preparation for this, the Thai government supported the training and exporting of Thai chefs as part of the Thai Kitchen to the World project. They have made it easier for restaurants outside of Thailand to hire Thai chefs. The vision was to move away from the model of Thais providing cheap labor to multinational corporations and instead use local skills to create products and services catering to affluent middle and upper-class global consumers.[91] The Institute of Food Research and Produce Development at Thailand's Kasetsart University has played a role in training Thai cooks "to manage the restaurants and to be professional restaurant entrepreneurs."[92] The workshops focus on teaching Thai cooks quality control, food safety, sanitation, and how to speak English. They are expected to work in other countries. The production and exporting of Thai cooks to Thai restaurants around the world (by 2008, there were twenty thousand Thai restaurants overseas in North America and Europe) has turned Thai cooks into guest workers.

On July 11, 2008, First Lady Laura Bush named Los Angeles's Thai Town a "Preserve America" community. George W. Bush signed the Preserve America initiative in 2003, an executive order that made the U.S. federal government a leader in "community efforts to preserve and enjoy our priceless cultural and natural heritage."[93] Spearheaded by the Thai CDC, which received continued support from Los Angeles elected officials and other city leaders, the national recognition marked Thai Town's cultural significance and meant that Thai Americans were "no longer an invisible community" in the United States. It also made Thai Town eligible for up to $250,000 in Preserve America grants as well as another $250,000 in matching funds.[94] Thai Town became one of twenty-two Preserve America communities in California, joining Chinatown and Little Tokyo as the only three located in Los Angeles. Sharon Lowe, a consultant to the Los Angeles Community Redevelopment Agency who helped with Thai Town's application stated, "As the city moves into the 21st century as a global city, a Pacific Rim city, it's important to preserve and promote our historic ethnic cultures and economically revitalize our communities."[95]

Conclusion

BEYOND COOKING AND EATING

AS A SECOND-GENERATION THAI AMERICAN born and raised in Los Angeles, I wrote *Flavors of Empire* because I was vexed by the hypervisibility of Thai food and the invisibility of Thai people in the United States. Without a doubt Thai food is an important part of Thai American life and community. It profoundly shaped my life even though my family never owned a Thai restaurant or grocery store. Growing up in the working-class Latino suburb of Pacoima in the San Fernando Valley in the 1980s, I spent a great deal of my childhood shopping with my mother and grandmother inside Thai grocery stores. I have vivid memories of eating at Thai restaurants with my parents and grandparents. I also remember spending entire days at the weekend food festivals at Wat Thai of Los Angeles, which was only a five-minute drive from our house, smelling and eating juicy grilled chicken skewers, noodle soups, and deep fried bananas—and washing it all down with my favorite drink, iced longan juice. Together, these places provided a tangible sense of ethnic identity and community, allowing us to taste what it meant to be Thai and to meet and stay connected with other Thais.

The problem was that Thai cuisine had by that time also effectively become a stand in for Thai people in American society. When I began writing this book in the mid-2000s Thai food culture was seemingly everywhere. Thai restaurants were plentiful in metropolitan areas and some started appearing in small, rural towns. Thai temples across the country held food festivals on a regular basis. Thai food was routinely featured in magazines, newspapers, and on popular television shows like Anthony Bourdain's *No Reservations* and Andrew Zimmern's *Bizarre Foods*. It was clear to me that the increased visibility of Thai food culture had helped American society fall in love with the *idea* of Thai people without having to deal with actual Thai people. It made Thais recognizable in a sanitized way that rendered real Thai people, with all of their complexities and contradictions, practically invisible. The little knowledge Americans had of Thai people seemed limited to Thai cuisine—that understandings of, interactions with, and feelings about Thais were filtered through people's experiences with Thai food. I experienced this first hand. Whenever I met a person for the first time and they learned of my ethnic background, they would, without fail, ask me if I cooked or if my parents owned a Thai restaurant or blurt out an enthusiastic "I love Thai food!" I'm sure many Thais would have welcomed such well-intentioned remarks. They were, after all, expressions of positive feelings toward Thai people and culture. Not me. I loved Thai food, too, but I did not enjoy having strangers reduce me to food, treating me like a plate of pad Thai.

I did not want to perpetuate this privileging of Thai cuisine over Thai people so I initially avoided food as a research path. I committed instead to writing a history of my community that would portray the "other side" of the community, outside of food. I quickly realized that was simply impossible, and that I could not adequately write a history of Thai Americans in Los Angeles without writing about Thai food. In addition to television shows and magazine articles celebrating Thai cuisine, I came across newspaper stories of Thai restaurant and food workers struggling under the boot of labor exploitation around the country.[1] I noticed that the Thai Community Development Center was centering Thai restaurants and culinary tourism to spur revitalization in Thai Town. In 2007, Thai food festivals at suburban Thai Buddhist temples in Berkeley and the one I grew up with in North Hollywood faced threats of being shut down by city officials because nearby residents were complaining of noise, parking, traffic, and smells. Also, the Thai government was ramping up efforts to train and export Thai chefs to different countries as part of their newly developed national economic development program, "Thai Kitchen to the World."[2]

As a result I began to see Thai food less as a diversion and more as an entry point into many of the pressing issues in the Thai American community I wished to examine: identity formation, community building, immigration, labor, globalization, class, gender, and race and ethnicity. So I decided to take America's fascination with Thai cuisine and turn it on its head: What made food central to Thai American identity and community formation in Los Angeles? How and why did Thai food culture come to stand in for actual Thai people in the United States? What impact did this have on Thai people's lives, their group position, and the way they understood themselves and their relationship to U.S. society?

As I have argued in this book, foodways became an indispensable part of the Thai American experience because of the confluence of U.S. Cold War intervention in Southeast Asia, the rise of discretionary leisure spending and consumer services, and the ascension of Los Angeles as a multicultural global city over the second half of the twentieth century. By joining these complicated narratives we see the way Thai food culture became a stand in for Thai people: it was a palatable and pleasurable means for Americans to get to know and understand Thais, a group that, given its relative small population numbers, was not widely represented in other arenas and thus was largely invisible to the American public outside of food. Thai food acted as a primary site for the construction of Thai Americans as an exotic racialized foreign other through taste and other human senses besides sight. For Thais in Los Angeles, food became a way for them to see themselves in relation to how America imagined them to be.

The fascination with Thai cuisine resulted in Thais remaking their sense of self through the perceived exoticness and sensuousness of Thai food. This negotiation of power—of U.S. empire, liberal multiculturalism, and Los Angeles' racialized spatial imaginaries—through foodways produced "Thai American" identity. The hypervisibility of Thai food also offered a chance for Thais to openly engage with and undermine their racialization as "Orientals" in the context of consumer culture. Using discourses of race, ethnicity, and nation along with the unique flavor profile of *yum* to differentiate Thai cuisine from other types of food, Thai effectively distinguished themselves from those within and outside of their racial and ethnic group, especially other Asians. While food brought Thais together and allowed them to remake and define Los Angeles as a multicultural, cosmopolitan place, it also created barriers to community mobilization against social and economic inequalities as Thai cuisine obscured many of the struggles and harsh realities faced by Thais throughout the city.

The story of food in the making of Thai America explored here opens onto larger threads and broader narratives of postwar U.S. history and Asian/ Pacific Islander American studies. What I have done is tried to present at once a history of U.S. empire, race, immigration, and Los Angeles. My hope is that this book can help us understand each of these histories in new ways and push our thinking in new directions. First, it deepens our knowledge of the postwar U.S. empire. The rise and development of the American empire has received enormous scholarly attention that has generated significant insight into how the United States emerged as a global leader, particularly after World War II, and the many ways it has wielded its power and projected its hegemony throughout the world. There has been an explosion of work that has taken up the task of interrogating the role of race as a central organizing principle of the postwar U.S. empire.[3] More specifically, it asks how race drove U.S. global expansion after World War II and how the postwar empire racialized others abroad and constructed racial hierarchies at home, especially amid decolonization and civil rights movements. Beyond cultural representations, some of the newer approaches examine the way race was shaped in the everyday life of U.S. empire by everyday people, both U.S. citizens and those on the receiving end of U.S. foreign policy. Treating "social history as diplomatic history," Adria Imada, Jana Lipman, Adrian Burgos, and Dennis Merrill, for example, have all illustrated that U.S. racial categories and systems were constituted in the textures of the everyday, from hula shows and red-light districts to baseball fields and hotel lobbies.[4]

My emphasis on foodways and culinary contact zones builds on this emerging scholarship on race and the everyday life of U.S. empire after World War II by highlighting new dimensions of this narrative. For one, the exploration of gustatory pleasures and sensory experiences suggests that other human senses besides sight played a critical role in the formation of race and racial hierarchies in the postwar era. In addition, we also learn more about the role American women played in supporting and advancing postwar U.S. imperial regimes. Although empire has been gendered as a masculine project of conquest and domination and centers men as the primary actors, women also participated in postwar U.S. global expansion as culinary tourists, cookbook authors, and suburban homemakers. Including women into the narrative is not simply about diversifying the cast of historical actors but adhering to an intersectional approach that underscores gender and power in the building and maintenance of the postwar U.S.

Finally, the growth of culinary tourism in Asia and the Pacific region coupled with the number of Oriental cookbooks published by white American women complicates our conceptions of cultural imperialism. It suggests that the postwar U.S. empire was characterized by the preservation, celebration, and promotion of local cultures (albeit in simplistic and static versions). So instead of outright imposition of American culture or forced assimilation to American norms evident in modernization efforts, the way Americans approached Thai food culture was, in many ways, influenced by a much more complicated yet deeply rooted imperial and colonial logic: the simultaneous attempt to homogenize and differentiate; to make natives more like Americans and at the same time keep them separate.

Taking into account these quotidian dimensions of the postwar U.S. empire permits a more accurate portrayal of the intertwined, transnational character of American history. It adds clarity to the many ways U.S. foreign policy intersects with domestic affairs to normalize empire as a "way of life" in the United States.[5] It also presents further evidence of U.S. racial formation as a transnational, global process determined not only by socio-political and economic factors contained inside the formal boundaries of the U.S. nation-state but also by U.S. empire—in all of its multiple expressions— abroad. While critics of the transnational approach to U.S. history claim that it does not draw a fine enough line around what constitutes "American history" and blurs the line between domestic and foreign to the point that it disappears, this book asserts that many of the key transformations in postwar American culture and society cannot be adequately understood without taking into account America's position in and actions around the world. Perhaps more importantly, as Simeon Man has written, it is to "seek to comprehend the discursive logic and technologies of empire and to unravel its entanglements with liberal modernity."[6]

The second intervention has to do with how race is made in the late twentieth century United States. When scholars think about racial formation in the United States (if we accept race as a social construction and not a biological fact) they rarely, if ever, think about foodways. After all there are a gamut of larger scale sites—capitalism, public health, mass media, law and politics— where racial categories are created, given meaning, and organized along a hierarchy and where racial ideologies are trafficked in. Yet I have shown that food informs the production of racial difference and racial knowledge. The book proves that race in America gets made in seemingly mundane and unexpected places like food culture. In an era of liberal multiculturalism (because the meaning of race is also historically specific and changes over time), foodways emerged as an especially potent site for racial and ethnic classification that muddled race, ethnicity, culture and nation. Of course, while food was about race it was never only about race. Food also hardened class distinctions, reinforced gender hierarchies, and bolstered ethnic and national divisions. The racialization of both Thais and whites through foodways, which was transnational, intersectional, and involved both top-down and bottom-up processes rooted heavily in senses other than sight, influenced the way they lived their lives and interacted with society.

Focusing on the practices of everyday life to examine the history of racial formation in the United States is a useful approach because it illuminates the connective tissue linking social structures, political economy, and individual lived experiences—or the interaction of the political with the social and cultural. If we are to believe that race permeates all aspects of U.S. society and that the structures of racial systems work most effectively when they are relatively invisible, taken for granted, and "natural" then it makes sense to give as much attention to the less obvious sites of racial formation as we do the more obvious ones. It is important to continue to trace and analyze the development of racial projects in supposedly insignificant places to make visible the invisible mechanisms of racial domination with the intent of denaturalizing and denormalizing them.

At the same time, a spectrum of political identities, many times oppositional, also emerge out of the quotidian as people resist, negotiate, and comply with the dominant racial order, racial ideologies, and their own racial and ethnic status. Food culture is but one example of how practices of everyday life are often critical to how people make sense of the world around them, where they fit into that world, who should belong in that world, and how they imagine and remake new worlds. Since definitions of citizenship and struggles over full rights are constituted by social participation, everyday practices should not be seen as a sideshow or a rehearsal for formal political action but instead as a set of interactions and exchanges that give rise to notions of race, gender, politics, history, community, and social position relative to others—which are inherently political acts. The mundane is not trivial or a mere distraction from "real issues." On the contrary, if we wish to understand race in America and how people engage and become shaped by racial structures we cannot ignore the ordinary and commonplace.

Third, this book nuances our conceptions of post-1965 immigration and immigrant lives. The explosion of immigration to the United States over the second half of the twentieth century has been well documented. By far the best scholarship takes a globalist and critical transnational perspective that centers on America's global power, foreign policy, war, and the expansion of global capitalism to explain late twentieth century migration to the United States.[7] Proponents argue that U.S. political, colonial, military, economic, and cultural and ideological ties in other countries, especially in Asia and Latin America, has produced the mass migration of millions of people to the country since World War II. Simply put, immigrants are "here" because America was "there."

This scholarship has been deeply enriched by studies of immigrant and refugee transnational and diasporic identities, communities, and cultures in the United States. Such studies have illustrated the multidirectional, complex nature of immigrant and refugee lives by showing how they forged identities and communities based on cultural practices and symbols across and within nation-state boundaries to establish cultural citizenship and a sense of belonging to many different "homes" (both imagined and geographically real) and as a way to negotiate domestic U.S. racism and the exercise of American global power.[8] Several scholars have even looked specifically at the role of foodways in the formation of immigrant transnational identities. Haiming Liu and Lianlian Lin, for example, have written that "food is an expression of ethnic resilience" and testify to how immigrants affirm ethnic identity, preserve cultural heritage, and construct and imagine "home" in new and often hostile societies.[9] Focusing on the "culinary identity" of Chinese immigrants in Los Angeles's San Gabriel Valley, they argue that rather than pursue "wholesale assimilation, post-1965 Chinese immigrants have selectively maintained some of their native cultural traditions such as food" to make transnational identity a tangible reality.[10]

As a product of U.S. Cold War intervention in Thailand, Thai migration to Los Angeles provides further empirical evidence that immigrants do not come to the United States from random spots around the world but from places where American military, economic, and cultural penetration has already established binational relations and thus a bridge between the sending and receiving nations. Continuing to foreground the uneven global relations of power between the United States and other countries counters conventional views of immigration as a "unidirectional phenomenon" in which, as Mae Ngai writes, "the hapless poor of the world clamor at the gates of the putatively disinterested wealthier nations."[11]

This book also shows how food, to expand on Liu and Lin, is indispensable to transnational community and identity making. To add depth to our understanding, however, we need to build on the work of scholars like Martin Manalansan, Rick Bonus, and David Sutton who help us see the heavy influence that sensory experiences have on the way people come to terms with displacement, movement, and forced migration.[12] We need to pay attention to not only the symbolic and social meaning of food but also the way smell, taste, and touch of cooking and eating evoke, neurologically, memories that are central to transnational culinary identities.

If we also engage the historical, more expansive view of food (beyond cooking and eating) taken up in this book, two key dimensions of transnational immigrant experiences become clearer. For one, nation-state power and borders did not necessarily erode or weaken in the late twentieth century. U.S. food policies, food systems, and global trade relations all boosted U.S. border making and border control, which in turn defined the look, feel, and livelihood of communities and lived experiences. The U.S. nation-state shaped Thai food culture in Los Angeles by enacting mechanisms—quotas, quality standards, and inspections—that determined whether Thai immigrants had access to the foods they wanted and needed. So immigrants do not just bring their foods with them—they bring only what they are allowed to. The myriad ways Thais acquired "authentic" ingredients to reproduce Thai flavors and nourish community shows what globalization looked like from below before NAFTA and the World Trade Organization.

It also leads to new ways of thinking about how transnational immigrant identities and communities manifested in physical places and what they meant for American society. Physical transnational sites—grocery stores, restaurants, temples, and designated ethnic neighborhoods (Thai Town)—allowed immigrants to recreate home, stay linked economically and politically to their homeland, and maintain their ethnic and national identity in the United States. At the same time, these places also facilitated the integration of immigrants into all facets of society. They transformed the cultural landscape and built environment of cities and suburbs in ways that often sparked heated confrontations between newcomers and long-time (mostly white) residents over land use, property values, race, culture, and assimilation.

Yet in spite of the pushback, transnational immigrant places persisted and have only continued to grow in number. While it is tempting to attribute this persistence solely to the resilient efforts of immigrants who, as agents of change, fought tenaciously for them to exist, that is only part of the story. We cannot adequately explain the histories of transnational immigrant places without taking into account that American society in many ways prompted and promoted transnational sites with a strong, visible ethnic assertiveness because it allowed them to celebrate and showcase multiculturalism, cosmopolitanism, and its relationship to the global capitalist economy. Foodways helps us to see that these places did not simply emerge out of immigrants' desire to create their own spaces to preserve ethnic culture and to feel safe and "at home" in a hostile, unwelcoming environment. Dominant society induced, incentivized, and accepted and celebrated them. Thus, transnational immigrant places (and the identities they embodied and produced) were not inherently resistant—they also functioned in the service of neoliberalism in ways that redefined the meaning of citizenship and belonging in the late twentieth century.

Finally, this book adds to the diverse and multilayered narratives of metropolitan history in the United States. Modern metropolitan areas, particularly global cities like Los Angeles, underwent a series of transformations over the later half of the twentieth century that had an immense impact not only on geography, economies, infrastructure, networks, and flows, but also on the lived experiences of its inhabitants. The most insightful work that examines the interplay between space and place—the abstract and the lived—during this period focuses on the agency and struggles of racial and ethnic groups, including immigrants, and their attempts to assert a right to live in, participate in, and remake metropolitan spaces.[13] These studies establish that communities of color used formal politics, legal tactics, protests, and myriad cultural and discursive practices to claim space and combat racial segregation, attacks on public space, and other forms of exclusion that barred them from being full-fledged participants in urban and suburban life. In the process these efforts generated racial identities, communities, physical places, and counter spatial imaginaries that defined regions.

Yet, fighting for a right to the city and suburb looked and played out differently in different places for different racial and ethnic groups—especially because their positions along the U.S. racial hierarchy varied by time and region. To expand our insight into the way people viewed and experienced cities and suburbs, and perhaps move toward historical synthesis, we need to continue paying attention to the unique ways communities confronted metropolitan inequality on the ground and its consequences on racial and ethnic formation. Ethnic food offers a useful analytic tool to make sense of the processes and factors involved in making claims on metropolitan space in large part because it accounts for space both lived and abstract. Food culture allowed Thais to anchor identity and community to urban and suburban spaces across Los Angeles, particularly through taste, and establish a sense of belonging to the region. Asserting a right to the global city through food, however, also reflected a negotiation of the increased privatization of everyday life and neoliberalism. This was especially evident at Wat Thai, where Thais used private property as public space to build community, and in the creation of Thai Town, where they promoted Thai cuisine and commodified Thai culture as heritage to stimulate collective mobilization, political activism, and capital investment from Thailand.

In addition, food accounts for regional identity formation. What we need are more studies of the role food plays in making cities and, in turn, how cities shape tastes and how Americans eat over time. Food culture helped cities form a sense of self, with restaurants and festivals acting as edible and sensory markers of multiculturalism, cosmopolitanism, provincialism, and "All Americanism." Moreover, food opens up metropolitan histories not fully explored in this book: interracial and interethnic relations in dining rooms (whites were not the only group to eat ethnic cuisine) and kitchens; how restaurants contributed to gentrification and displacement; and restaurant health inspections and food safety regulations, including ordinances on street food vending aimed at banning or curtailing the selling of food on sidewalks that targeted immigrants and ignited debate over cultural differences in cooking practices, race, food handling, and cleanliness.[14]

One of the goals of this book is to make a case to include Thai Americans in historical narratives of Asian/Pacific Islander America. As I finish writing this book, the Thai American experience is completely absent in nearly all the seminal syntheses of Asian/Pacific Islander American histories.[15] The continued absence is striking considering the field's recognition of the exploding diversity of Asian/Pacific Islander America, the transnational and cultural turns in the scholarship, critiques of the field's East Asian bias, and the inclusion of other Southeast Asians into the master narrative. That Thais are among the more recent arrivals and are numerically smaller than other Asian/Pacific Islander groups—at 237,583 (not including the tens of thousands outside of legal status) they are only the 10th largest Asian population according to the 2010 U.S. census—are not factors.[16] The main problem has been that historical treatments of Thai Americans do not exist.

I hope this book addresses this problem and establishes why narratives of Asian/Pacific Islander American history need to engage Thai Americans. The most obvious reason is that it expands our knowledge of the heterogeneity and diversity of post-1965 Asian/Pacific Islander America by documenting the experiences of a "new" group. Yet beyond an additive, Thai American history expands our understanding of central themes and events in Asian/Pacific Islander American history from the Cold War and U.S. intervention in Southeast Asia to post-1965 immigration patterns, ethnic entrepreneurship, and suburbanization. More importantly, it turns the narrative in original directions. For example, the experiences of Thais who entered the United States through the "side door" with student and tourist visas and overstayed opens up the understudied history of exdocumented Asian/Pacific Islander

Americans. This is especially relevant as recent debates around undocumented immigrants obsess over Mexican "illegals" and focus almost exclusively on the U.S.-Mexico border—while nearly 40 percent of undocumented people currently living in the United States entered from various parts of the world with valid documents, such as student visas.[17] In this way, Thai American history is relevant to Asian/Pacific Islander American history and American history more broadly but also a range of other fields and disciplines. Of course, Thai Americans should be studied in their own right. But my aim has been to demonstrate that there is a great deal to be learned about the human condition through the experiences of Thai people—and other peoples considered unimportant and irrelevant to our understanding of the past because of size and time.

The other main goal has been to prove that food is a dynamic analytic tool to make sense of key turning points that changed everyday life in the United States. Food is a stimulus for and register of larger transformations. Its intrinsic value, notably the way it engages all the human senses, allows us to not only tell more evocative stories but also interpret and explain historical change in fresh ways. Equally important, food is an effective means of historical investigation because it evokes warm feelings and nostalgia that are central to our consumer habits and personal identities. It acts as a familiar, intimate, and therefore tangible reference and point of entry into the past that and allows us to link the past with the present. In short, food is serious, legitimate subject worthy of intellectual thought and energy. Food is also a powerful "entrée" to the central themes and broader narratives of American history. As an expression of cultural heritage, traditions, and ethnic resilience it is a window into identity and community making—especially for peoples who grappled with and tried to survive U.S. conquest, white settler colonialism, slavery, Jim Crow, war, displacement and migration. Yet food is also deeply rooted in political economy and not simply cultural heritage. I have tried to make this clear by illustrating how U.S. global power, rather than just cultural values and abilities, set the terms on which Thais entered, incorporated themselves into, and negotiated American society through foodways. For Thai Americans food became more than a way to retain and express culture—it became intimately intertwined with U.S. foreign policy, trade, labor, urbanization, civic engagement, and political visibility.

The relationship between food and Thai Americans is one that is still evolving. In 2013, the Royal Thai Consulate in Los Angeles appointed Jet

Tilakamonkul as the first-ever "Thai Culinary Ambassador" to represent and further promote Thai food on behalf of the Thai government.[18] The appointment signals that Thai cuisine in Los Angeles will continue operating as culinary diplomacy between Thailand and the United States. It also points to the Thai government's persistent attempt to thrust Thai food into the forefront of its economic and national development policies. The Thai Kitchen to the World project, which has been revamped and renamed quite a few times since it was introduced in 2001, remains the flagship in Thailand's effort to become a leading food exporter and expand the number of Thai restaurants worldwide to stimulate tourism to Thailand and establish a global standard for Thai taste and flavors.[19] This will have important ramifications not just on Thai foodways but also Thai American and Thai diasporic identities and communities more broadly, especially in terms of race, gender, and class as Thai chefs—trained under the Thai Kitchen to the World project—will essentially be exported as guest workers to cities throughout the world.

Thai Town has also strengthened its commitment to food as an engine for economic growth, urban revitalization, and social integration. In addition to culinary tourism via restaurants and festivals, however, there has been growing attention to issues of food security and access to healthy foods for the multiracial and multiethnic working-class immigrant residents of the area. In 2016, the Thai Community Development Center broke ground for its Thai Town Marketplace. The $29.5 million, 5,000 square foot Marketplace—a decade in the making—sits on the southeast corner of Hollywood Boulevard and Western Avenue and will house 18 food retail and artisan vendor stalls and a local farmer's market.[20] While much of the impetus for the Marketplace is to spur entrepreneurship and economic self-sufficiency, what is most compelling is that the project has been inclusive, since its inception, of the views and needs of not just Thais but the neighborhood's Latino and Armenian residents, many of whom also lack job skills and are underemployed. Existing residents had direct input in how Thai Town should look and who it should serve. As such the Marketplace reflects what appears to be an alternative form of urban redevelopment that is both cognizant of and pushes back against gentrification and displacement—the hallmarks of "urban renewal"—offering timely insight into present day and future struggles for a right to the global city.

In North Hollywood, the conflict over food festivals at the Wat Thai of Los Angeles that took place in the 1980s also has a more contemporary postscript. Nearly twenty-five years later, in 2007, Los Angeles city officials placed a moratorium on the sale of food on weekends at Wat Thai. Nearby homeowners once again blamed temple's festivities for parking problems, trash, and noise, claiming it was "unfair" that their "quality of life was horrible on the weekends."[21] The residents discovered the original zoning ordinance and submitted it to the city. City officials ruled that Wat Thai was essentially a "food festival" that inconvenienced nearby residents. The moratorium was permanent. It restricted the selling of food to the courtyard at the bottom level of the temple's school building on weekends, which attracts far smaller crowds. Many of the vendors went elsewhere to sell their food. But as I finish this book Wat Thai has been able to host food festivals on major holidays in addition to the weekend food court. Still, the power of zoning to regulate and exclude remained powerfully durable in Los Angeles, demanding further exploration as the story of competing racialized spatial imaginaries continues to evolve.[22]

One thing, however, is clear: Thai food festivals in suburban Los Angeles have built community and social networks to great ends at precisely the moment in which authentic "American" community was supposedly in decline. They stand as a powerful counterpunch to those who lament nonwhite populations, particularly immigrants, for fracturing an otherwise unified American culture or sense of togetherness. Suburbanization, specifically the desire for a privatized suburban ideal constructed through exclusionary mechanisms like zoning, play a more significant role in both the diminishing of public spaces and undermining more inclusive notions of community in late twentieth century U.S. society than immigrants who are unwilling to assimilate.

Analyzing the history of food in the making of Thai America can also help us understand the broader implications of food and racism in the United States today. There is no doubt that the taste, smell, texture, and sight of food continues to be a means to degrade people of color. As it has been at numerous points throughout American history, food is an effective way to draw boundaries around and between who is and is not civilized, assimilable, and American (white). Ethnic cooking and eating practices remain, in other words, an incredibly effective way to racialize groups as foreign, nonnormative, repulsive, offensive, backwards, savage, and unfit for and a threat to American society and culture.[23] Communities of color know this all too well.

At the same time, for a generation conditioned under liberal multiculturalism and neoliberalism, cooking and eating the cuisine of others has also come to be seen as a way to alleviate racism, a sort of discrimination therapy.

Cuisine-driven multiculturalism has flourished. It gains more momentum with the increasing exposure of U.S. consumers to a diverse array of ethnic cuisines. By tracing the historical origins and development of cuisine driven multiculturalism, this book pushes the contemporary conversation around food and racism forward by shining more light on how food buttresses white supremacy through well-meaning, liberal racism exemplified by a love and passion for ethnic food. Systemic racism, namely white racial privilege, has neither worked nor persisted entirely because of ignorance or racist bigots with crude beliefs about the inferiority of people of color (even when they mask with code words). Genuine curiosity, appreciation, and a willingness to experience and accept other cultures through foodways also insidiously reinforces structural racism rooted in imperialism and colonialism.

The phenomenon of white chefs appropriating ethnic cuisines in the United States has sparked intense debate over the role of cultural appreciation and racism, colonialism and imperialism.[24] Countless white chefs—Andy Ricker, Rick Bayless, Fucshia Dunlop, Sean Brock, Carolyn Phillips, Nina Simonds, and Taylor Akins, to name but a few—have recently been in the crosshairs for gaining fame and fortune cooking food from a culture not their own. Critics have accused them of "columbusing," of having only a shallow understanding of the cultures they "borrow" from, and for erasing chefs of color who cook the same food by virtue of centering themselves.[25] Critics are especially outraged about the fact that white culinary appropriators win prestigious awards, are deemed authority figures, and get more opportunities in top food media outlets to share their knowledge of how to cook ethnic dishes because of their whiteness.

For instance, Andy Ricker, chef and owner of the wildly popular Pok Pok restaurants, author of *Pok Pok*, and winner of two James Beard awards (2011 for best chef northwest, 2014 for "cooking, recipes, or instruction" for his writing on Thai curries), has emerged as Thai America's resident culinary appropriator.[26] Ricker has been taken to task for building his empire cooking and selling "authentic" northern-style Thai street food for non-Thai foodies.[27] The chefs, as well as their defenders, have responded by saying that they, indeed, have a deep knowledge, understanding, and respect for the cultures they are benefitting from and by giving credit to "natives" who taught them the craft.[28] Some defenders have even blamed people of color for letting "foreigners pawn themselves off to the Western media as 'the authority'" on ethnic cuisines and that marginalized groups cared little about capitalizing on their culinary traditions until white chefs started becoming famous for it.[29]

As the debate rages on without an end in sight, it is important to keep the focus on histories of racialization, imperialism, and colonialism in the United States rather than fixate on the intent and attitudes of individual white chefs and their knowledge of the culture and histories surrounding the dishes they prepare. Thai restaurateurs have cared about Thai food, just like other ethnic restaurateurs, and have been preparing equally delicious dishes for decades without fanfare, and when fanfare came it was only when whites started eating and writing about it. Unlike white chefs, chefs of color do not have unbridled freedom to serve street-style or "authentic" dishes with obscure ingredients for U.S. consumers because their food is, as it always has been, associated with their bodies. Due to the history of food and racialization in America, chefs of color must refine dishes (yet keep them exotic and different) to not only make them more palatable but to shield themselves and their communities from being labeled as disgusting, diseased, and not fully human. The kinds of dishes they serve have real consequences on how society views and treats them as people—not just as chefs. The opposite is true for Ricker and other white chefs, who, because of their whiteness, can cook and serve dishes on the bizarre end of exotic, especially ones that satiate the quest for "unknown" (previously unpalatable to whites) dishes currently fueling foodie culture today, without any consequence on how they live their everyday lives. White America will not suffer any consequences from white chefs cooking "street style." In fact, their whiteness "elevates" cuisines and makes them fashionable, trendy, and award winning.

My point is not to determine if the likes of Andy Ricker—and historical predecessors like Marie Wilson and Jennifer Brennan—are racists, colonizers, liberal multiculturalists, or all of the above. Their encounters with ethnic food consist of more than feelings and attitudes toward others. Focusing on specific individuals erases not only the deeply entrenched histories of racialization but also the structural underpinnings of U.S. imperial and neocolonial interventions that made culinary appropriation possible. This is why, as Uma Narayan has argued, demanding white chefs and foodies to be more aware of whiteness and colonialism as they cook and devour the cuisine of others is not enough. There is no amount of concerned reflection, she contends, that will "undo the fact that mainstream [white] eaters would remain privileged consumers, benefiting from the structural inequalities and unpleasant material realities that often form the contexts in which 'ethnic food' is produced and consumed."[30] The relationship between white culinary appropriators and the groups they extract from are deeply embedded in historically constituted relationships of power that will only change in meaningful ways with large-scale, systemic changes in these relations of power.[31]

As ethnic cuisine becomes more popular in foodie culture, it is imperative not to lose sight of the fact that there are real people who cook and serve the food we consume in eateries across the United States. The quest for new and exciting dishes in restaurants, festivals, and food stalls and food trucks has generated an obsession with the eater's experience and the food on the plate in ways that render food service workers invisible. This invisibility has real consequences. Centering the foodie's experience and desires—for quality taste, service, setting, and cleanliness—only reinforces our privileged position as consumers benefiting from the structural inequities and legacies of U.S. colonialism and neocolonialism that created the conditions for the availability of ethnic cuisines. The marginalization and erasure also further dehumanizes people of color and immigrant workers, who make up the majority of the labor behind the kitchen door, making it easier for us to lambaste them—in person and in reviews—when they make a mistake that diminishes the sanctity of our dining experiences. Our $10 should not be worth more than a person's dignity.

My hope is that this book counters this trend by finding the humanity of people on the receiving end of the consumption of ethnic cuisine. The goal, however, is not to tell these histories just to help us be more reflective and aware of how we treat food service workers. It is to spur action. Treating workers with dignity, respect, and kindness is good, but it does not change material realities or alter relations of power. Recognizing the humanity of food service workers should also mean supporting labor policies and practices that lead to concrete changes that improve peoples' lives.

Only through writing this book have I been able to realize that food is not merely a distraction from mobilization around real issues. The proliferation of commercial ethnic foodways can potentially spark radical, social justice-based political activism within the Thai American community and, more importantly, across marginalized racial and ethnic groups. This will not magically happen from breaking bread together or eating each other's cuisines. Rather, it will happen from recognizing that, for communities of color, our proximity to food culture has been shaped and defined by similar forces that have made our relationship with food unique yet familiar. We share the experience of using food to deal with migration and displacement; of going to extraordinary lengths for the right ingredients; of having little choice but to peddle our culture in restaurants; of toiling in kitchens without legal status; of being ridiculed for food; of being romanticized through it; of having it "columbused"; of living in a country that sees food service as our proper place in society; and of having America love our food but not our people. There are critical differences in our histories, to be sure, but food is at least one nexus where our histories converge to offer a basis for interracial and interethnic solidarity across gender, class, and citizenship. *Flavors of Empire* presents one strand of history to help build and sustain collective challenges against the existing neoliberal racial order.

NOTES

INTRODUCTION

1. I use *Thais* and *Thai Americans* interchangeably throughout the book to refer to both Thais from Thailand and Thais in the United States because it captures the ever-changing nature of transnational identity processes. Given that Thailand itself is home to various ethnic groups, here the terms encompass each of these groups unless otherwise specified (such as "ethnic Chinese"). While Thais did not refer to themselves as Thai American, I choose to do so because it speaks to the power of U.S. influence on their lives not just in the United States but also in Thailand, specifically U.S. racial and ethnic categories. I do not mean to overlook the significance of state defined immigration categories. Legal statuses informed relations inside families, within the Thai American community, and between Thais and the U.S. nation-state. As such, I make distinctions ("Thai immigrants and Thai Americans") in places where I believe these statuses operated most saliently.

2. I am indebted to Mary Louise Pratt for her concept of "cultural contact zone"—a modern social space where different cultures meet, often in highly asymmetrical power relationships. Mary Louise Pratt, "Arts of the Contact Zone," *Profession* (1991), 34. At the same time, I am also indebted to James Farrer, who has already refashioned Pratt's concept of a cultural contact zone into the concept of culinary contact zones. See James Farrer's "Shanghai's Western Restaurants as Culinary Contact Zones in a Transnational Culinary Field," in *The Globalization of Asian Cuisines: Transnational Networks and Culinary Contact Zones,* James Farrer ed. (New York: Palgrave McMillan, 2015), 104.

3. Rachel Slocum, "Race in the Study of Food," *Progress in Human Geography* 35, no. 3 (2011): 303. I also borrow from Lucy M. Long, who defines the concept of foodways as a "network of behaviors, traditions, and beliefs concerning food, and involves all the activities surrounding a food item and its consumption, including the procurement, preservation, preparation, presentation, and performance of that food." To highlight this network I also use the terms foodways, food culture, food

practices, and cuisine synonymously unless otherwise specified. Lucy M. Long ed., *Culinary Tourism* (Lexington: University of Kentucky, 2004), 8.

4. Carole Counihan and Penny Van Esterik, *Food and Culture: A Reader,* 2nd ed. (New York: Routledge Press, 2008); Linda Brown Keller, *Ethnic and Regional Foodways in the United States: The Performance of Group Identity* (Knoxville: University of Tennessee Press, 1984). Donna R. Gabaccia, *We Are What We Eat: Ethnic Food and the Making of Americans* (Cambridge, MA: Harvard University Press, 1998).

5. Robert Ji-Song Ku, Martin F. Manalansan, and Anita Mannur, ed., *Eating Asian America: A Food Studies Reader* (New York: New York University Press, 2013), 1.

6. In addition to *Eating Asian America*, there is growing work on food and race: Anita Mannur, *Culinary Fictions: Food in South Asian Diasporic Culture* (Philadelphia: Temple University Press, 2010); Anita Mannur and Valerie Matsumoto, eds., *Amerasia Journal 32: Meat versus Rice: New Research on Asian American Foodways* (Los Angeles: University of California–Los Angeles, 2006); Melanie DuPuis, *Nature's Perfect Food: How Milk Became America's Drink* (New York: New York University Press, 2002); Psyche Williams-Forson, *Building Houses Out of Chicken Legs: Black Women, Food, and Power* (Chapel Hill: University of North Carolina Press, 2006); Frederick Douglass Opie, *Hog and Hominy: Soul Food from Africa to America* (New York: Columbia University Press, 2008); Vicki Ruiz, "Citizen Restaurant: American Imaginaries, American Communities," *American Quarterly* 60 (March 2008): 1–21; Kyla Wazana Thompkins, *Racial Indigestion: Eating Bodies in the 19th Century* (New York: New York University Press, 2012). For useful overviews of the literature on food and race, see Jennifer Jensen Wallach, "Food and Race" in *The Routledge History of American Foodways* Michael D. Wise and Jennifer Jensen Wallach, eds. (New York: Routledge Press, 2016), 293–310, and John M. Burdick, "Race, Racial Identity, and Eating," in *Encyclopedia of Food and Agricultural Ethics*, Paul B. Thompson and David M. Kaplan, eds. (Springer Netherlands, 2014), 1573–1583. Other excellent works that look at race and the production of food include Matt Garcia, *A World of Its Own: Race, Labor, and Citrus in the Making of Greater Los Angeles, 1900–1970* (Chapel Hill: University of North Carolina Press, 2001); and Jose Alamillo, *Making Lemonade Out of Lemons: Mexican Labor and Leisure in a California Town, 1880–1960* (Urbana: University of Illinois Press, 2006).

7. Mark M. Smith, *How Race is Made: Slavery, Segregation, and the Senses* (Chapel Hill: University of North Carolina Press, 2006); Mark M. Smith, *Sensing the Past: Seeing, Hearing, Smelling, Tasting, and Touching in History* (Berkeley: University of California Press, 2007); Connie Y. Chiang, "Monterey-by-the-Smell: Odors and Social Conflict on the California Coastline," *Pacific Historical Review* 73 (May 2004): 183–214; David Sutton, *Remembrance of Repasts: An Anthropology of Food and Memory* (London: Berg Publishers, 2001); Constance Classen, *Worlds of Sense: Exploring the Senses in History and Across Cultures* (New York: Routledge Press, 1993); Jennifer Lynn Stoever, *The Sonic Color Line: Race and the Cultural Politics of Listening* (New York: New York University Press, 2016).

8. Smith, *How Race is Made*; *Sensing the Past*; Camille Bégin, *Taste of the Nation: The New Deal Search for America's Food* (Chicago: University of Illinois Press, 2016); Emily Walmsley, "Race, Place and Taste: Making Identities Through Sensory Experience in Ecuador," *Etnofoor* 18, no. 1, *SENSES* (2005).

9. Kanjana Thepboriruk, "Thai in Diaspora: Language and Identity in Los Angeles, California" (PhD dissertation, University of Hawaii-Manoa, 2015); Nuttawadee Changboonchu, "Thai Foodways in the Nation's Capital: Enterprise, Religious Practice, and Community" (Master's Thesis: Chatham University, 2015); Jacqueline Desbarats, "Thai Migration to Los Angeles," *Geographical Review* 69, no. 3 (1979): 302–318; Orapan Footrakoon, "Lived Experiences of Thai War Brides in Mixed Thai-American Families in the United States" (PhD dissertation, University of Minnesota, Minneapolis), 1999; Nutta Vinijnaiyapak, "Institutions and Civic Engagement: A Case Study of Thai Community in Los Angeles" (PhD dissertation, University of Southern California, 2004); Narong Kaeonil, "The Thai Community in Los Angeles: An Attitudinal Study of Its Socio-Economic Structure" (PhD dissertation, United States International University); Ladda Kitivipart, "Communication and Interaction Styles in Thai-American Cross-Cultural Marriages" (PhD dissertation, United States International University, 1988); Narissara Taweekuakulkit, "Thai-North American Intercultural Marriage in the United States: A Qualitative Study of Conflict from Thai Wives' Perspectives" (PhD dissertation, Wayne State University, 2005); Mindy Jitmanowan, "Effects of Acculturation and Adaptation on Psychological Well-Being in the Thai Population Residing in the United States" (PhD dissertation, Alliant International University, 2016); Danny Anuphong Dechartivong, "Who, Wat, Where, and Wai: The History of Wat Thai Los Angeles" (master's thesis, University of California Los Angeles, 2012); Ajjima Utaravichien, "Maintaining the Mother Language: Perceptions of Thai Parents in the United States" (PhD dissertation, Sam Houston State University, 2014); Tiffany Reed, "Negotiating Identity for Mixed Thai-Americans" (PhD dissertation, Northern Illinois University, 2008); Chulalak Nutgirasuwan, "Thai Community Development and Civic Engagement in Los Angeles: Local Business Characteristics and Perspectives" (PhD dissertation, University of LaVerne, 2010); Pamanee Chaiwat, "Maintaining Authenticity in Ethnic Enclaves: Chinatown, Koreatown, and Thai Town, Los Angeles" (PhD dissertation, University of Washington, 2015).

10. Jiemin Bao, *Creating a Buddhist Community: A Thai Temple in Silicon Valley* (Philadelphia: Temple University Press, 2015). Bao's other works include, *Marital Acts: Gender, Sexuality, and Identity among the Chinese Thai Diaspora* (Honolulu: University of Hawaii Press, 2005); "Merit-Making Capitalism: Re-Territorializing Thai Buddhism in Silicon Valley, California," *Journal of Asian American Studies* 8, no. 2 (2005); "Thai Middle-Classness: Forging Alliances with Whites and Cultivating Patronage from Thailand's Elite," *Journal of Asian American Studies* 12, no. 2 (2009).

11. U.S. aid estimate is by U.S. Senate for the period 1949–1969 and taken from Patricia Norland et al., *The Eagle and the Elephant: Thai-American Relations Since 1833* (Bangkok: United States Information Service), 104. The figures are

substantiated in David Wyatt's *Thailand: A Short History* (New Haven: Yale University Press, 274).

12. Charlotte Brooks, *Alien Neighbors, Foreign Friends: Asian Americans, Housing, and the Transformation of California* (Chicago: University of Chicago Press, 2009); Catherine Ceniza-Choy, *Global Families: A History of International Adoption in America* (New York: New York University Press, 2013); Cindy I-Fen Cheng, *Citizens of Asian America: Democracy and Race During the Cold War* (New York: New York University Press, 2013); Madeline Y. Hsu, *The Good Immigrants: How the Yellow Peril Became the Model Minority* (Princeton: Princeton University Press, 2015); Christina Klein, *Cold War Orientalism: Asia in the Middlebrow Imagination, 1945–1961* (Berkeley: University of California Press, 2003); Simeon Man, *Soldiering Through Empire: Race and the Making of the Decolonizing Pacific* (Berkeley: University of California Press, forthcoming); Naoko Shibusawa, *America's Geisha Ally: Reimagining the Japanese Enemy* (Cambridge: Harvard University Press, 2006); Robert G. Lee, *Orientals: Asian Americans in Popular Culture* (Philadelphia: Temple University Press, 2001), chapter 5.

13. A few examples of this vast body of work include Jason M. Colby, *The Business of Empire: United Fruit, Race, and U.S. Expansion in Central America* (Ithaca, NY: Cornell University Press, 2011); Nick Cullather, "The Foreign Policy of the Calorie," *The American Historical Review* 112, no. 2 (2007): 337–364; Rachel Laudan, *Cuisine and Empire: Cooking in World History* (Berkeley: University of California Press, 2013); Sidney W. Mintz, *Sweetness and Power: The Place of Sugar in Modern History* (New York: Penguin, 1985); Philip McMichael ed., *The Global Restructuring of Agro-Food Business* (Ithaca, NY: Cornell University Press, 1994); Raj Patel, *Stuffed and Starved: Markets, Power, and the Hidden Battle for the World Food System* (London: Portobello, 2007); Jeffrey M. Pilcher, *Que Vivan Los Tamales! Food and the Making of Mexican Identity* (Albuquerque: University of New Mexico Press, 1998); Krishnendu Ray and Tulasi Srinivas eds., *Curried Cultures: Globalization, Food, and South Asia* (Berkeley: University of California Press, 2012); Andrew Rimas and Evan Fraser, *Empires of Food: Feast, Famine, and the Rise and Fall of Civilizations* (New York: Simon & Schuster, 2010); John C. Super, *Food, Conquest, and Colonization in Sixteenth-Century Spanish America* (Albuquerque: University of New Mexico, 1988); and Eric Williams, *Capitalism & Slavery* (Chapel Hill: University of North Carolina Press, 1944).

14. Studies that adopt such an approach include Troy Bickham, "Eating the Empire: Intersections of Food, Cookery, and Imperialism in Eighteenth-Century Britain," *Past and Present* 198 (2008): 71–109; Katarzyna J. Cwiertka, *Cuisine, Colonialism, and Cold War: Food in Twentieth Century Korea* (Chicago: University of Chicago Press, 2012); Rebecca Earle, *The Body of the Conquistador: Food, Race, and the Colonial Experience in Spanish America* (New York: Cambridge University Press, 2012); Rebecca Earle, "If You Eat Their Food … Diets and Bodies in Early Colonial Spanish America," *American Historical Review* 115, no. 3 (2010): 688–713; Erica J. Peters, *Appetites and Aspirations in Vietnam: Food and Drink in the Long Nineteenth Century* (Lanham: AltaMira Press, 2012).

15. Uma Narayan, *Dislocating Cultures: Identities, Traditions, and Third-World Feminism* (New York: Routledge Press, 1997), 162.

16. Peters, *Appetites and Aspirations in Vietnam*, 11, xiv.

17. Farrer, ed., *The Globalization of Asian Cuisines*, 8.

18. Ibid., 9.

19. Jodi Kim, *Ends of Empire: Asian American Critique and the Cold War* (Minneapolis: University of Minnesota Press, 2010), 237.

20. The macrohistorical approaches to food and empire I am referring to include the works of Cullather, Mintz, Patel, Rimas and Fraser, and Super, along with parts of Jared M. Diamond's *Guns, Germs, and Steel: The Fate of Human Societies* (New York: W.W. Norton & Company, 1997).

21. I add to the work of Adria Imada, Christina Klein, Jana Lipman, Dennis Merrill, Penny Von Eschen, and others who have explored the "everyday life of U.S. empire" to challenge traditional notions of empire and colonialism as a totalizing system of domination. Adria Imada, *Aloha America: Hula Circuits through the U.S. Empire* (Durham: Duke University Press, 2012); Klein, *Cold War Orientalism*; Lipman, *Guantanamo*; Dennis Merrill, *Negotiating Paradise: U.S. Tourism and Empire in Twentieth Century Latin America* (Chapel Hill: University of North Carolina Press, 2009); and Penny Von Eschen, *Satchmo Blows Up the World: Jazz Ambassadors Play the Cold War* (Cambridge: Harvard University Press, 2004).

22. Julian Go, *Patterns of Empire: The British and American Empires, 1688 to the Present* (New York: Cambridge University Press, 2011), 12. Drawing on Go, I define empire as a sociopolitical formation, often arranged hierarchically based on socially constructed categories, wherein a central political authority or center exercises control or unequal influence over the political processes of subordinated territories, peoples, and societies through a variety of means and methods. Ibid., 7.

23. It is important to keep in mind that, as William Deverell and Greg Hise remind us, there is a much longer history of Los Angeles as a global city. Or, in the words of Louis Pubols, "Los Angeles was born a global city," a crossroads of migration and a multiracial/ethnic place since its inception. So I say "full-fledged" because the 1970s marked a significant turning point in the development of Los Angeles as a global city both in terms of the intensified connection to the global economy and in its embrace of multiculturalism and diversity. See Introduction and Part I of William Deverell and Greg Hise eds., *A Companion to Los Angeles* (Oxford: John Wiley & Sons, 2014). Louise Pubols, "Born Global: From Pueblo to Statehood," in *A Companion to Los Angeles*, William Deverell and Greg Hise, eds. (Oxford: John Wiley & Sons, 2014), 21.

24. On the twin processes of deindustrialization and reindustrialization in Los Angeles, see Manuel Pastor Jr., "Economics and Ethnicity: Poverty, Race, and Immigration in Los Angeles County," in *Asian and Latino Immigrants in a Restructuring Economy: The Metamorphosis of Southern California,* Marta Lopez-Garza and David R. Diaz, eds. (Palo Alto: Stanford University Press, 2002), 104–106; Edna Bonacich and Richard P. Applebaum, *Behind the Label: Inequality in the Los Angeles Apparel*

Industry (Berkeley: University of California, 2000), 4–5; Edward W. Soja, *My Los Angeles: From Urban Restructuring to Regional Urbanization* (Berkeley: University of California Press), 34; Michael J. Dear, H. Eric Schockman, and Greg Hise, *Rethinking Los Angeles* (Thousand Oaks, CA: Sage Publications, 1996), 10–11.

25. Lisa Lowe uses the term "racialized feminization of labor" to describe the exploitation of gendered and racialized labor in the service sector economy under global capitalism. Lowe, *Immigrant Acts: On Asian American Cultural Politics* (Durham, NC: Duke University Press, 1996), 158. In addition, Pierette Hondagneu-Sotelo has also argued that income polarization in the 1980s and 1990s, coupled with the increased migration to the United States, a legacy and product of U.S. imperialism, colonialism, war, and global capitalist expansion, fueled spending on consumer products and services provided by immigrant women of color. In terms of food and restaurant services, she points out that the growth of professional opportunities for women resulted in them outsourcing to immigrants the work that men had previously outsourced to them. Pierette Hondagneu-Sotelo, *Doméstica: Immigrant Workers Cleaning and Caring in the Shadow of Affluence* (Berkeley: University of California Press, 2007).

26. Roger Waldinger, "From Ellis Island to LAX: Immigrant Prospects in the American City," *IMR*, 1081.

27. Ngai argues that the Immigration Act of 1965, which is largely seen as an act that opened up immigration, "comprised a complex of measures that promoted both greater inclusions and greater exclusions." One of the exclusionary measures was the continued numerical restriction via the allotment of quotas. Mae Ngai, *Impossible Subjects: Illegal Aliens and the Making of Modern America* (Princeton: Princeton University Press, 2004), 230, 263.

28. Krishnendu Ray, *The Ethnic Entrepreneur* (New York: Bloomsbury Academic, 2016); See also Ray's "The Immigrant Restaurateur and the American City: Taste, Toil, and the Politics of Inhabitation," in *Social Research* 81, no. 2 (2014): 374.

29. Natalia Molina, "The Importance of Place and Place-Makers in the Life of a Los Angeles Community: What Gentrification Erases from Echo Park," *Southern California Quarterly* 97, no. 1 (2015): 71.

30. Ray uses "creatures of political economy" to describe the way academic scholarship on ethnic entrepreneurship tend to treat immigrant entrepreneurs. Ray, "The Immigrant Restaurateur and the American City," 374. The body of literature on ethnic entrepreneurship, ethnic economies, and enclave economies is vast. Here is a small sample of the work that focus specifically on Asian immigrants: Kimberly Kay Hoang, "Nailing Race and Labor Relations: Vietnamese Nail Salons in Majority-Minority Neighborhoods," *Journal of Asian American Studies* 18, no. 2 (2015): 113–139; Erin M. Curtis, "Cambodian Donut Shops and the Negotiation of Identity in Los Angeles," in *Eating Asian America*, ed. Ku, Manalansan, and Mannur, 13–29; Pyong Gap Min, *Caught in the Middle: Korean Communities in New York and Los Angeles* (Berkeley: University of California Press, 1996); Jennifer Lee, "Striving for the American Dream: Struggle, Success, and Intergroup Conflict among Korean

Immigrant Entrepreneurs," in *Contemporary Asian America: A Multidisciplinary Studies Reader,* ed. Min Zhou and J. V. Gatewood (New York: New York University Press, 2007), 243–258.

31. One of the more well known cases of anti-Asian sentiment in Los Angeles during this period was the English-Only Movement in suburban Monterey Park, California in the mid 1980s, which sought to ban the use of Chinese language on business signs (without any English translation) and tried to make English the city's official language. See Timothy Fong, *The First Suburban Chinatown: The Remaking of Monterey Park, California* (Philadelphia, PA: Temple University Press, 1994) and Leland T. Saito, *Race and Politics: Asian Americans, Latinos, and Whites in a Los Angeles Suburb* (Champaign: University of Illinois Press, 1998).

32. Yen Le Espiritu, *Asian American Panethnicity: Bridging Institutions and Identities* (Philadelphia, PA: Temple University Press, 1992), Chapter 6; See also Dana Frank, *Buy American: The Untold Story of Economic Nationalism* (Boston: Beacon Press, 1999), Chapter 7.

33. I do not mean to suggest that the presence and impact of immigrants and the "colonized" on U.S. society is identical to the impact of U.S. imperialism and colonialism on the Third World, or what Gordon Lewis has called "colonialism in reverse." As Uma Narayan states, the presence of "many people of Third-World origins in Western societies is rooted in the injustices of colonialism and racism." Gordon Lewis, *Slavery, Imperialism, and Freedom: Studies in English Radical Thought* (New York: Monthly Review Press, 1978), 304; Narayan, *Dislocating Cultures,* 185.

34. Scott Kurashige, *The Shifting Grounds of Race: Black and Japanese Americans in the Making of Multiethnic Los Angeles* (Princeton, NJ: Princeton University Press, 2008), 7–8; See also Kurashige, "Between 'White Spot' and 'World City': Racial Integration and the Roots of Multiculturalism," in *A Companion to Los Angeles,* ed. Deverell and Hise, 56–71, and Charlotte Brooks, *Alien Neighbors, Foreign Friends: Asian Americans, Housing, and the Transformation of Urban California* (Chicago: University of Chicago Press, 2009), Chapter 2.

35. Kurashige, *The Shifting Grounds of Race,* 8.

36. Ibid., 260.

37. See Avery Gordon and Christopher Newfield, *Mapping Multiculturalism* (Minneapolis: University of Minnesota Press, 1996); Arif Dirlik, *Third World Criticism in the Age of Global Capitalism* (Boulder, CO: Westfield Press, 1997), Preface and Introduction; Lalaie Ameeriar, "The Sanitized Sensorium," *American Anthropologist* 114, no. 3 (2012): 509–520; Vijay Prashad, "Multiculturalism Kills Me," April 26, 2007, https://zcomm.org/zcommentary/multiculturalism-kills-me-by-vijay-prashad/; Karin Aguilar-San Juan, *Little Saigons: Staying Vietnamese in America* (Minneapolis: University of Minnesota Press, 2009), Chapter 4.

38. Lowe, *Immigrant Acts,* 86, 90; Lowe's quote on pluralism and the status quo, she is paraphrasing Hal Foster, "The Problem of Pluralism," *Art in America,* January 1982, 9–15; reprinted as "Against Pluralism" in Hal Foster, *Recodings: Art, Spectacle, Cultural Politics* (Seattle, WA: Bay Press, 1985).

39. Sneja Gunew, "Feminism and the Politics of Irreducible Differences: Multiculturalism/Ethnicity/Race," in *Feminism and the Politics of Difference,* ed. Sneja Gunew and Anna Yeatman (Boulder, CO: Westview Press, 1993), 13, 16.

40. Lisa Heldke, xv–xviii; Roger Abrahams, "Equal Opportunity Eating: A Structural Excursus on Thins of the Mouth," in *Ethnic Foodways in the United States,* ed. Keller Brown and Mussell eds., 34; Perhaps one of the more well-known critiques of the consumption of ethnic food as a challenge to racism is bell hooks's "Eating the Other: Desire and Resistance," in which she is weary of the way cultural, racial, and ethnic differences get commodified and "offered up as new dishes to enhance the white palate." bell hooks, *Black Looks: Race and Representation* (Boston: South End Press, 1992), 21–39; For more on the culinary imperialism, see Anne Goldman, "I Yam What I Yam: Cooking, Culture and Colonialism," in *De/Colonizing the Subject: The Politics of Gender in Women's Autobiography*, ed. Sidonie Smith and Julia Watson (Minneapolis: University of Minnesota Press, 1992).

41. Narayan, *Dislocating Cultures,* 184

42. Ibid., 180.

43. Robin D. G. Kelley, *Race Rebels: Culture, Politics, and the Black Working Class* (New York: Free Press, 1996), 13.

44. Frank H. Wu, *Yellow: Race in America Beyond Black and White* (New York: Basic Books, 2002), 216; Anita Mannur and Manalansan used a "carefully calibrated balance of acceptable multiculturalism" in the piece, "Dude, What's that Smell? The Sriracha Shutdown and Immigrant Excess," *NYU press blog,* January 16, 2014, http://www.fromthesquare.org/dude-whats-that-smell-the-sriracha-shutdown-and-immigrant-excess/#.WE833SMrK2x.

45. Edward W. Soja, "Los Angeles, 1965–2002: From Crisis-Generated Restructuring to Restructuring Generated-Crisis," in *The City: Los Angeles and Urban Theory at the End of the Twentieth Century,* ed. Allen J. Scott and Edward W. Soja (Berkeley: University of California Press, 1996), 434.

46. Jack Rosenthal, "The Outer City: US in Suburban Turmoil," *New York Times,* May 30, 1971; Rob Kling, Spencer C. Olin Jr, and Mark Poster, *Postsuburban California: The Transformation of Orange County since World War II* (Berkeley: University of California Press, 1995); Christopher B. Leinberger and Charles Lockwood, "How Business is Reshaping America," *Atlantic Monthly* 258, no. 10 (1986): 43–52; Joel Garreau, *Edge City: Life on the New Frontier* (Norwell: Anchor Press, 2011); Edward W. Soja, "Inside Exopolis: Scenes from Orange County," in *Variations on a Theme Park: The New American City and the End of Public Space*, ed. Michael Sorkin (New York: Hill and Wang, 1992): 94–122.

47. Mike Davis, *City of Quartz: Excavating the Future in Los Angeles* (New York: Verso, 1990), 323–324.

48. Soja, "Los Angeles, 1965–2002," 428.

49. George Lipsitz, "The Racialization of Space and the Spatialization of Race: Theorizing the Hidden Arhitecture of Landscape," *Landscape Journal* 26, no. 1 (2007): 10–23; George Lipsitz, *How Racism Takes Place* (Philadelphia, PA: Temple University Press, 2011), Introduction.

50. Pauline Lipman, *The New Political Economy of Urban Education: Neoliberalism, Race, and the Right to the City* (New York: Routledge Press, 2011), 12; Stephen Nathan Haymes, *Race, Culture, and the City: A Pedagogy for Black Urban Struggle* (Albany: SUNY Press, 1995), 20.

51. Lawrence D. Bobo, Melvin L. Oliver, James H. Johnson Jr., and Abel Valenzuela Jr., "Analyzing Inequality in Los Angeles," in *Prismatic Metropolis: Inequality in Los Angeles*, ed. Lawrence D. Bobo, Melvin L. Oliver, James H. Johnson Jr., and Abel Valenzuela Jr. (New York: Russell Sage Foundation, 2002), 21–22. See also Kurashige, *The Shifting Grounds of Race*, Chapter 1; George J. Sanchez, "'What's Good for Boyle Heights Is Good for the Jews': Creating Multiracialism on the Eastside during the 1950s," *American Quarterly* 56, no. 3 (2004): 634–636; Josh Sides, *LA City Limits: African American Los Angeles from the Great Depression to the Present* (Berkeley: University of California Press, 2003), Chapter 4; Josh Sides, "Straight into Compton: American Dreams, Urban Nightmares, and the Metamorphosis of a Black Suburb" *American Quarterly* 56, no. 3 (2004): 583–605; and Brooks, *Alien Neighbors, Foreign Friends*, Chapter 2.

52. To be clear, this does not mean that all white people consciously or purposefully embrace the white spatial imaginary. As Lipsitz writes: "not all whites endorse the white spatial imaginary, and some Blacks embrace it and profit from it. Yet every white person benefits from the association of white places with privilege, from the neighborhood race effects that create unequal and unjust geographies of opportunity." Lipsitz, *How Racism Takes Place*, 28.

53. Lipsitz, *How Racism Takes Place*, 13.

54. Lipsitz, *How Racism Takes Place*, 12, Chapter 2; The following sample of works, while they do not use the concept of "spatial imaginaries" explicitly, are excellent examples of the way communities of color in Los Angeles constructed physical places and engaged racialized spaces: Garcia, *A World of Its Own*, Chapter 2; George J. Sanchez, "'What's Good for Boyle Heights Is Good for the Jews'"; Phoebe S. Kropp, "Citizens of the Past?: Olvera Street and the Construction of Race and Memory in 1930s Los Angeles," *Radical History Review* 81 (Fall 2001): 35–60; Laura Barraclough, "Contested Cowboys: Ethnic Mexican Charros and the Struggle for Suburban Public Space in 1970s Los Angeles," *Aztlan: A Journal of Chicano Studies* 37, no. 2 (2012): 95–124; Jerry Gonzalez, "'A Place in the Sun': Mexican Americans, Race, and the Suburbanization of Los Angeles, 1940–1980," (PhD dissertation, University of Southern California, 2009); Douglas Flamming, *Bound for Freedom: Black Los Angeles in Jim Crow America* (Berkeley: University of California Press, 2005), Chapter 3; Eric Avila, *Popular Culture in the Age of White Flight: Fear and Fantasy in Suburban Los Angeles* (Berkeley: University of California Press, 2004); Wendy Cheng, *The Changs Next Door to the Díazes: Remapping Race in Suburban California* (Minneapolis: University of Minnesota Press, 2013); Linda Espana-Maram, *Creating Masculinity in Los Angeles's Little Manila: Working Class Filipinos and Popular Culture, 1920s–1950s* (New York: Columbia University Press, 2006); Rick Bonus, *Locating Filipino Americans: Ethnicity and the Cultural Politics of Space* (Philadelphia: Temple University Press, 2000); Nhi Lieu, *The American Dream in*

Vietnamese (Minneapolis: University of Minnesota Press, 2011); and Hillary Jenks, "'Home is Little Tokyo': Race, Community, and Memory in Twentieth-Century Los Angeles" (PhD dissertation, University of Southern California, 2008).

55. For an excellent overview of Asian American suburbanization in the United States, which includes some discussion of Asian American suburbanization in Los Angeles, see Becky Nicolaides, "Introduction: Asian American Suburban History," in *Journal of American Ethnic History* 34, no. 2 (2015): 5–17; For general overviews of racial, ethnic, and class diversification in American suburbs, see Becky Nicolaides and Andrew Wiese, eds., *The Suburb Reader*, 2nd Edition (New York: Routledge Press, 2016), Chapter 6 and Chapter 14.

56. Genevieve Carpio, Clara Irazábal, and Laura Pulido, "Right to the Suburb? Rethinking Lefebvre and Immigrant Activism" *Journal of Urban Affairs* 33, no. 2 (2011): 189.

57. Wei Li, *Ethnoburb: The New Ethnic Community in Urban America* (University of Hawaii Press, 2009), 3–6;

58. Cheng, *Citizens of Asian America*; Saito, *Race and Politics*; Cheng, *The Changs Next Door to the Díazes*; Karen Tongson, *Relocations: Queer Suburban Imaginaries* (New York: New York University Press, 2011); Emily Skop and Wei Li, "Asians in America's Suburbs: Patterns and Consequences of Settlement," *Geographical Review* 95, no. 2 (2005): 167–188; James Zarsadiaz, "Where the Wild Things Are: 'Country Living,' Asian American Suburbanization and the Politics of Space in Los Angeles' East San Gabriel Valley, 1945–2005," (PhD dissertation, Northwestern University, 2014).

59. Lipsitz, "Racialization of Space and the Spatialization of Race," 12.

60. Bonus, *Locating Filipino Americans*; Jenks, "'Home is Little Tokyo'"; Lieu, *The American Dream in Vietnamese*; Joseph Bernardo, "From Little Brown Brothers to Forgotten Americans: Race, Space, and Empire in Filipino Los Angeles" (PhD dissertation, University of Washington, 2014); Espana-Maram, *Creating Masculinity in Los Angeles's Little Manila*; Dawn Mabalon, *Little Manila is in the Heart: The Making of the Filipina/o American Community in Stockton, California* (Durham: Duke University Press, 2013); Haiming Liu and Lianlian Lin, "Food, Culinary Identity, and Transnational Culture: Chinese Restaurant Business in Southern California," *Journal of Asian American Studies* 12, no. 2 (2009): 135–162; Karin Aguilar-San Juan and Linda Trinh Vo, "Fields of Dreams: Place, Race, and Memory in Boston's Vietnamese American Community," *Amerasia Journal* 29, no. 1 (2003): 80–96; Chiou-Ling Yeh, *Making an American Festival: Chinese New York in San Francisco's Chinatown* (Berkeley: University of California Press, 2008).

61. Quote is from Bonus, *Locating Filipino Americans*, 4.

62. The concept of "right to the global city" is from Mark Purcell, "Citizenship and the Right to the Global City: Reimagining the Capitalist World Order," *International Journal of Urban and Regional Research* 27, no. 3 (2003): 564–590.

63. Henri Lefebvre, "The Right to the City," in *Writings on Cities* (Oxford: Blackwell, 1996): 63–181; Don Mitchell, *The Right to the City: Social Justice and the Fight for Public Space* (New York: Guilford Press, 2003); Peter Marcuse, "From

Critical Urban Theory to the Right to the City" *City* 13, no. 2–3 (2009): 185–197; David Harvey, "The Right to the City," *International Journal of Urban and Regional Research* 27, no. 4 (2003): 939–941; Clara Irazábal, *Ordinary Places/Extraordinary Events: Citizenship, Democracy and Public Space in Latin America* (New York: Routledge Press, 2008).

64. In addition to Carpio, Irazábal, and Pulido's "Right to the Suburb?," Jerry Gonzalez and Laura Barraclough have also offered important insight to the way ethnic Mexican cultural practices in suburban public spaces posed a direct challenge to the dominant white spatial imaginary. Gonzalez, "'A Place in the Sun,'" 204; Barraclough, "Contested Cowboys," 99.

65. Lipman, *The New Political Economy of Urban Education*, 6.

66. Carpio, Irazábal, and Pulido, "Right to the Suburb?," 188.

CHAPTER ONE

1. Marie Wilson, *Siamese Cookery* (Rutland and Tokyo: Tuttle Press, 1965), 15.

2. Ibid., 16.

3. I use *Oriental* to place in front of readers the exact terminology used to describe Asian and Pacific Islander food and peoples during this period. I replace *Oriental* with *Asian/Pacific* when possible, but I have kept it where I believe it is useful for understanding white Americans' attitudes and assumptions about Thailand specifically and Asia and the Pacific more broadly.

4. Borrowing from Thongchai Winichakul, I use the terms *Siam, Siamese, Thailand*, and *Thai* throughout the book based on basic criteria: *Siam* and *Siamese* are used for the country and its people before the change of the country's name in 1939. *Thailand* and *Thai* are used for the post-1939 context. Thongchai Winichakul, *Siam Mapped: A History of the Geo-Body of a Nation* (Honolulu: University of Hawaii Press, 1994), 18.

5. United States Department of State, *Treaty of Amity and Commerce between his Majesty the Magnificent King of Siam, and the United States of America*, December 04, 1837.

6. David B. Sickels, *Bangkok Despatches*, March 12, 1877, quoted in Benjamin A. Batson, "American Diplomats in Southeast Asia in the Nineteenth Century: The Case of Siam," *Journal of the Siam Society*, 64.2 (1976): 105. Sickels also described the Siamese as "ignorant and superstitious" but not "bigoted or intolerant"; Jacob T. Child, Minister to Siam, wrote "the outlawry and demoralization prevailing here" in *Bangkok Despatches*, September 30, 1887, quoted in Batson, 105. Moreover, many despised what they considered to be the slow and "tardy" pace of Siamese government affairs. In 1896, Minister John Barrett, one of the youngest in American history, complimented the Siamese for its "acceptance of approved foreign ideas of progress" that placed them "equal to the Japanese and in most respects ahead of the Chinese," but believed "they [Siamese] lack apparently ambition, and the power of action and achievement to carry out plans and promises." At one point during his

stint, Barrett also became confused by a Belgian advisor to Siam who treated "the Siamese in all his letters and remarks as if they were a people like and equal to the chief races of Europe and America." When the Siamese government responded to a rebellion in 1902, American diplomat Hamilton King observed, "Little Siam is doing all she can do or all she thinks she can, but oriental methods are not Anglo-Saxon methods." Sempronius H. Boyd, *Siam Despatches*, November 20, 1891, quoted in Batson, 105; John Barrett, *Siam Despatches*, May 10, 1895, quoted in Batson, 106; Hamilton King, *Siam Despatches*, August 6, 1902, quoted in Batson, 107.

7. Chaophraya Thiphakorawong, a member of King Mongkut's entourage and group of elites and who wrote articles for a nascent Thai press, referred to Christianity as a "foolish religion." Chris Baker and Pasuk Phongpaichit, *A History of Thailand* (Cambridge: Cambridge University Press, 2005), 41–42.

8. Winichakul, *Siam Mapped*, 117–118, 121–122.

9. Thongchai Winichakul, "The Quest for 'Siwilai': A Geographical Discourse of Civilizational Thinking in the Late Nineteenth and Early Twentieth-Century Siam," *The Journal of Asian Studies* 59, no. 3 (2000): 528.

10. David Wyatt, *Thailand: A Short History* (New Haven: Yale University Press, 2003), 246–247.

11. Wyatt, *Thailand*, 247; Baker and Phongpaichit, *A History of Thailand*, 135.

12. Baker and Phongpaichit, *A History of Thailand*, 137; David Wyatt, *Thailand*, 247–251; Patricia Norland et al., *The Eagle and the Elephant: Thai-American Relations Since 1833* (Bangkok: United States Information Service), 82–83.

13. T.L. Goodman, "Siamese Feel Anxious About Peace Terms," *The Sydney Morning Herald*, October 8, 1945.

14. King Mongkut expressed his positive attitudes toward Americans and approval of U.S.-Siamese relations through symbolic gestures of goodwill. In 1861 the King wrote a friendly letter to U.S. president James Buchanan and sent him a sword, a photograph of the King and his daughter, and later offered to send multiple pairs of elephants (the most prestigious animals in Siam) for breeding so that they might be used to clear "woods" and "matted jungles" in the service of U.S. continental expansion. Buchanan's successor, Abraham Lincoln, accepted the sword and photograph but politely declined the elephants; Wongduen Narasuj, "Siamese-American Relations in the Nineteenth Century" (Ph.D. dissertation, Illinois State University, 1988), 49; King of Siam Letter to President James Buchanan, February 14, 1861, Series: Communications from Heads of Foreign States, 1789–1909, File Unit: Ceremonial Letters from Siam, General Records of the Department of State, 1763–2002, Record Group 59 (National Archives and Records Administration, Washington, D.C.).

15. "San Marinan Impressed by Thailand Democracy" *Los Angeles Times*, November 2, 1952.

16. R. Sean Randolph, *The United States and Thailand: Alliance Dynamics, 1950–1985* (Berkeley, CA: Institute of East Asian Studies, University of California, Berkeley, 1986), 26–27.

17. Ibid.

18. In September of 1954, the United States, France, Great Britain, New Zealand, Australia, the Philippines, Thailand, and Pakistan formed SEATO. Once the communist threat seemed to change from military attacks to internal subversion, SEATO began promoting modernization efforts and "economic progress and social well-being," in Southeast Asia. The organization also participated in cultural exchanges. The Manila Pact and Pacific Charter, September 8, 1954. Presidential Paper, President's Office Files, Thailand: General, 1961–1963, Box 124a, John F. Kennedy Presidential Library, Boston, MA.

19. Jennifer M. Taw, *Thailand and the Philippines: Case Studies in U.S. IMET Training and Its Role in Internal Defense and Development* (Santa Monica: Rand Corporation, 1994), 20.

20. Christina Klein, *Cold War Orientalism: Asia in the Middlebrow Imagination, 1945–1961* (Berkeley: University of California Press, 2003), 194.

21. Ibid, 194.

22. Ibid, 191.

23. For an excellent account of the most influential architects of modernization theory, see Michael Latham, *Modernization as Ideology: American Social Science and "Nation Building" in the Kennedy Era* (Chapel Hill: University of North Carolina Press, 2000), chapter 2; Klein, *Cold War Orientalism*, 197–198.

24. Randolph, *The United States and Thailand*, 109.

25. Eleanor Billmyer, "Specialists in the Problems and Needs of Southeast Asia: Shortage of Experts Rockefeller Foundation Grant," *Christian Science Monitor*, April 19, 1952.

26. To be sure, the academic interest on Thais was minimal at the time. But the research did reflect the growth and legitimacy of area studies and the social sciences in the United States, which influenced U.S. government officials and policymakers looking for reasons to intervene in Thailand. Here is a small sample of the variety of early research conducted: Hazel M. Hauck, "Aspects of Health, Sanitation, and Nutritional Status in a Siamese Rice Village: Studies in Bang Chan, 1952–1954" (Cornell University Data Paper Series, 1956); Rose Kohn Goldsen, "Factors Related to Acceptance of Innovations in Bang Chan, Thailand: An Analysis of a Survey Conducted by the Cornell Cross-Cultural Methodology Project" (Cornell University Data Paper Series, 1957); Jane Richardson Hanks, "Maternity and its Rituals in Bang Chan" (Cornell University Data Paper Series, 1964); Laurence Judd, "Dry Rice Agriculture in Northern Thailand" (Cornell University Data Paper Series, 1964); and Lucien M. Hanks, ed,, "Ethnographic Notes on Northern Thailand" (Cornell University Data Paper Series, 1965); Anthropologist Ruth Benedict produced a notable ethnographic study of Thai culture during World War II, published posthumously in 1952, in which she concluded that the lack of Thai parental authority and discipline toward infants and adolescents led to "Thai cheerfulness, easy conviviality, and non-violence" and could explain why Thais "gamble with pleasure, are indolent rather than hard-working and accept easily subordinate positions in a hierarchy." See Ruth Benedict, *Thai Culture and Behavior: An Unpublished War-Time Study Dated September, 1943*

(Ithaca, NY: Southeast Asia Program Department of Far Eastern Studies, Cornell University, 1952).

27. Benedict, 44.

28. David Price's *Cold War Anthropology* explores in more depth the way American anthropologists not only produced knowledge about Thai people, culture, and history but also the way that knowledge was used in the service of U.S. neocolonialism in the region, particularly counterinsurgency operations in northern Thailand via Southeast Asian Development Advisory Group (SEADAG) and Academic Advisory Committee for Thailand (AACT), and USAID; David Price, *Cold War Anthropology: The CIA, the Pentagon, and the Growth of Dual Use Anthropology* (Durham, NC: Duke University Press, 2016).

29. For an overview of the impact of U.S. education and programs in Thailand, see: Peter Kundstadter, "Impact of American Education on Thailand," *Educational Perspectives* 21, no. 4 (1982): 19–26.

30. Norland et al., *The Eagle and the Elephant*, 91.

31. Warner Montgomery, "The Purpose and Problems of A.I.D. Educational Assistance to Thailand" (PhD dissertation, University of Michigan, 1968), 35.

32. Ibid., 49.

33. "U.N. Peace Corps Suggested by U.S.," *New York Times*, April 26, 1961.

34. Norland et al., *The Eagle and the Elephant,* 106.

35. Ann Frank, "Don't Be Upset a Way of Life, Observes Peace Corps Veteran," *Los Angeles Times,* February 3, 1966.

36. Jerolyn "Jerri" Minor interview with Susan Luccini on March 27, 2008, Returned Peace Corps Volunteer Oral History Collection, Container Series 091 (Thailand, John F. Kennedy Presidential Library and Museum, Boston, MA).

37. Ibid.

38. Baker and Phongpaichit, *A History of Thailand*, 148–149.

39. William Warren, "The Most Beautiful Word in English? Bangkok Says, 'Progress,'" *New York Times*, August 7, 1966.

40. Terence Smith, "Bangkok School Has Stamp of Teen-Age America," *New York Times*, December 8, 1968.

41. Teresia Teaiwa uses the term *militourism* to describe the way military and paramilitary force lubricates and strengthens a tourist industry—and in turn how that tourist industry masks the military force supporting it. Teresia Teaiwa, "Reading Paul Gauguin's Noa Noa with Epeli Hau'ofa's Kisses in the Nederends: Militourism, Feminism, and the 'Polynesian' Body," in *Inside Out: Literature, Cultural Politics, and Identity in the New Pacific*, ed. Vilsoni Hereniko and Rob Wilson (Lanham: Rowman & Littlefield, 1999).

42. Lloyd Shearer, "Thailand is a Man's World—and the G.I.'s Like It," *Parade Magazine*, March 24, 1968, 10.

43. James Jouppi journal, Returned Peace Corps Volunteer Oral History Collection, Container Series 091(Thailand), Box 12-13, John F. Kennedy Presidential Library and Museum, Boston, MA, 35.

44. Ibid., 135.

45. Ibid., 268.

46. Warren, "The Most Beautiful Word in English?"

47. Jouppi journal, 321–322; Mike Schmicker, "Land of Smiles" memoir, p. 62, Returned Peace Corps Volunteer Personal Papers, Box 80.

48. Pasuk Phongpaichit, *From Peasant Girls to Bangkok Masseuses* (Geneva: International Labour Office, 1982), 6, 24; Penny Van Esterik, *Materializing Thailand* (Oxford: Berg Publishers, 2000), 175; Smith, "Bangkok School Has Stamp of Teen-Age America."

49. Randolph, *The United States and Thailand*, 62; Schmicker, "Land of Smiles" memoir, 63.

50. Susan Cooper, interviewed by Lorie Burnett, May 12, 2005, Returned Peace Corps Volunteer Oral History Collection, Series 091, Thailand.

51. Warren, "The Most Beautiful Word in English? Bangkok Says, 'Progress'"; Baker and Phongpaichit, *A History of Thailand*, 150.

52. Jouppi journal, 133.

53. Cynthia Enloe, *Maneuvers: The International Politics of Militarizing Women's Lives* (Berkeley: University of California Press, 2000), 69.

54. Schmicker, "Land of Smiles" memoir, 159.

55. Enloe, *Maneuvers*, 70.

56. Quoted in Enloe, *Maneuvers*, 69.

57. Shearer, "Thailand is a Man's World—and the GI's Like It."

58. Joyce Wadler, "Lloyd Shearer, Longtime Celebrity Columnist, Dies at 84," *New York Times*, May 27, 2001.

59. Shearer, "Thailand is a Man's World—and the GI's Like It"

60. Ibid.

61. Paul Raffaele, "G.I. Children in Thailand—Some Can Now Be Adopted," *Parade Magazine*, May 29, 1977.

62. Ibid.

63. Kathleen Barry, *The Prostitution of Sexuality: The Global Exploitation of Women* (New York: New York University Press, 1995), chapter 4.

64. Enloe, *Maneuvers,* 71.

65. Cited in Klein, *Cold War Orientalism*, 104.

66. Christina Klein offers a sound overview of the writing and cultural production on Asia and the Pacific. She focuses primarily on writer James Michener, who became famous for not only writing about the region but "for narrating America's encounter with Asia and the Pacific." Klein, *Cold War Orientalism*, 117–135.

67. Klein, *Cold War Orientalism*, 110.

68. Ibid.

69. "Travel Agent Puts in Time on Move," *Los Angeles Times*, January 10, 1958; "R. W. Hemphill Named Travel Agents Chief," *Los Angeles Times*, November 11, 1956; Cordell Hicks, "Hotels Big Factor," *Los Angeles Times,* April 6, 1958.

70. Ibid.

71. R. W. Hemphill, "Guatemala Preparing to Welcome Tourists," *Los Angeles Times,* November 16, 1946.

72. R. W. Hemphill, "Travel Notes: Darkest Africa Now Just a Day's Flight," *Los Angeles Times,* February 20, 1949.

73. "Tourist Boom Establishes Hawaii Records," *Los Angeles Times,* October 31, 1954.

74. Chuck Y. Gee and Matt Lurie, eds, *The Story of the Pacific Asia Travel Association* (San Francisco: Pacific Asia Travel Association, 1993), xiii.

75. Harry G. Clement, *The Future of Tourism in the Pacific and Far East* (Washington DC: U.S. Department of Commerce, Bureau of Foreign Commerce, 1961), iii.

76. Cordel Hicks, "Travel Agents' Banquet," *Los Angeles Times,* June 4, 1959.

77. Pacific Area Travel Association, Pacific Area Travel Handbook (Menlo Park, CA: Lane Publishing Company, 1955), 70.

78. Ibid., 70.

79. Ibid., 69–70, 78–79.

80. Ibid., 70.

81. Baker and Phongpaichit, *A History of Thailand,* 149; Clement, "The Future of Tourism in the Pacific and Far East," 127.

82. Clement, "The Future of Tourism in the Pacific and Far East," 127.

83. Porphant Ouyyanont, "The Vietnam War and Tourism in Bangkok's Development, 1960–1970," *Southeast Asian Studies* 39 (September 2001):166.

84. Clement, "The Future of Tourism in the Pacific and Far East," 135.

85. Ouyyanont, "The Vietnam War and Tourism in Bangkok's Development, 1960–1970," 165.

86. Ibid., 174.

87. Walter Meyer, *Beyond the Mask: Toward a Transdisciplinary Approach of Selected Social Problems Related to the Evolution and Context of International Tourism in Thailand* (Saarbrucken, Germany: Verlag Breitenbach Publishers, 1988), 71.

88. Schmicker, "Land of Smiles" memoir, 87.

89. Warren, "The Most Beautiful Word in English? Bangkok Says, 'Progress.'"

90. Philip Cornwel-Smith, *Very Thai: Everyday Popular Culture* (Bangkok, Thailand: River Books), 18; Penny Van Esterik, *Food Culture in Southeast Asia* (Westport, CT: Greenwood Press, 2008), 90.

91. Al Ricketts, "On the Town," *Pacific Stars and Stripes,* August 4, 1965.

92. Van Esterik, *Food Culture in Southeast Asia,* 90.

93. Peter Lee, interview conducted by Robert Klein, August 4, 2004, Returned Peace Corp Volunteer Oral History Collection; Minor interview.

94. Marianne May Apple, July 26, 1966, Returned Peace Corps Volunteer Personal Papers, Box 12, pp. 8–9.

95. Ibid., 33.

96. Barbara Hansen, tape-recorded interview by Mark Padoongpatt, July 22, 2010 (in author's possession).

97. Jean Murphy, "She's Gung Ho for Oriental Cookery," *Los Angeles Times,* August 31, 1967.

98. Cecil Fleming, "A Happy Task—Getting to Know Thai Cuisine," *Los Angeles Times,* January 6, 1966.

99. Ibid.

100. Wilson, *Siamese Cookery,* 16.

101. Barbara Hansen, "Students Learn By Doing: Thai Cookery With a British Accent," *Los Angeles Times,* May 12, 1977.

102. Jennifer Brennan, *The Original Thai Cookbook* (New York: Perigree Books, 1984), preface.

103. Wilson, *Siamese Cookery,* 13.

104. Brennan, *The Original Thai Cookbook,* 28; Wilson, *Siamese Cookery,* 14.

105. Brennan, *The Original Thai Cookbook,* 51.

106. Ibid., 37–39; Wilson, Siamese Cookery, 15.

107. Klein, *Cold War Orientalism,* 23, 41–49.

108. In his seminal "Imperialist Nostalgia," Renato Rosaldo argues that imperialist nostalgia revolves around a paradox: "A person kills somebody and then mourns the victim. In more attenuated form, someone deliberately alters a form of life, and then regrets that things have not remained as they were prior to the intervention. At one more remove, people destroy their environment, and then they worship nature." See Renato Rosaldo, "Imperialist Nostalgia," in *Representations* 26 (Spring 1989): 108.

109. Brennan, *The Original Thai Cookbook,* 6.

110. Ibid, 6.

111. Wilson, *Siamese Cookery,* 10.

112. Brennan, *The Original Thai Cookbook,* 26.

113. Ibid, 6.

114. Ibid, 6.

115. In addition, in the northeast or Isaan, which contained about one-third of Thailand's population, a number of leaders who resisted the increasing centralization of power in Bangkok were jailed or killed during the late 1940s for advocating communism and separatism. Moreover, since the 1930s, Phibun's government had tried to impose Thai language and Thai dress and close down local community schools and Islamic courts. Baker and Phongpaichit, *A History of Thailand,* 173.

116. Van Esterik, *Food Culture in Southeast Asia,* 74.

117. Heldke, *Exotic Appetites,* 105–110.

118. Parama Roy, "Reading Communities and Culinary Communities: The Gastropoetics of the South Asian Diaspora," in *positions: east asia cultures critique* 10 (Fall 2002), 480.

119. For more on ersatz nostalgia—"armchair nostalgia" or "nostalgia without lived experience or collective historical memory," see Arjun Appadurai's analysis of nostalgia as the product and motor of late capitalist consumerism in Arjun Appadurai, *Modernity at Large: Cultural Dimensions of Globalization* (Minneapolis: University of Minnesota, 1996), 77–78.

120. Jennifer Brennan, *Curries and Bugles: A Memoir and Cookbook of the British Raj* (London: Viking, 1990).

121. Renato Rosaldo, "Imperialist Nostalgia."

122. Brennan, *The Original Thai Cookbook*, 3, 4; Lisa Heldke, *Exotic Appetites: Ruminations of a Food Adventurer* (New York: Routledge Press, 2003), 101.

123. Hansen, "Students Learn By Doing: Thai Cookery with a British Accent."

124. Andrew Coe, *Chop Suey: A Cultural History of Chinese Food in the United States* (Oxford: Oxford University Press, 2009), 147.

125. Ibid.

126. Mark Padoongpatt, "Oriental Cookery: Devouring Asian Cuisine in the Cold War," in *Eating Asian America: A Food Studies Reader*, Robert Ku, Martin Manalansan IV, and Anita Mannur eds. (New York: NYU Press, 2013), 186–207.

127. Edna Beilenson, *Simple Oriental Cookery* (New York: Peter Pauper Press, 1960), title page; Padoongpatt, "Oriental Cookery," 200–203.

128. "Oriental Theme Selected," *Los Angeles Times*, February 14, 1963.

129. Hicks, "Travel Agents' Banquet."

130. See Adria L. Imada, *Aloha America: Hula Circuits through the U.S. Empire* (Durham: Duke University Press, 2012; Jana Lipman, *Guantanamo: A Working-Class History between Empire and Revolution* (Berkeley: University of California Press, 2008); and Dennis Merrill, *Negotiating Paradise: U.S. Tourism and Empire in Twentieth-Century Latin America* (Chapel Hill: University of North Carolina Press, 2009).

131. Brennan, *The Original Thai Cookbook*, 29.

132. Wilson, *Siamese Cookery*, 12.

133. Lisa Lowe, *Immigrant Acts: On Asian American Cultural Politics* (Durham: Duke University Press, 1996), 16; Yen Le Espiritu, *Home Bound: Filipino American Lives Across Cultures, Communities, and Countries* (Berkeley: University of California, 2003), 5; and Oscar V. Campomanes, "New Formations of Asian American Studies and the Question of U.S. Imperialism," *Positions* 5, no. 2 (1997): 534; Also see Paul Ong, Edna Bonacich, and Lucie Cheng, eds, *The New Asian Immigration in Los Angeles and Global Restructuring* (Philadelphia: Temple University Press, 1994).

CHAPTER TWO

1. Colman Andrews, "Fare of The Country: With Satay and Tiger Prawns, Fiery Thai Food Is a Hit in L.A.," *New York Times*, July 6, 1990.

2. By using the term "authentic" to describe the sought after Thai ingredients, I do not wish to suggest that these ingredients are objectively authentic. Rather, I use it to refer to what Thais considered or believed to be authentic Thai ingredients—defined largely by taste and flavor profile as well as by country of origin and/or region (Southeast Asia). David Sutton's use of the concept of "wholeness" builds on James Fernandez's work on "returning to the whole," which Fernandez developed by studying the way groups in West Africa used religious revitalization to try and combat alienation and become whole under conditions of colonialism. See David E. Sutton, "Synesthesia, Memory, and the Taste of Home," in Carolyn Korsmeyer ed.,

The Taste Culture Reader: Experiencing Food and Drink (New York: Berg Publishers, 2005), 305; and James Fernandez, *Bwiti: An Ethnography of Religious Imagination in Africa* (Princeton, NJ: Princeton University Press, 1982).

3. I use "ingredients" and "foodstuffs" interchangeably to refer to the food or substances used in cooking. This includes packaged and canned goods like coconut milk and curry paste, as well as fresh fruit and vegetables such as kaffir lime and lemon grass.

4. Jacqueline Desbarats, "Thai Migration to Los Angeles," *Geographical Review,* 69 (July 1979): 302. The total numbers are from Nutta Vinijnaiyapak, "Institutions and Civic Engagement: A Case Study of Thai Community in Los Angeles," (Ph.D. dissertation: University of Southern California, 2004), 15. Nutta Vinijnaiyapak cites Narong Kaeonil, "The Thai Community in Los Angeles: An Attitudinal Study of Its Socio-Economic Structure" (Ph.D. dissertation: United States International University).

5. Desbarats, "Thai Migration to Los Angeles," 305.

6. Aroon Seeboonruang, tape-recorded interview by Mark Padoongpatt, December 16, 2008 (in author's possession).

7. Madeline Y. Hsu, *The Good Immigrants: How the Yellow Peril Became the Model Minority* (Princeton, NJ: Princeton University Press, 2015), 4.

8. Immigration and Nationality Act, 66 Stat. 173 (1952); Mae Ngai, *Impossible Subjects: Illegal Aliens and the Making of Modern America* (Princeton, NJ: University of Princeton Press, 2004), 37–38.

9. David Gutierrez, *Walls and Mirrors: Mexican Americans, Mexican Immigrants, and the Politics of Ethnicity* (Berkeley: University of California Press, 1995), chap. 5; Ngai, *Impossible Subjects,* 263.

10. Hsu, *The Good Immigrants,* 5.

11. Frank Auerbach, *Immigration Laws of the United States* (Indianapolis, IN: Bobbs-Merrill, 1961), 377.

12. Mae Ngai, *Impossible Subjects: Illegal Aliens and the Making of Modern America* (Princeton, NJ: Princeton University Press, 2004), 230, 263.

13. U.S. Department of State, 1974; Immigration and Naturalization Service, 1974, Washington D.C.; taken from Kaeonil, "The Thai Community in Los Angeles," 31.

14. Kaeonil, "The Thai Community in Los Angeles," 33–34.

15. Surasak Wongskhaluang, tape-recorded interview by Mark Padoongpatt, March 18, 2009 (in author's possession).

16. Urai Ruenprom, tape-recorded interview by Mark Padoongpatt, December 18, 2008 (in author's possession). Naturalization Index Cards of the U.S. District Court for the Southern District of California, Central Division (Los Angeles), 1915–1976 (microfilm: roll 94), series M125 (National Archives and Records Administration).

17. Wanit Jarungkitanan, "Michigan Test," in Benedict R. Anderson and Ruchira C. Mendiones, eds., *In the Mirror: Literature and Politics in Siam in the American Era* (Ithaca, NY: Cornell University Press, 1985), 18. 143.

18. Jarungkitanan, "Michigan Test," 152.

19. Warner Montgomery, "The Purpose and Problems of A.I.D. Educational Assistance to Thailand" (Ph.D. Dissertation, University of Michigan, 1968), 51.

20. Amara Raksasataya, "An Open University," in *Education in Thailand: Some Thai Perspectives*, Amnuay Tapingkae and Louis J. Setti eds., (Washington D.C.: U.S. Office of Education, Institute of International Studies, 1973), 108.

21. Desbarats, "Thai Migration to Los Angeles," 306.

22. Keyes Beech, "U.S. Consuls: Visa Issuing—The Strain of Playing God," *Los Angeles Times*, May 13, 1981.

23. Evan Maxwell, "Student Visa System Found Riddled with Gaps, Flaws," *Los Angeles Times*, August 13, 1979.

24. Beech, "U.S. Consuls."

25. Ibid.

26. Sudarat Disayawattana, *The Craft of Ethnic Newspaper-Making: A Study of the Negotiation of Culture in the Thai-language Newspapers of Los Angeles* (Ph.D. dissertation, University of Iowa, 1993), 54.

27. Ibid., 59.

28. Myrna Oliver, "Foreign Students Must Pay Tuition Hike, Judge Rules," *Los Angeles Times*, May 16, 1972; Gene I. Maeroff, "Foreign Students Face a Cost Squeeze in U.S." *New York Times*, June 25, 1972.

29. Parsomsee Ruenprom, "Seventy-Two Year Anniversary Memoir," p. 12, letter in Celebration of Urai Ruenprom's 72nd birthday, February 21, 1999 (in Mark Padoongpatt's possession)

30. Jirah Krittayapong, "Robin Hood in the Land of the Free? An Ethnographic Study of Undocumented Immigrants from Thailand in the U.S." (Ph.D. dissertation: Ohio University, 2012), 5.

31. Kaeonil, "The Thai Community in Los Angeles," 7.

32. *Sombat Kamheangpatiyooth, Petitioner, v. Immigration and Naturalization Service, Respondent.*

33. Beech, "U.S. Consuls."

34. Kaeonil, "The Thai Community in Los Angeles," 34.

35. Ibid.

36. Beech, "U.S. Consuls."

37. Ibid.

38. Beech, "U.S. Consuls."

39. Desbarats, "Thai Migration to Los Angeles," 305.

40. War Brides Act, Public Law 721 (1945).

41. Susan Koshy, *Sexual Naturalization: Asian Americans and Miscegenation* (Palo Alto: Stanford University Press, 2004), 12.

42. Carl L. Bankston III and Danielle Antoinette Hidalgo, "The Waves of War: Immigrants, Refugees, and New Americans from Southeast Asia," in Min Zhou and J. V. Gatewood, eds., *Contemporary Asian America: A Multidisciplinary Reader, 2nd edition* (New York: New York University Press, 2007), 139–157, esp. 149.

43. Desbarats, "Thai Migration to Los Angeles," 313; For a fascinating look into the lived experiences of Thai war brides in the United States, see Orapan Footrakoon, *Lived Experiences of Thai War Brides in Mixed Thai-American Families in the United States* (Ph.D. dissertation, University of Minnesota, 1999).

44. Desbarats, "Thai Migration to Los Angeles," 317.

45. Anderson and Mendiones, *In The Mirror*, 24.

46. Disayawattana, *The Craft of Ethnic Newspaper-Making*, 54.

47. Malulee Pinsuvana, *Cooking Thai Food in American Kitchens* (Bangkok: Thai Watana Panich Press Co., Ltd, 1976), preface.

48. Andrew Coe, *Chop Suey: A Cultural History of Chinese Food in the United States* (Oxford: Oxford University Press, 85–87).

49. Not all Thai people enjoy the same types of dishes, as people in most communities do not all eat the same foods in the same ways. That said, Thai cuisine is often characterized by this flavor combination, or *yum*. Chef Jet Tilakamonkul once said at one of his many cooking demonstrations that "'yum' is the perfect balance between hot, sour, salty, and sweet" and that in cooking Thai food, one must "chase the *yum* and use the country-specific ingredients, and you will make authentic food." Canda Fuqua, "Chef Tila Chases the 'Yum,'" *Corvallis-Gazette Times,* February 8, 2013; See also Penny Van Esterik, *Food Culture in Southeast Asia* (Westport and London: Greenwood Press, 2006), 39.

50. Meredith Abarca, *Food Across Borders*, Matt Garcia, Don Mitchell, and Melanie DuPuis eds., (New Brunswick: Rutgers University Press, 2017); Sutton, "Synesthesia, Memory, and the Taste of Home," 305; See also C. Nadia Seremetakis' "The Breast of Aphrodite," pp. 297-303, and Deborah Lupton, "Food and Emotion," in *The Taste Culture Reader: Experiencing Food and Drink*, Carolyn Korsmeyer ed., (New York: Berg Publishers, 2005), 317–324.

51. Abarca, *Food across Borders.*

52. Ibid.

53. Lois Dwan, "Roundabout," *Los Angeles Times,* February 27, 1972; Jean Barry, *Thai Students in the United States: A Study in Attitude Change* (Ithaca, NY: Cornell University Department of Asian Studies, 1967), 30.

54. Prakas Yenbamroong, tape-recorded interview by Mark Padoongpatt, January 13, 2010 (in author's possession).

55. Dwan, "Roundabout."

56. Carol Soucek, "Thai Culture Spices L.A. Melting Pot," *Los Angeles Herald-Examiner,* July 20, 1975.

57. Cecil Fleming, "A Happy Task—Getting to Know Thai Cuisine," *Los Angeles Times,* January 6, 1966.

58. Marie Wilson, *Siamese Cookery* (Rutland and Tokyo: Tuttle Press, 1965), 35.

59. Ibid., 36.

60. Jet Tilakamonkul, tape-recorded interview by Mark Padoongpatt, October 16, 2007 (in author's possession).

61. Tilakamonkul, interview.

62. The "golden triangle" refers to the geographic area where the borders of Thailand, Burma, and Laos meet, which during the 1960 and 1970s emerged as the world's major cultivator of opium and heroin. U.S. intervention in Southeast Asia during the Cold War sparked the explosion of an illegal flow of heroin into the U.S. that drew the attention of U.S. drug enforcement agencies and U.S. Customs. See Ron Chepesiuk, *Bangkok Connection: Trafficking Heroin from Asia to the USA* (Dublin, Ireland: Maverick House, 2014); and Ko-lin Chin, *Golden Triangle: Inside Southeast Asia's Drug Trade* (Ithaca, NY: Cornell University Press, 2009).

63. I understand that the term "kaffir" is a racial slur commonly used outside of the United States. White colonialists used it as a derogatory term to insult Black Africans, and its power to offend grew more intense in apartheid era-South Africa. While I recognize its history as a derogatory term, I use it to place in front of readers the exact terminology used.

64. U.S. Department of Agriculture and ARS National Genetic Resources Program, *Germplasm Resources Information Network* (National Germplasm Resources Laboratory, Beltsville, MD), online database available at http://www .ars-grin.gov.4/cgi-bin/npgs/acc/display.pl?1434184, accessed July 3, 2015; Tilaka-monkul, interview; the availability of "exotic" citrus in the region appears to be true. See "History and Scope," *Citrus Variety Collection,* accessed July 3, 2015, http:// www.citrusvariety.ucr.edu/history/index.html.

65. Tilakamonkul, interview.

66. Tilakamonkul, interview; Andrews, "Fare of the Country."

67. Tilakamonkul, interview.

68. Kathleen Squires, "The Next Generation: Jet Tila, The Charleston LA," *Zagat,* September 27, 2013, accessed July 3, 2015, https://www.zagat.com/b/the -next-generation-jet-tila-the-charleston-la.

69. Kelly DiNardo, "Travel Q&A: Chef Jet Tila Talks about Travel's Influence on His Cooking and the Importance of Getting Lost," Dec. 2, 2014, *MapQuest Discover,* accessed May 21, 2015, http://www.mapquest.com/travel/articles/chef-jet -tila-food-network-los-angeles-21001185; Squires, "The Next Generation."

70. Jet Tila has mentioned on multiple occasions that this family was able to come to Los Angeles because of his Mexican aunt who sponsored them to come to the United States. Mar Yvette, "Q&A: Chef Jet Does Bistronomics," *MarPop,* accessed July 3, 2015, http://www.marpop.com/whats-new/qa-chef-jet-tila/. In a recent inter-view, he mentions: "I have a natural affinity toward Mexican food and culture, but mine goes deeper than my native city to my family tree. When my uncle moved to the U.S. from Thailand, he fell in love with a woman named Dora Lucero and married her almost instantly. Soon there were Thai/Chinese/Mexican cousins running around." "Jet Tila: Favorite Local Spots," *Travels in Taste,* accessed July 4, 2015, http://www .travelsintaste.com/jet_tila__favorite_local_spots__antojos_df-listing2616.aspx.

71. Squires, "The Next Generation."

72. John H. Jackson, "The General Agreement of Tariffs and Trade in the United States Domestic Law," *Michigan Law Review* 66 (1967), 250; Charles S. Pearson, *United States Trade Policy: A Work in Progress* (Hoboken: Wiley Press, 2004), 7.

73. Jackson, "The General Agreement of Tariffs and Trade in the United States Domestic Law," 250.

74. Eugene T. Rossides, *U.S. Import Trade Regulation* (Edison, NJ: BNA Books, 1986), 56–57.

75. Carole Sugarman, "A Matter of Imports: The Challenge of Tracking the Rising Tide of Foreign Foods," *Washington Post,* December 6, 1989.

76. World Trade Organization, "Provisional Accession of Thailand, Memorandum on Foreign Trade Regime," p. 3, April 24, 1979, *General Agreement on Tariffs and Trade,* accessed December 2, 2016, https://www.wto.org/gatt_docs/English /SULPDF/90990450.pdf.

77. Japan was the top buyer of Thai exports, bringing in about 25% of Thailand's total exports each year between 1968 and 1977. Ibid., 4.

78. Ibid., 2; Yanee Srimanee and Jayant Kumar Routray, "The Fruit and Vegetable Marketing Chains in Thailand: Policy Impacts and Implications," *International Journal of Retail & Distribution Management* 40 (2012): 658, 666–67.

79. World Trade Organization, "Provisional Accession of Thailand," 8.

80. Sugarman, "A Matter of Imports"; For a useful overview on the origins of federal oversight and the responsibilities of the USDA and the FDA regarding domestic food supply and imports, see Marion Nestle, *Safe Food: Bacteria, Biotechnology, and Bioterrorism* (Berkeley: University of California Press, 2003), 50–61 and chap. 3.

81. Sugarman, "A Matter of Imports"; U.S. Department of Agriculture and Animal and Plant Health Inspection Service, *A 40-year Retrospective of APHIS, 1972–2012* (Washington D.C: USDA, 2013), 4.

82. Rossides, *U.S. Trade Import Regulation*, 489.

83. Sugarman, "A Matter of Imports."

84. In *Buy American*, historian Dana Frank explains that this increased global competition was a matter of "chickens coming home to roost." She writes that at the same time the American Century seemed limitless in the early 1960s, the billions of dollars the United States spent to bring Japan and Germany into the capitalist orbit resulted in competition and the rise of industrial powerhouses—steel, auto, machine tools, electrical manufacturing—which ultimately led to the crisis of the 1970s and 1980s. Moreover, the allied powers agreed not to allow these countries to spend money on military endeavors. Dana Frank, *Buy American: The Untold Story of Economic Nationalism* (Boston: Beacon Press, 1999), 126.

85. Ibid., 132.

86. Sugarman, "A Matter of Imports."

87. Stein, "As Trade Grows, Customs Service Controls Flow through Ports," *Los Angeles Times,* March 20, 1988; U.S. Department of Agriculture and Animal and Plant Health Inspection Service, *A 40-year Retrospective of APHIS,* 5.

88. Barbara Hansen, "Thai Markets Short on Kaffir Lime Leaves," *Los Angeles Times,* June 30, 1999.

89. Stein, "As Trade Grows, Customs Service Controls Flow through Ports."

90. Ibid.

91. Sugarman, "A Matter of Imports."

92. The Comprehensive Crime Control Act of 1984 and the Trade and the Tariff Act of 1984 authorized customs officers to carry firearms and make arrests. Prior to 1984, the authority of customs agents to make arrests was limited, as they could only do so for breach of navigation laws, or for violations of the narcotic drug and marijuana laws. See Rossides, *U.S. Import Trade Regulation*, 512–13.

93. Peter Coates's *American Perceptions of Immigrant and Invasive Species: Strangers on the Land* (Berkeley: University of California Press, 2006) offers an insightful analysis of how this type of border making process played out in U.S. history but within the context of flora and fauna instead of food. Coates argues that U.S. fears over its "ecological identity," and how that anxiety helped construct American national identity, dates back to the mid-1800s when ideas and discourses about "invasive" species intersected with national identity, nativism, and cultural nationalism.

94. Sugarman, "A Matter of Imports."

95. Stein, "As Trade Grows, Customs Service Controls Flow through Ports."

96. Peter S. Greenberg, "Customs is Cracking Down on Forbidden Fruits," *Los Angeles Times,* March 22, 1987.

97. For example, the U.S. Customs Service published a pamphlet called "Know Before You Go" to inform overseas travelers about what foods they were not allowed to bring back. In addition, the USDA also published a seventeen-page booklet called "Traveler's Tips" that listed food items that were acceptable to bring back into the United States. See Greenberg, "Customs is Cracking Down on Forbidden Fruits."

98. Stein, "As Trade Grows, Customs Service Controls Flow through Ports."

99. This was consistent with other agencies as well. For example, in 1970 the FDA in was able to inspect about 20% of the 500,000 imported entries. But by 1987, the FDA-regulated imports reached 1.5 million, and the agency was only able to check the documents of only 9% of the goods and physically sample 2% in their labs—40% of which did not meet FDA standards. Sugarman, "A Matter of Imports."

100. Stein, "As Trade Grows, Customs Service Controls Flow through Ports."

101. Charlyne Varkonyi, "Major Ingredients in Thai Food Harder to Find," *Los Angeles Times,* July 12, 1990.

102. Hansen, "Thai Markets Short on Kaffir Lime Leaves."

103. Tilakamonkul, interview.

104. Squires, "The Next Generation."

105. A public or private corporation had to submit an application to the Foreign-Trade Zones Board and have it approved to establish, operate, and maintain a zone. Rossides, *U.S. Import Regulation,* 73.

106. Ibid., 70.

107. Tilakamonkul, interview.

108. Dara Orenstein, "Foreign-Trade Zones and the Cultural Logic of Frictionless Production," *Radical History Review,* 109 (Winter 2011): 48.

109. Ibid., 54; There is not enough evidence to suggest that Bangkok Market exploited Mexican workers, although labor exploitation and low wages are characteristic of FTZs.

110. Rossides, *U.S. Import Regulation,* 70.

111. Orenstein, "Foreign-Trade Zones and the Cultural Logic of Frictionless Production," 47.

112. Joel Millman, "Stir Fry: Mexican Vegetables in U.S. Woks—Fewer Import Controls, Lower Costs Increase Demand for Bok Choy," *Wall Street Journal,* March 5, 1998.

113. Natalia Molina, "The Importance of Place and Place-Makers in the Life of a Los Angeles Community: What Gentrification Erases from Echo Park," *Southern California Quarterly* 97, no. 1 (2015): 71.

114. Ibid.

115. Chanchanit "Chancee" Martorell, tape-recorded interview by Mark Padoongpatt, December 18, 2009 (in author's possession); James Paul Allen and Eugene Turner, *The Ethnic Quilt: Population Diversity in Southern California* (Northridge, CA: Center for Geographical Studies, 1997), 159–60.

116. Allen and Turner, *The Ethnic Quilt,* 101, 102, 104, 105; 1960 United States Census Tract Record 90029, Los Angeles County; 1970 United States Census Tract Record 90029, Los Angeles County; 1980 United States Census Tract Record 90029, Los Angeles County, *Social Explorer & U.S. Census Bureau* (Washington, D.C.: U.S. Government Printing Office).

117. Jet Tila, quoted in David Pierson and Anna Gorman, "A New Take on Thai Town," *Los Angeles Times,* August 2, 2007.

118. Desbarats, "Thai Migration to Los Angeles," 316.

119. According to Min Zhou, the difference between an ethnic economy and an enclave economy is that an ethnic economy consists of enterprises that are either owned, or supervised, or staffed by racial/ethnic minority group members regardless of size, type, and locational clustering and does not necessarily require intense ethnic marking of their businesses (such as Korean liquor stores). An enclave economy, on the other hand, is bounded by location and coethnicity—a physical concentration within an ethnically identifiable area, such as East Hollywood. Min Zhou, "Revisiting Ethnic Entrepreneurship: Convergencies, Controversies, and Conceptual Advancements," *IMR* 32, no. 2 (2004): 1042–1046.

120. Wat Thai of Los Angeles, *Phra Tamrachanuwat* (North Hollywood, CA: Wat Thai of Los Angeles), 151.

CHAPTER THREE

1. Daniel Herron, "Thailand's Tommy Tang, Celebrity Chef—From Bangkok to Hollywood!," *Splash Magazines,* accessed December 4, 2016, http://www.lasplash.com/publish/Celebrity_Talk_102/thailand-s-tommy-chef-celebrity-chef.php.

2. Janice Schindeler, "Tommy Tang: The Chef that Brought Thai to the Table," *Houston Chronicle,* April 14, 2004.

3. Susan Jacques, "Variety is the Tang of Life; Thai Restaurant Owner Rides a Wave of Interest in Ethnic Food," *Los Angeles Times,* April 19, 1997. Many of these dishes were not on the menu from 1987, so they might have been specials or featured on previous menus.

4. Irene S. Virbila, "The New Tommy Tang's Thai: Modest Tastes for the Young," *Los Angeles Times,* February 3, 1995; Restaurants, *New York Times,* December 5, 1986.

5. Rose Dosti, "Spicy and Sweet: Tommy Tang's Duck Dish Suits Western Tastes but Respects its Asian Roots," *Los Angeles Times,* October 16, 1988.

6. Barry Siegel, "Immigrants' Story Not Always a Tale of Success," *Los Angeles Times,* December 13, 1982.

7. On the twin processes of deindustrialization and reindustrialization in Los Angeles, see Manuel Pastor Jr., "Economics and Ethnicity: Poverty, Race, and Immigration in Los Angeles County" in *Asian and Latino Immigrants in a Restructuring Economy: The Metamorphosis of Southern California,* Marta Lopez-Garza and David R. Diaz, eds. (Palo Alto: Stanford University Press, 2002), 104–106; Edna Bonacich and Richard P. Applebaum, *Behind the Label: Inequality in the Los Angeles Apparel Industry* (Berkeley: University of California, 2000), 4–5; Edward W. Soja, *My Los Angeles: From Urban Restructuring to Regional Urbanization* (Berkeley: University of California Press), 34; Michael J. Dear, H. Eric Schockman, and Greg Hise, *Rethinking Los Angeles* (Thousand Oaks, CA: Sage Publication, 1996), 10–11.

8. Immigration and Nationality Act, 79 Stat. 911 (1965).

9. Victor Sodsook, *I Love Thai Food* (Los Angeles: Spice Market Studio, 1989).

10. There is an extensive body of research on how immigrants seek self-employment in greater proportion than U.S. citizens because of discrimination in the primary labor market and disadvantages associated with immigrant status (although there are differences between ethnic and racial groups). See Min Zhou, "Revisiting Ethnic Entrepreneurship: Convergencies, Controversies, and Conceptual Advancements," *International Migration Review* 38 (September 2004): 1047; Edna Bonacich, "A Theory of Middleman Minorities," *American Sociological Review* 38, no. 5 (1973): 583–594; Fernando Mata and Ravi Pendakur, "Immigration, Labor Force Integration and the Pursuit of Self-Employment," *The International Migration Review* 33, no. 2 (1999): 378–402; Bernard P. Wong, *Patronage, Brokerage, Entrepreneurship, and the Chinese Community of New York* (New York: AMS Press, 1988); Jennifer Lee, "Striving for the American Dream: Struggle, Success, and Intergroup Conflict among Korean Immigrant Entrepreneurs," in *Contemporary Asian America: A Multidisciplinary Reader,* Min Zhou and J. V. Gatewood eds., (New York: New York University Press, 2007), 245.

11. Thomas Bailey, "A Case Study of Immigrants in the Restaurant Industry," *Industrial Relations* 24 (March 1985): 216.

12. Paul Ong and Evelyn Blumenberg, "Income and Racial Inequality in Los Angeles," in *The City: Los Angeles and Urban Theory at the End of the Twentieth*

Century, Allen John Scott and Edward W. Soja eds. (Berkeley: University of California Press, 1996), 318.

13. Roger Waldinger, "From Ellis Island to LAX: Immigrant Prospects in the American City," *International Migration Review* 30 (Winter 1996): 1081.

14. Kongkiat Chantarangsu, tape-recorded interview by Mark Padoongpatt, March 25, 2016 (in author's possession).

15. Ivan H. Light, *Business and Welfare Among Chinese, Japanese, and Blacks* (Berkeley: University of California, 1972); Ivan Light, Im Jung Kwuon, and Deng Zhong, "Korean Rotating Credit Associations in Los Angeles," *Amerasia Journal* 16, no. 2 (1990): 35–54; Mark Arax, "Pooled Cash of Loan Clubs Key to Asian Immigrant Entrepreneurs," *Los Angeles Times,* October 30, 1988.

16. Alejandro Portes and Min Zhou define "bounded solidarity" as a process by which immigrants, realizing that they are phenotypically and culturally different, develop a greater sense of solidarity with coethnics within the U.S. nation-state. This shared experience, often grounded in experiences with discrimination, leads to mutual support among immigrant employers and employees. Alejandro Portes and Min Zhou, "Gaining the Upper Hand: Economic Mobility among Immigrant and Domestic Minorities," *Ethnic and Racial Studies* 15, no. 4 (1992): 491–522.

17. Jet Tilakamonkul, tape-recorded interview by Mark Padoongpatt, October 16, 2007 (in author's possession).

18. I draw on Krishendu Ray here, who points out that immigrants are more than "creatures only of political economy" but also people who think about "taste, beauty, and how such things might intersect with their practical moral universe." See Krishnendu Ray, *The Ethnic Restauranteur* (New York: Bloomsbury Publishing, 2016) and Krishnendu Ray, "The Immigrant Restauranteur and the American City," *Social Research* 81 (Summer 2014), 374.

19. Prakas Yenbamroong, tape-recorded interview by Mark Padoongpatt, January 13, 2010 (in author's possession).

20. Joshua Lurie, "Interview: Chef Kris Yenbamroong," December 14, 2012, *Food GPS,* accessed December 3, 2016, http://foodgps.com/interview-chef-kris-yenbamroong-night-market/.

21. Yenbamroong interview.

22. Colman Andrews, "Talesa's Finely Made Thai Food," *Los Angeles Times,* September 23, 1983.

23. Jane Greenstein, "A Taste of Thai," *Los Angeles Times,* July 26, 1987.

24. Colman Andrews, "Thai One On," *Los Angeles Times,* November 30, 1976

25. Nuanta Dejakaisaya, chief of Los Angeles office of Tourist Organization of Thailand, quoted in Bobbie Justice, "Going Native: Where Foreigners Go in L.A. When They Want Home Cooking," *Los Angeles Times,* July 26, 1977.

26. U.S. Department of the Interior, Census Office, *Compendium of the Twentieth Census: 1980* (Washington D.C.: U.S. Government Printing Office, 1981).

27. The entrance of Jews into exclusive white postwar suburbs not only secured their whiteness but also constructed whiteness. For example, George J. Sanchez asserts in his study of Jews in Boyle Heights, California, that after World War II

Jews were able to move out of Boyle Heights and into areas that excluded them previously, such as the Westside and the San Fernando Valley, whereas Mexicans and Japanese could not. And Deborah Dash Moore's study of Jewish suburbanization in the San Fernando Valley makes clear that Jews bought homes in the west and south valley—bulwarks of whiteness in the region. Being able to purchase a home and live in the suburbs for European ethnics before the Fair Housing Act of 1968 meant one had, in the suburban context, gained entry into whiteness. George J. Sanchez, "What's Good for Boyle Heights is Good for the Jews," *American Quarterly: Los Angeles and the Future of Urban Cultures* 56 (2004): 638; Deborah Dash Moore, *To The Golden Cities: Pursuing the American Jewish Dream in Miami and L.A.* (Cambridge, MA: Harvard University Press, 1994).

28. Tilakamonkul, interview.

29. Jacqueline Desbarats, "Thai Migration to Los Angeles," *Geographical Review* 69, no. 3 (1979): 317.

30. "New American Eating Pattern: Dine Out, Carry In," *New York Times*, October 30, 1985.

31. Fran Zell, "Restaurant Business Up, for Many Vittle Reason," *Chicago Tribune*, May 17, 1975.

32. Lois Dwan, "Roundabout: Ginger Man Comes West," *Los Angeles Times*, August 27, 1978.

33. Barbara Hansen, tape-recorded interview by Mark Padoongpatt, July 22, 2010 (in author's possession).

34. Kamolmal Pootaraksa and William Crawford, *Thai Home Cooking from Kamolmal's Kitchen* (New York: Plume, 1986).

35. Yupa Holzner, *Great Thai Cooking for My American Friends: Creative Thai Dishes Made Easy* (Royal House, 1989).

36. Rose Dosti, "Let's Eat Out," ibid.

37. Tilakamonkul, interview.

38. Sodsook, *I Love Thai Food*, 30.

39. Ibid.

40. Rose Dosti, "The Search for LA's Thai Cuisine Pioneers," *Los Angeles Times*, December 22, 1988. Between 1982 and 1989, eight Awards of Excellence were given to Victor Sodsook and Siamese Princess (one each year). The California Restaurant Writers Association honored him with four consecutive three-star awards for food for the years 1985, 1986, 1987, and 1988. Between 1985 and 1988, the association also awarded him three consecutive three-star ratings for wine (1985, 1986, 1987) and with a four-star rating (the highest) in 1988. In addition, *Wine Spectator* magazine granted the restaurant four total awards of excellence (1986, 1987, 1988, 1989). Moreover, Sodsook received the "Outstanding Award" from the Dining Professionals of America in 1988 and 1989.

41. For a discussion of the growing appeal of ethnic food and eating healthy among white Americans at a national scale, see Donna R. Gabaccia, *We Are What We Eat: Ethnic Food and the Making of Americans* (Cambridge, MA: Harvard University Press, 1998), chap. 8.

42. Consella A. Lee, "Healthy Profits: Gym Chains Don't Sweat Recession as Working Out Becomes a Way of Life," *Los Angeles Times,* October 16, 1992.

43. Harvey Levenstein, *Revolution at the Table: The Transformation of the American Diet* (Berkeley: University of California Press, 2003), 205.

44. Tilakamonkul, interview.

45. Dosti, "Let's Eat Out."

46. Levenstein, *Revolution at the Table,* 205.

47. Ibid.

48. Otis M. Wiles, "All Nations Food Served Here," *Los Angeles Times,* January 15, 1922; Bertha Anne Houck, "Gastronomic Adventures," *Los Angeles Times,* May 13, 1928.

49. Lois Dwan, "Calendar: Toward a Distinct L.A. Style," *Los Angeles Times,* January 2, 1983.

50. According to leading food critics, another food revolution was taking place that discarded continental cuisine in favor of locally and regionally sourced ingredients and accessible dining. This middle- and upper-class revolution, known as "California cuisine" and embodied by Wolfgang Puck and others, gained more notoriety than the immigrant-infused ethnic food revolution. Calvin Trillin, "The Traveling Man's Burden," 456–457; Ruth Reichl, "Dinosaur Under Glass," *Los Angeles Times,* January 4, 1987; Lois Dwan, "L.A.'s Creative Chefs—The Main Ingredient," *Los Angeles Times,* September 17, 1978.

51. Ruth Reichl, "Restaurants in the Eighties," *Los Angeles Times,* December 29, 1989, p. 16.

52. James Farrer, *The Globalization of Asian Cuisines: Transnational Networks and Culinary Contact Zones* (Basingstoke, England: Palgrave Macmillan, 2015), 8.

53. It is my understanding that Chinese Thai in the United States strongly identify with "Thai," in part because of the impact of Thai nationalism and efforts (sometimes violent) to assimilate ethnic Chinese in Thailand during the nineteenth and mid-twentieth centuries. So while it is possible that Chinese Thai in Los Angeles opened Thai-Chinese restaurants to highlight their ethnic Chinese identity alongside their Thai identity, my point is that it is most important to think about how they imagined the connection between Chinese and Thai, especially in relation to U.S. racial categories. Ibid.; Justice, "Going Native."

54. Barbara Hansen, "Let's Eat Out: Up a Notch for Thai Food," *Los Angeles Times,* March 10, 1983.

55. Jennie Germann Molz, "Tasting an Imagined Thailand: Authenticity and Culinary Tourism in Thai Restaurants," in *Culinary Tourism,* Lucy Long, ed. (Lexington: University of Kentucky, 2004): 53–75; See also Gary Alan Fine and Jenny Ungbha Korn, "Arun's: A Review," *Contexts* 4, no. 1 (2005): 63–65.

56. Beverly Beyer and Ed Rabey, "Footloose in Bangkok: Grace, Charm Abound in the Siamese Style," *Los Angeles Times,* April 12, 1987.

57. Jitlada Restaurant circa 1980s menu; Pin Tong Thai Café circa 1980s menu, Menu Collection, Los Angeles Central Public Library.

58. Pin Tong Thai Café circa 1980s menu; Café '84 1984 menu, Menu Collection, Los Angeles Central Public Library.

59. Siamese Princess 1977 menu, Menu Collection, Los Angeles Central Public Library.

60. Charles Perry, "Restaurant Review: Showcase for Thai Cuisine, Culture," *Los Angeles Times*, February 15, 1985; Beverly Bush Smith, "Delights of Thai Cuisine," *Los Angeles Times*, September 13, 1984.

61. Charles Perry, "Restaurant Review: Showcase for Thai Cuisine, Culture."

62. Michelle Huneven, "Restaurants Review: Thai Restaurants Offer Home Spices Amid Mild Fare for Americans," *Los Angeles Times,* September 2, 1988.

63. Dosti, "The Search for LA's Thai Cuisine Pioneers."

64. Bush Smith, *Los Angeles Times*, September 13, 1984.

65. Rose Dosti, "Chan Dara: It's Worth It," *Los Angeles Times,* August 27, 1981; Rose Dosti, "Chan Dara Rates A Plus," *Los Angeles Times*, September 1, 1983.

66. Yenbamroong, interview.

67. Dwan, "Roundabout."

68. Kris Yenbamroong, "That One Time I Nearly Destroyed the Family Business," *Bon Appetit*, February 23, 2017.

69. Colman Andrews, "Talesa's Finely Made Thai Food."

70. Dosti, "Let's Eat Out."

71. Ruth Reichl, "Restaurants in the Eighties," *Los Angeles Times,* December 29, 1989.

72. Charles Perry, "It's a Personal Place to Savor the Unusual: Charles Perry on Restaurants," *Los Angeles Times,* August 23, 1985.

73. Dick Roraback, "The Valley of the Thais," *Los Angeles Times,* April 12, 1981.

74. Ruth Reichl, "Thai Food—Walk on the Gentler Side," *Los Angeles Times,* April 19, 1987.

75. Hansen, "Let's Eat Out."

76. Ibid.

77. Barbara Hansen, "Hot, Spicy Thai Dishes," *Los Angeles Times,* October 21, 1982.

78. Dosti, "Let's Eat Out."

79. Roraback, "The Valley of the Thais."

80. Colman Andrews, "Thai One On," *Los Angeles Times,* November 30, 1976.

81. Bush Smith, *Los Angeles Times*, September 13, 1984.

82. Roraback, "The Valley of the Thais." The reference to "odd little mushroom from Fantasia" was Orientalist. The 1940s cartoon featured dancing Chinese mushrooms—with slanted eyes, no mouth, and mushroom heads as the Chinese straw hat.

83. Colman Andrews, "Restaurants: Thailand's Food—A Well-Defined Cuisine of its Own," *Los Angeles Times,* April 12, 1981.

84. Ibid.

85. For instance, the 1980 U.S. census did not have a separate category for "Thai" as it did for Chinese, Japanese, Asian Indian, Korean, Vietnamese, Guamanian, and

Samoan. The 1990 U.S. census, however, did allow immigrants to report their race by offering a revised list of examples next to the "other API" write-in line, with "Thai" being one of the listed examples. Beverly M. Pratt, Lindsay Hixson, and Nicholas A. Jones, "Measuring Race and Ethnicity across the Decades, 1790–2010," (Infographic), Population Division, U.S. Census Bureau, 2010.

86. Lois Dwan, "Thai Food from North: Balanced," *Los Angeles Times,* March 7, 1982.

87. Charles Perry, "It's a Personal Place to Savor the Unusual: Charles Perry on Restaurants," *Los Angeles Times,* August 23, 1985.

88. "A Waitress at Arunee Thai House, Michelle Huneven," *Los Angeles Times,* September 2, 1988.

89. Tilakamonkul, interview; Yenbamroong, interview. Dwan, "Roundabout."

90. Sirijit Sunanta, "The Globalization of Thai Cuisine," paper presented at the Canadian Council for Southeast Asian Studies, October 14–16, 2005, York University, Toronto, Canada; Tilakamonkul, interview; Yenbamroong, interview; Sodsook, *I Love Thai Food,* 12.

91. Penny Van Esterik, *Materializing Thailand* (Oxford: Berg Press, 2000), 9.

92. Pootaraksa and Crawford, *Thai Home Cooking from Kamolmal's Kitchen*, 1.

93. Yenbamroong, interview.

94. Ibid.

95. According to Patrick Jory, Thailand witnessed a resurgence in expressions of ethnic and regional cultures and identities from the 1960s through the 1990s. He argues that this resurgence did not reflect a rejection of or resistance to "hegemonic constructions of Thai identity but rather an expansion of the concept of Thai identity to include a more pluralistic notion of what it means to be Thai." Patrick Jory, "Political Decentralisation and the Resurgence of Regional Identities in Thailand," *Australian Journal of Social Issues* 34 (November 1999): 348–349.

96. Linda Burum, "It Makes a Tiger Cry: Thailand's Isaan Cooking Hits L.A.," *Los Angeles Times,* June 25, 1989. Linda Burum writes that Isaan fare had become popular in Bangkok because rural northeastern Thais migrated to work in central Bangkok and some started opening up stalls to sell the food to these workers. Soon, Bangkok's upper- and middle-class urbanites started eating it and grew to love the flavor.

97. Dwan quotes Rafael Steinberg's *Pacific and Southeast Asian Cooking* (New York: Time Life Books, 1970), 190.

98. Burum, "It Makes a Tiger Cry."

99. Ibid.

100. Dwan, "Thai Food from North."

101. J. D. Gold was quick to point out that even Kaiswai's central-style Bangkok dishes—sate, pad thai, mee grob—is "prepared masterfully well." Gold, "Monkgorn Kawasai's Searingly Hot Thai Food is Flavorful, But Not for the Meek," Los Angeles Times, April 15, 1988.

102. Of course, at this point, almost all the food served in Thai restaurants in Los Angeles was Americanized Thai food in the sense that it featured a Western

dining sequence of courses, substituted ingredients like tofu and brown rice, and so on.

103. Kaiswai, for instance, minimized his use of nam plah in favor of a soy and wine concoction; This was not due to lack of ingredients, nor was it generational, because second-generation Thais had not come of age yet, and even newly arrived Isaan were already making concessions.

104. Perry, "Restaurant Review."

105. Jacques, "Variety is the Tang of Life." Many of these dishes were not on the menu from 1987, so they must have been specials or featured on previous menus.

106. Dosti, "Spicy and Sweet."

107. Tommy Tang, *Modern Thai Cuisine* (Garden City Park, NY: Square One Publishing), xi.

108. I borrow the phrase "behind the kitchen door" from Saru Jayaraman, whose *Behind the Kitchen Door* boldly illustrates the way investigations of the U.S. restaurant industry raises important questions about not just "eating out," the enchantment with "exotic" ethnic cuisines, or sustainability in terms of sourcing organic, fair-trade, and free-range ingredients, but also the neglected yet vital issues of labor exploitation, unsanitary work conditions, low wages, racism and sexism, customers' inhumane treatment of food service workers, and struggles to improve workers' rights. Saru Jayaraman, *Behind the Kitchen Door* (Ithaca: Cornell University Press, 2013).

109. Somkiat Cramer, tape-recorded interview by Mark Padoongpatt, March 15, 2009 (in author's possession)

110. Mike Davis, *City of Quartz: Excavating the Future in Los Angeles* (New York: Verso, 2006), 227.

111. Kaeonil, "The Thai Community in Los Angeles," 6; Cramer interview.

112. Charles Keely Jr., "Asian Restaurateurs Secrets of Success," *Los Angeles Times*, May 26, 1985.

113. Keely Jr., "Asian Restaurateurs Secrets of Success."

114. When Wandee first started working in Los Angeles in 1985, the minimum wage stood at $3.35. The minimum wage was raised to $4.25 in 1988. Henry Weinstein, "Minimum Wage in State Goes to $4.25: Increase of 27% from $3.35 an Hour Makes It Nation's Highest Pay Floor," *Los Angeles Times*, December 19, 1987.

115. She was on official payroll later at Arunee's House so that she could receive paystubs and be eligible for a green card.

116. Wandee Pathomrit, tape-recorded interview by Mark Padoongpatt, March 25, 2016 and May 20, 2016 (in author's possession).

117. Wandee Pathomrit, interview.

118. Ibid.

119. Ibid.

120. Wanda Pathomrit, tape-recorded interview by Mark Padoongpatt, May 20, 2016 (in author's possession).

121. Wanda Pathomrit, interview.

122. Ibid.

123. Wandee Pathomrit, interview.

CHAPTER FOUR

1. Barbara Hansen, "Thais in Southern California Celebrate a Bicentennial," *Los Angeles Times*, April 22, 1982.

2. Robert Janovici, "Case Nos. ZA20952 and 21272 Modification (Revocation Hearing January 28, 1983)," 7, January 19, 1984, City of Los Angeles, Department of City Planning, Office of Zoning Administration Papers, Los Angeles City Archives and Records Center.

3. Ibid., 6.

4. For example, Timothy Fong, *The First Suburban Chinatown: The Remaking of Monterey Park, California* (Philadelphia: Temple University Press, 1994) and Leland T. Saito, *Race and Politics: Asian Americans, Latinos, and Whites in a Los Angeles Suburb* (Champaign: University of Illinois Press, 1998); and Wei Li, *Ethnoburb: The New Ethnic Community in Urban America* (University of Hawaii Press, 2009), 95.

5. George Lipsitz, *How Racism Takes Place* (Philadelphia, PA: Temple University Press, 2011), 28–41.

6. Kenneth T. Jackson, *Crabgrass Frontier: The Suburbanization of the United States* (New York: Oxford University Press, 1985); Robert Fishman, *Bourgeosie Utopias: The Rise and Fall of Suburbia* (New York: Basic Books, 1987). For excellent critiques and a standard literature review of the "old suburban history," see Thomas J. Sugrue and Kevin M. Kruse, eds., *The New Suburban History* (Chicago: University of Chicago Press, 2006), introduction; and Nicolaides and Wiese, eds., *The Suburb Reader*, 5–9.

7. George J. Sanchez, "What's Good for Boyle Heights is Good for the Jews," *American Quarterly: Los Angeles and the Future of Urban Cultures* 56 (September 2004): 638; Josh Sides, *LA City Limits: African American Los Angeles from the Great Depression to the Present* (Berkeley: University of California Press, 2003), 104–105.

8. Kevin Roderick, *The San Fernando Valley: America's Suburb* (Los Angeles: Los Angeles Times Books, 2001), 139. The San Fernando Valley's multiracial and multiethnic suburbs have received greater attention in the last several years. See Laura Barraclough, "Ethnic Mexican Charros and the Struggle for Suburban Public Space in 1970s Los Angeles." *Aztlán: A Journal of Chicano Studies* 37 (2012): 95–124; and Laura Barracough, *Making the San Fernando Valley: Rural Landscapes, Urban Development, and White Privilege* (Athens: University of Georgia Press, 2011); Jean-Paul R. deGuzman, "Race, Community, and Activism in Greater Los Angeles: Japanese Americans, African Americans and the Contested Spaces of Southern California's Post-World War II San Fernando Valley," in *The Nation and Its Peoples: Citizens, Denizens, Migrants,* ed. Shannon Gleeson and John S. W. Park (New York: Routledge, 2014); Sides, *LA City Limits.*

9. Sides, *LA City Limits*, 104.

10. Ibid., 104.

11. Sanchez, "What's Good for Boyle Heights is Good for the Jews," 638.

12. Roderick, *The San Fernando Valley,* 137; Barraclough, "Contested Cowboys," 105.

13. Barraclough, "Contested Cowboys," 105; George Garrigues, "Comfort Is an $8,000 Income," *Los Angeles Times,* November 13, 1963.

14. Nicolaides, *My Blue Heaven: Life and Politics in the Working-class Suburbs of Los Angeles, 1920–1965* (Chicago: University of Chicago Press, 2002); Andrew Weise, *Places of Their Own: African American Suburbanization in the Twentieth Century* (Chicago: University of Chicago Press, 2004), 7.

15. James P. Allen and Eugene Turner, *The Ethnic Quilt: Population Diversity in Southern California* (Northridge, CA, 1997), chaps. 4 and 5; DeGuzman, "Race, Community, and Activism in Greater Los Angeles."

16. Roderick, *The San Fernando Valley,* 140.

17. "White" is used here as a racial category that encompasses different European ethnic groups including but not limited to Armenians, Jews, Italians, and Germans. Being able to purchase a home and live in the suburbs for European ethnics before the Fair Housing Act of 1968 meant one had, in the suburban context, gained entry into whiteness. For more on the whiteness of many of these European ethnic groups and how their suburbanization in the San Fernando Valley secured and constructed their whiteness, see Sanchez, "What's Good for Boyle Heights is Good For the Jews"; Deborah Dash Moore, *To The Golden Cities: Pursuing the American Jewish Dream in Miami and L.A.* (Cambridge: Harvard University Press, 1994).

18. U.S. Census Bureau, "Race" for Census Tract 1214-1215, Los Angeles County, 1980 Census, available at Social Explorer Dataset.

19. Ibid.

20. U.S. Census Bureau, "Foreign Born" for Census Tract 1220, Los Angeles County, 1980 Census, available at Social Explorer Dataset.

21. Ibid. Foreign-Born: 38.4% (no citizenship status); 12.8% naturalized citizen; 25.6% not a citizen.

22. The largest group of Asian/Pacific Islanders in this tract was Filipinos (28.8%), followed by Thais, Japanese (8.9%), Chinese (6.1%), and Vietnamese (4%). "Race" for Census Tract 1214-1215, Los Angeles County, Social Explorer Dataset (SE), Census 1990, Social Explorer, U.S. Census Bureau.

23. The 1990 U.S. census counted 9,270 Thais in Los Angeles, with 24,191 identifying themselves as Thai in the 1990 census questionnaire. The estimates I provide are from Thai community leaders who have taken into account Thais who are outside of legal status and those who did not wish to be counted. Allen and Turner, *The Ethnic Quilt,* 140; Jake Doherty, "Westlake Thai Group Strives for Greater Cohesion," *Los Angeles Times,* June 19, 1994.

24. Jacqueline Desbarats, "Thai Migration to Los Angeles," *Geographical Review* 69, no. 3 (1979): 315–317

25. Allen and Turner, *The Ethnic Quilt,* 160.

26. John Dart, "Thais Seek Backing for Buddhist Temple Here," *Los Angeles Times,* September 28, 1969.

27. Wendy Cadge, "Thai Buddhism in America: An Historical and Contemporary Overview," *Contemporary Buddhism* 6 (May 2005), 14.

28. Danny Anuphong Dechartivong, "Who, Wat, Where, and Wai: The History of Wat Thai Los Angeles" (master's thesis, University of California Los Angeles, 2012), 23–24.

29. Dechartivong, "Who, Wat, Where, and Wai," 25;

30. Prah Rajavaramuni, *Thai Buddhism in the Buddhist World* (Bangkok, Thailand: Unity Progress Press, 1984), 11; Jiemin Bao, *Creating a Buddhist Community: A Thai Temple in Silicon Valley* (Philadelphia: Temple University Press, 2015), 8; Charles F. Keyes, "Buddhism and National Integration in Thailand," *Journal of Asian Studies* 30, no. 3 (1971): 551–568; For a historical overview of Theravada Buddhism in the United States, see Wendy Cadge, *Heartwood: The First Generation of Therevada Buddhism in America* (Chicago: University of Chicago Press, 2004) and Wendy Cadge and Sidhorn Sangdhanoo, "Thai Buddhism in America: An Historical and Contemporary Overview," *Contemporary Buddhism* 6, no. 1 (2005): 7–35; See also Paul David Numrich, *Old Wisdom in the New World: Americanization in Two Immigrant Theravada Buddhist Temples* (Knoxville: University of Tennessee Press, 1996).

31. Bao, *Creating a Buddhist Community,* 97–98.

32. Ibid., 97–98; Donald S. Lopez Jr., *The Story of Buddhism: A Concise Guide to Its History and Teachings* (San Francisco, CA: Harper Collins, 2001), 10.

33. Dechartivong, "Who, Wat, Where, and Wai," 25–26.

34. Rajavaramuni, *Thai Buddhism in the Buddhist World,* 154.; Dechartivong, "Who, Wat, Where, and Wai," 26

35. Dechartivong, "Who, Wat, Where, and Wai"; Urai Ruenprom, tape-recorded interview by Mark Padoongpatt, December 18, 2008 (in author's possession); Rajavaramuni, *Thai Buddhism in the Buddhist World,* 155; Ken Lubas, "It's Unique in U.S.," *Los Angeles Times,* August 10, 1980.

36. Rajavaramuni, *Thai Buddhism in the Buddhist World,* 154; Markel, "Culture Clash," *Los Angeles Times,* April 24, 1983.

37. Dechartivong, "Who, Wat, Where, Wai," 27–28.

38. Markel, "Culture Clash."

39. Punsak Sosothinkul was so committed that he continued to borrow money from his parents sustain the temple in its early stages. Tragically, he did not live to see its entire completion, as he was shot and killed in 1974 as an innocent bystander in what was described as a gang shootout. "Police Trying to Chart Background of Gunfight: Three Thais Sought in Connection with Restaurant Slayings," *Los Angeles Times,* November 4, 1974.

40. Janovici, "Case Nos. ZA20952 and 21272 Modification (Revocation Hearing January 28, 1983)," 7, January 19, 1984, City of Los Angeles, Department of City Planning, Office of Zoning Administration Papers, Los Angeles City Archives and Records Center.

41. Lubas, "It's Unique in the U.S."

42. Markel, "Culture Clash."

43. Ibid.

44. Cadge, "Thai Buddhism in America"; Markel, "Culture Clash."

45. Lubas, "It's Unique in the U.S."

46. Dechartivong, "Who, Wat, Where, and Wai," 28–29.

47. James J. Crisp, Case Numbers CUZ 84-228, BZA 3282, and CF 85-1376, 1987, Plan Approval, Department of Building and Safety, December 18, 1987, City of Los Angeles, Department of City Planning, Office of Zoning Administration Papers, Los Angeles City Archives and Records Center.

48. Jiemin Bao, "Merit-Making Capitalism: Re-territorializing Thai Buddhism in Silicon Valley, California," *Journal of Asian American Studies* 8 (June 2005): 125. See also Bao, *Creating a Buddhist Community*.

49. Bao, "Merit-Making Capitalism," 154.

50. Rajavaramuni, *Thai Buddhism in the Buddhist World,* 154.

51. Timothy L. Smith, "Religion and Ethnicity in America," *The American Historical Review* 83, no. 5 (1978): 1161. Carolyn Chen, *Getting Saved in America: Taiwanese Immigration and Religious Experience* (Princeton, NJ: Princeton University Press, 2008). Carolyn Chen points to the importance of both Christian churches and Buddhist temples in Taiwanese immigrant adjustment to life in contemporary suburban Southern California. She argues that Taiwanese immigrants become American through religion, no matter if it is Christianity or Buddhism. She also discusses the way Taiwanese immigrants converted to Buddhism as a response to the increasing, and overpowering, number of Christian converts within the Taiwanese community.

52. Theravada Buddhist Center, Articles of Incorporation, 2, copy in author's possession.

53. Supachai Surongsain and Linda Mabalot, "Wat Thai of Los Angeles: More Than a Place of Worship," in *The Life of Phra Tamrachanuwat* (Los Angeles, California 1991), 156, in author's possession.

54. Ibid.

55. Dechartivong, "Who, Wat, Where, and Wai," 37–39.

56. Ibid.

57. John Nielsen, "Temple in Sun Valley Takes Root as Cultural Center for Thai Buddhists," *Los Angeles Times*, October 29, 1984.

58. Ibid.

59. Ibid.

60. Surongsain and Mabalot, "Wat Thai of Los Angeles," 153.

61. Bruce J. Schulman, "The Privatization of Everyday Life: Public Policy, Public Services, and Public Space in the 1980s," in *Living in the Eighties,* ed. Gil Troy and Vincent J. Cannato (New York: Basic Books, 2009), 169–175.

62. Dechartivong, "Who, Wat, Where, and Wai," 40.

63. Sawangchit Karschamroon, tape-recorded interview by Mark Padoongpatt, November 1, 2016 (in author's possession)

64. Karschamroon interview. By the late 1990s and early 2000s, temple officials believed the quality of the food had declined so they began holding cooking compe-

titions in which 8–10 potential vendors would cook-off and a judge would determine which vendor could sell their dish at the temple.

65. Hansen, "Thais in Southern California Celebrate a Bicentennial."

66. Sara Terry, "Thai Food with a California Twist," *Christian Science Monitor,* December 4, 2002.

67. Hansen, "Thais in Southern California Celebrate a Bicentennial."

68. Karschamroong interview

69. Hansen, "Thais in Southern California Celebrate a Bicentennial."

70. Ibid.

71. Norman Sklarewitz, "Thais That Bind," *Westways Magazine,* August 1992, 28.

72. For more on racialized and classed discourses of smell and the relationship between food, smell, and place, see Martin Manalansan, "The Empire of Food: Place, Memory and Asian Ethnic Cuisines," in *Gastropolis: Food and New York City,* Jonathan Deutch and Annie Hauck-Lawson eds., (New York: Columbia University Press, 2009), 93–107 and "Immigrant Lives and the Politics of Olfaction in the Global City," in *The Smell Culture Reader,* Jim Drobnick ed., (Oxford: Berg, 2006), 41–52.

73. Tanit Karschamroong, tape-recorded interview by Mark Padoongpatt, November 1, 2016 (in author's possession)

74. Uma Narayan, *Dislocating Cultures: Identities, Traditions, and Third-World Feminism* (New York: Routledge Press, 1997), 184.

75. Ibid.

76. Narayan adds that we risk "privileging the mind too much if we ignore the ways in which a more carnal relish may sometimes contribute to appreciation in ways as powerful as intellectual understanding." Ibid., 184.

77. Jiemin Bao, "Thai American Middle-Classness," *Journal of Asian American Studies* 12 (June 2009): 185.

78. Personal letter from Arthur Lurvey and Susan Lurvey to Phra Thepsophon, circa 1991, reprinted in *The Life of Phra Tamrachanuwat* (Los Angeles, California, 1991), in author's possession.

79. Janovici, "Case Nos. ZA20952 and 21272 Modification (Revocation Hearing January 28, 1983)," 7.

80. I will use the terms "residents" and "homeowners" to describe the suburban homeowners as well as members of the Neighborhood Committee. Of course, this does not mean that Thais were not homeowners or residents, but where appropriate, I will use "Thai resident" or "Thai homeowner" for clarification.

81. Ibid., 9–10.

82. Ibid., 11.

83. Ibid.

84. Janovici, "Case Nos. ZA20952 and 21272 Modification (Revocation Hearing January 28, 1983)," 7.

85. Case No. CUZ 84-228, 4, December 5, 1984, City of Los Angeles, Department of City Planning-Community Planning Case Review and Comment, Office of Zoning Administration Papers.

86. Ibid.

87. Markel, "Culture Clash."

88. Ibid.

89. John Nielsen, "City Carves Compromise on Noise, Crowds, at Temple," *Los Angeles Times*, March 22, 1984.

90. George Lipsitz, *How Racism Takes Place* (Philadelphia, PA: Temple University Press, 2011), 13.

91. Viola L. Smith to Office of Zoning Administration, December 28, 1984, City of Los Angeles, Department of City Planning, Office of Zoning Administration Papers, Los Angeles City Archives and Records Center.

92. Frank E. Manuel and Fritzie P. Manuel, *Utopian Thought in the Western World* (Cambridge: Harvard University Press, 1974), 27.

93. Ibid.

94. Schulman, "The Privatization of Everyday Life," 167–180; Henry A. Giroux, *Public Spaces, Private Lives: Beyond the Culture of Cynicism* (Lanham, MD: Rowman and Littlefield, 2001); Gerald Frug, "The Legal Technology of Exclusion in Metropolitan America," in *The New Suburban History*, edited by Kevin M. Kruse and Thomas J. Sugrue.

95. Frug, "The Legal Technology of Exclusion in Metropolitan America," 211.

96. Let me further clarify what I mean by "private" and "public," and why I use them in opposition when discussing space, culture, and the suburban ideal. On the one hand, "private" refers not simply to property ownership or profit motive, but also a turning inward into one's own private life, a withdrawal or "checking out" from community and society. In addition to abdication it also promotes homogeneity, conformity, exclusion, separation, and a desire to escape conflict instead of finding ways to deal with it collectively. "Public," on the other hand, is intended to mean open and equal access for everyone. It encourages active social engagement and community in that different people are forced to interact and learn to get along whether they like it or not. It also values diversity, openness, conflict resolution, and democratic practices and sensibilities. Though the historical actors in this story did not use this exact terminology, they capture many of the characteristics that defined the opposing conceptions of an ideal suburb.

97. Mike Davis, *City of Quartz: Excavating the Future in Los Angeles* (New York: Verso, 1990), 227, 257–60.

98. For more on the complexities of white suburbanites political views and diversity of discourse they mobilized during the 1970s and 1980s to exclude based on race, see Daniel Ho Sang, *Racial Propositions: Ballot Initiatives and the Making of Postwar California* (Berkeley: University of California Press, 2010); Robert Self, *American Babylon: Race and the Struggle for Postwar Oakland* (Princeton, NJ: Princeton University Press, 2003); Lisa McGirr, *Suburban Warriors: The Origins of the New American Right* (Princeton, NJ: Princeton University Press, 2001); Matthew Lassiter, *The Silent Majority: Suburban Politics in the Sunbelt South* (Princeton, NJ: Princeton University Press, 2006); Matthew F. Delmont, *Why Busing Failed: Race, Media, and the National Resistance to School Desegregation* (Berkeley:

University of California Press, 2016); Fong, *The First Suburban Chinatown*, chap. 5; Saito, *Race and Politics;* and Barraclough, *Making the San Fernando Valley.*

99. Mark Purcell, "The Decline of the Political Consensus for Urban Growth: Evidence from Los Angeles," *Journal of Urban Affairs* 22 (Spring 2000): 191; Michan Connor, "'These Communities Have the Most to Gain from Valley Cityhood': Color-Blind Rhetoric of Urban Secession in Los Angeles, 1996–2002," *Journal of Urban History* 40 (January 2014): 48–64. See also Michan Connor, "The Emotional Economy of Color-Blind Racism (Updated)," July 1, 2015, https://metro politanhistory.wordpress.com/2015/07/01/the-emotional-economy-of-color-blind -racism/.

100. Nicolaides, *My Blue Heaven,* 275.

101. Marc Weiss explores the urban origins of zoning and the way community builders used it to supplement private restriction deeds. He also discusses the relationship between zoning and class as well as industrial development strategies. Marc A. Weiss, *The Rise of Community Builders: The American Real Estate Industry and Urban Land Planning* (Frederick, OH: BeardBooks, 2002).

102. Since the early 1900s, zoning laws allowed urban planners and homeowners to use class codes to pursue visual signs of a prosperous quality of life. Equally important, city planners also made wide use of racial zoning for racial exclusion and to maintain segregation. Charles J. McLain, *In Search of Equality: The Chinese Struggle against Discrimination in Nineteenth-Century America* (Berkeley: University of California Press, 1994), 223–233; See also Colin Gordon, *Mapping Decline: St. Louis and the Fate of the American City* (Philadelphia: University of Pennsylvania Press, 2008), chapter 3 and Christopher Silver, "The Racial Origins of Zoning: Southern Cities from 1910–40," *Planning Perspectives* 6, no. 2 (1991): 189–205.

103. Frug, "The Legal Technology of Exclusion," 206.

104. Michael Jones-Correa, "Reshaping the American Dream: Immigrants, Ethnic Minorities, and the Politics of the New Suburbs," in *The New Suburban History,* ed. Kruse and Sugrue, 198–99.

105. The conflict over Hsi Lai Buddhist Temple in Hacienda Heights, California during the 1980s also stands out. Wei Li, *Ethnoburb: The New Ethnic Community in Urban America* (Honolulu: University of Hawaii Press, 2008), 95.

106. The vice president of the board tried to reassure the neighbors, but the police had to intervene. The temple lay people were issued parking tickets, even when other residents parked the same way but did not received tickets. Bao, "From Wandering to Wat: Creating a Thai Temple and Inventing New Space in the United States," *Amerasia Journal* 34, no. 3 (2006): 6; Bao, *Creating a Buddhist Community,* 61.

107. Bao, "From Wandering to Wat," 6.

108. Fong, *The First Suburban Chinatown,* 5.

109. Anita Mannur and Martin F. Manalansan, "Dude, What's That Smell?" The Sriracha Shutdown and Immigrant Excess," *From the Square,* NYU Press blog, accessed December 23, 2016, www.fromthesquare.org/dude-whats-that-smell-the -sriracha-shutdown-and-immigrant-excess/#.WE833SMrK2x.

110. Markel, "Culture Clash."

111. Nielsen, "City Carves Compromise on Noise, Crowds, at Temple."

112. Openly racist comments could have potentially ended the homeowners' case against Wat Thai festivals since discriminatory intent would have been found unconstitutional.

113. David Freund has illustrated how "property values" and "quality of life" were racialized concepts that afforded suburbanites during this period a useful language to participate in maintaining white privilege and power without appearing racist. See David Freund, *Colored Property: State Policy and White Racial Politics in Suburban America* (Chicago: University of Chicago, 2010).

114. Lipsitz, *How Racism Takes Place,* 35.

115. See Lalaie Ameeriar, "The Sanitized Sensorium," *American Anthropologist* 114, no. 3 (2012): 509–520.

116. Viola Smith, "Department of City Planning Community Planning Case Review and Comments: Case No. CUZ 84-228," December 17, 1984 (review and approval date), City of Los Angeles Department of City Planning, Office of Zoning Administration, Los Angeles City Archives and Records Center.

117. Ibid.

118. Appraisal Report: Case No. CUZ 84-228, Standard Offer for Agreement and Purchase, March 11, 1984, City of Los Angeles Department of City Planning, Office of Zoning Administration, Los Angeles City Archives and Records Center.

119. Janovici, "Case Nos. ZA20952 and 21272 Modification (Revocation Hearing January 28, 1983)," 13.

120. Ibid.

121. Markel, "Culture Clash."

122. Phra Thepsopon to David Wygand, August 28, 1984, Case No. CUZ 84-228, Office of Zoning Administration Papers.

123. Bao, "Thai American Middle-Classness," 171–173.

124. Markel, "Culture Clash."

125. Ethnic groups in the United States have long used ethnicity as a strategy for class advancement, with elite members of the group using ethnicity to secure power they otherwise could not obtain and with poorer members using ethnicity to secure solidarity from elites. For examples, see April Schultz *Ethnicity on Parade: Inventing the Norwegian American through Celebration* (Amherst: University of Massachusetts Press, 1994) and Michael Miller Topp, *Those Without a Country: The Political Culture of Italian American Syndicalists* (Minneapolis: University of Minnesota Press, 2001).

126. Nielsen, "City Carves Compromise on Noise, Crowds at Temple."

127. David P. Christianson, tape-recorded interview by Mark Padoongpatt, March 15, 2007 (in author's possession).

128. Christianson interview.

129. Ibid.

130. Janovici, "Case Nos. ZA20952 and 21272 Modification (Revocation Hearing January 28, 1983)," 1.

131. John Nielsen, "Board Rules Buddhist Temple Can Add School," *Los Angeles Times,* June 5, 1985.

132. David Wygand to City of Los Angeles Zoning Administration, December 23, 1984, Case No. CUZ 84-228, 2–3, Office of Zoning Administration Papers.

133. Nielsen, "Board Rules Buddhist Temple Can Add School."

134. Christianson interview.

135. Scott Kurashige, *The Shifting Grounds of Race: Black and Japanese Americans in the Making of Multiethnic Los Angeles* (Princeton, NJ: Princeton University Press, 2008), 279.

136. Ibid., 280; Purcell, "The Decline of the Political Consensus for Urban Growth: Evidence from Los Angeles," 88.

137. Christianson interview.

138. Letter from David P. Christianson to Wat Thai of Los Angeles, January 2, 1991, reprinted in *The Life of Phra Tamrachanuwat* (Los Angeles, California, 1991), in author's possession.

CHAPTER FIVE

1. Thai Community Development Center, "Surveying East Hollywood: A Profile and Needs Assessment of the Business Community," (Los Angeles: Thai Community Development Center, 2002), 3.

2. U.S. Census Data Set: 2000 Summary File 1 (SF 1) 100-Percent Data. The 2000 census did not have a count for Armenians, although it is very likely that they may have identified themselves under the "White" category.

3. Ibid.

4. Sudarat Disayawattana, *The Craft of Ethnic Newspaper-Making: A Study of the Negotiation of Culture in the Thai-Language Newspapers of Los Angeles* (Ph.D. dissertation, University of Iowa, 1993), 155.

5. Ibid., 157.

6. George J. Sanchez, "Face the Nation: Race, Immigration, and the Rise of Nativism in Late Twentieth Century America," *International Migration Review* 31 (1997): 1009–1030.

7. Connie Kang, "Asian American Groups Organize to Fight Measure," *Los Angeles Times,* Oct. 9, 1994. For an excellent analysis of the racial politics of California ballot measures, see Daniel Ho Sang, *Racial Propositions: Ballot Initiatives and the Making of Postwar California* (Berkeley: University of California Press, 2010).

8. Peter Hong, "Speaking Up for the Silent," *Los Angeles Times,* Aug. 23, 1995.

9. Chanchanit Martorell, interview.

10. Ibid.

11. Chanchanit Martorell, Course Syllabus, Spring 1995, copy stored at Thai Community Development Center, Los Angeles, California.

12. Ibid.

13. Martha Nakagawa, "UCLA Ushers in a New Thai American Era," *Asianweek*, May 14, 1993.

14. Jake Doherty, "Westlake Thai Group Strives for Greater Cohesion," *Los Angeles Times*, June 19, 1994.

15. Ibid.

16. Doherty, "Westlake Thai Group Strives for Greater Cohesion."

17. Henry A. Giroux, *Public Spaces, Private Lives: Beyond the Culture of Cynicism* (Lanham: Rowman and Littlefield, 2003), 4–5.

18. Robert D. Putnam, *Bowling Alone: The Collapse and Revival of American Community* (New York: New York University Press, 2000).

19. Karen Robinson-Jacobs, "From Virtual Slavery to Being Boss," *Los Angeles Times*, Oct. 25, 2001.

20. Ibid.

21. Ibid.

22. Julie Su and Chanchanit Martorell, "Exploitation and Abuse in the Garment Industry: The Case of the Thai Slave-Labor Case in El Monte," in *Asian and Latino Immigrants in a Restructuring Economy,* edited by Marta Lopez-Garza and David Diaz (Stanford: Stanford University Press, 2001), 27.

23. Ibid., 22.

24. Patrick J. McDonnell, "Thai Sweatshop Workers Savor Freedom's Joys," *Los Angeles Times,* Aug. 13, 1995.

25. Su and Martorell, "Exploitation and Abuse in the Garment Industry," 26.

26. Kenneth B. Noble, "Thai Workers Are Set Free in California," *New York Times,* Aug. 4, 1995.

27. Su and Martorell, "Exploitation and Abuse in the Garment Industry," 26.

28. Patrick Lee and George White, "INS Got Tip on Sweatshop 3 Years Ago," *Los Angeles Times,* Aug. 4, 1995.

29. Karl Schoenberger and Shawn Hubler, "Asian Leaders Call for Release of Thai Workers," *Los Angeles Times,* Aug. 10, 1995.

30. Department of Justice Press Release, "Ten Thai Nationals [Indicted] On New Charges of Slavery and Kidnapping," Nov. 9, 1995, copy stored at Thai Community Development Center, Los Angeles, California.

31. Schoenberger and Hubler, "Asian Leaders Call for Release of Thai Workers."

32. Patrick J. McDonnell, "Thai Sweatshop Workers Savor Freedom's Joys," *Los Angeles Times,* Aug. 13, 1995.

33. Kenneth Chang, "Not Home Free," *Los Angeles Times,* June 19, 1996.

34. Karl Schoenberger, Patrick McDonnell, and Elson Trinidad, "Feasting on Kindness," *Los Angeles Times,* August 20, 1995.

35. Thai Community Development Center, "The Ongoing Struggle by the Thai Community Development Center to Abolish Human Trafficking and Modern Day Slavery," n.d., accessed Jan. 4, 2017, at http://thaicdc.org/cms/assets/Uploads/human-trafficking/Thai-CDC-Appeal.pdf.

36. Christopher Scheer, "Thailand to L.A., A Life of Debasement Thai Slaves," *Los Angeles Times,* Aug. 14, 1995.

37. Schoenberger and Hubler, "Asian Leaders Call for Release of Thai Workers."

38. Karl Schoenberger, "Sweatshop Workers' Plight Splits Thai Community," *Los Angeles Times,* Aug. 23, 1995.

39. Schoenberger, "Sweatshop Workers' Plight Splits Thai Community."

40. Ibid.

41. Scheer, "Thailand to L.A., A Life of Debasement Thai Slaves."

42. Eric Slater, Claire Vitucci, and Julie Tamaki, "Servitude a Fact of Life, Thais Say," *Los Angeles Times,* April 3, 1998.

43. Ibid.

44. Chanchanit Martorell and Beatrice "Tippe" Morlan, *Images of America: Thais in Los Angeles* (Charleston: Arcadia Publishing, 2011), 111.

45. Thai Smakom of UCLA, "Thai Town Survey" (Los Angeles: University of California Los Angeles and Office of Councilman Michael Woo, 1992), 5.

46. Ibid.

47. Thai Town Formation Committee Members' Mini-Manual, "Synopsis of the Thai Town Meeting," Thai Community Development Center, May 28, 1998, 13. Copy stored at Thai Community Development Center, Los Angeles, California.

48. Ibid., 14.

49. Martorell interview.

50. "Synopsis of the Thai Town Meeting," 5.

51. Ibid.

52. This is disputable because a "no reply" from some of the businesses could very well be a sign of opposition, which means the Thai CDC may have also ignored them to build consensus—or "community."

53. Thai Community Development Center, "Steps Taken By Thai CDC to Establish Thai Town," stored at Thai Community Development Center, Los Angeles, California.

54. "Nation's First Thai Town Designated," *Rafu Shimpo,* Feb. 7, 2000.

55. Deborah Belgum, "Thai Town: New Designation Brings High Hopes to Area," *Los Angeles Business Journal,* Jan. 23–30, 2000, p. 83.

56. "Introduction to Entrepreneurship, Student Workbook," n.d., accessed June 25, 2011, http://www.thaicdchome.org/cms/thai-town-development/.

57. Belgum, "Thai Town: New Designation Brings High Hopes to Area," 83.

58. Ibid., 9–10.

59. Ibid, 7.

60. Maria Elena Fernandez, "A Thai-Style Piece of the American Pie," *Los Angeles Times,* July 2, 2002.

61. Ibid.

62. For insight into the racial politics of urban renewal in Los Angeles specifically, see Dana Cuff, *The Provisional City: Los Angeles Stories of Architecture and Urbanism* (Cambridge: MIT Press, 2000); and Eric Avila, *Popular Culture in the Age of White Flight: Fear and Fantasy in Suburban Los Angeles* (Berkeley: University of California Press, 2006).

63. Rachel Benioff, "Profiles of Engagement: Public Markets as Engines for Urban Revitalization," University of California, Los Angeles Center for Community Partnerships (Los Angeles: University of California Regents, 2008), 1.

64. Ibid., 2.

65. David Pierson and Anna Gorman, "A New Take on Thai Town," *Los Angeles Times*, Aug. 2, 2007; Benioff, "Profiles of Engagement," 2.

66. Benioff, "Profiles of Engagement," 2–3.

67. Ibid, 2.

68. Ernesto J. Vigoreaux, "Thai Town Atlas and Community Analysis Research Project" (MA thesis, University of California, Los Angeles, 2000), 36–40.

69. Vinijnaiyapak, "Institutions and Civic Engagement," 291–295, 305.

70. Thai Community Development Center, "Preserve America Communities Program Neighborhood Application," 2008, 12, stored at Thai Community Development Center, Los Angeles, California.

71. Martorell and Morlan, *Images of America*, 77.

72. Thai Community Development Center, "Former Human Trafficking Victims Won the Curry King Title in the LA Curry Festival," Thai CDC Press Release, April 18, 2008, accessed Jan. 4, 2016, at http://www.thaicdc.org/cms/assets/Uploads/Curry-Festival/Curry-King-Contest-press-release-040909.pdf.

73. Thai New Year Festival Corporation, Reservation form for Food and Merchandise Booths, 5th Annual Thai New Year Songkran Festival, April 13, 2008, Thai Town, Los Angeles, California, in author's possession.

74. Wongskhaluang interview, March 18, 2009.

75. Ibid.

76. Ibid.

77. Ibid.

78. Thai Community Development Center, "Preserve America Communities Program Neighborhood Application," 12.

79. Wongskhaluang, interview.

80. Ibid.

81. Rothman, *Devil's Bargains*, 12.

82. Anthony J. Stanonis, ed., *Dixie Emporium: Tourism, Foodways, and Consumer Culture in the American South* (Athens: University of Georgia Press, 2008), 3.

83. Rothman, *Devil's Bargains*, 12.

84. Thai Community Development Center, "Preserve America Communities Program Neighborhood Application," 12.

85. Anthony Bourdain's No Reservations, "Los Angeles," Travel Channel, aired Feb. 5, 2007, Zero Point Zero Production Inc., written and hosted by Anthony Bourdain, episode produced by Tracey Gudwin, and executive producer Myleeta Aga.

86. Ibid., Feb. 5, 2007.

87. Kavi Chongkittavorn, "Globalisation of Thai Food," *Thailand Monitor* 12 (January–April 2006), 17–20.

88. Van Esterik, *Food Culture in Southeast Asia,* 93; *Thai Food to the World,* accessed June 26, 2011, http://www.thaifoodtoworld.com/home/governmentpol .php.

89. Royal Thai Consulate General Los Angeles, "Thai Cuisine" Los Angeles Press Release, Aug. 3, 2005, in author's possession.

90. Ibid.

91. Daniel Lian, "Thaksin's Model: The Thai Prime Minister's Economic Paradigm Offers A New Role for Thailand in the Global Economy," *Asiaweek,* Aug. 17, 2001.

92. "An Interview: Dr. Warunee Varanyanond, Institute of Food Research and Product Development (IFRPD)," *Thai Food to the World,* Nov. 30, 2005, accessed June 25, 2011, http://www.thaifoodtoworld.com/home/interviewdetail.php?cms _id=61&language=EN.

93. *Preserve America,* accessed June 25, 2011, http://www.preserveamerica.gov /EO.html.

94. Teresa Watanabe, "A Boost for Thai Town," *Los Angeles Times,* August 3, 2008.

95. Watanabe, "A Boost for Thai Town."

CONCLUSION

1. "Port Hueneme Eatery 1 of 2 Ordered to Pay Workers Back Wages," *McClatchy—Tribune Business News,* September 10, 2009; Brent Hunsberger; "Typhoon Discriminated Against Thai Chefs, Oregon Workplace Investigators Conclude," *The Oregonian,* May 11, 2011.

2. "Thailand: Commerce Minister to Revive 'Thai Kitchen to the World' Project," *Asia News Monitor,* January 14, 2009.

3. Here is a brief list: Laura Briggs, *Reproducing Empire: Race, Sex, Science, and U.S. Imperialism in Puerto Rico* (Berkeley: University of California Press, 2003); James T. Campbell, Matthew Pratt Guterl, and Robert G. Lee, eds., *Race, Nation, and Empire in American History* (Chapel Hill: University of North Carolina Press, 2007); Takashi Fujitani, *Race for Empire: Koreans as Japanese and Japanese as Americans During World War II* (Berkeley: University of California Press, 2011); Matthew Frye Jacobson, *Barbarian Virtues: The United States Encounters Foreign Peoples at Home and Abroad* (New York: Hill and Wang, 2000); and Paul Kramer, *The Blood of Government: Race, Empire, the United States, and the Philippines,* (Chapel Hill: University of North Carolina Press, 2006).

4. Jana Lipman writes that "social history is, in fact, diplomatic history." Jana K. Lipman, *Guantanamo: A Working-Class History between Empire and Revolution* (Berkeley: University of California Press, 2008), 6. Adria Imada, *Aloha America: Hula Circuits through the U.S. Empire* (Durham, NC: Duke University Press, 2012); Klein, *Cold War Orientalism;* Dennis Merrill, *Negotiating Paradise: U.S. Tourism and Empire in Twentieth Century Latin America* (Chapel Hill: University of North

Carolina Press, 2009). Adrian Burgos, *Playing America's Game: Baseball, Latinos, and the Color Line* (Berkeley: University of California Press, 2007).

5. William Appleman Williams, *Empire as a Way of Life* (New York: Oxford University Press, 1980).

6. Simeon Man, "Transpacific Connections between Two Empires," *American Quarterly* 66, no. 2 (2014): 441–451.

7. Yen Le Espiritu, *Home Bound: Filipino American Lives Across Cultures, Communities, and Countries* (Berkeley: University of California Press, 2003); Stephen Castles, "Migration and Community Formation under Conditions of Globalization," *International Migration Review* 36, no. 4 (2002): 1143–1168; Paul Ong, Edna Bonacich, and Lucie Cheng, eds., *The New Asian Immigration in Los Angeles and Global Restructuring* (Philadelphia: Temple University Press, 1994); Lisa Lowe, *Immigrant Acts: On Asian American Cultural Politics* (Durham, NC: Duke University Press, 1996), chapter 7; Aihwa Ong, *Buddha is Hiding: Refugees, Citizenship, the New America* (Berkeley: University of California Press, 2003); Saskia Sassen, *The Mobility of Labor and Capital: A Study of International Investment and Labor Flows* (New York: Cambridge, 1988); and Linda Basch, Nina Glick Schiller, and Cristina Blanc, *Nations Unbound: Transnational Projects, Postcolonial Predicaments, and Deterritorialized Nation-States* (USA: Gordon and Breach, 1994).

8. Espiritu, *Home Bound*, 10.

9. Haiming Liu and Lianlian Lin, "Food, Culinary Identity, and Transnational Culture: Chinese Restaurant Business in Southern California," *Journal of Asian American Studies* 12, no. 2 (2009): 150; See also Martin Manalansan, "The Empire of Food: Place, Memory, and Asian 'Ethnic Cuisines,'" in *Gastropolis: Food & New York City*, edited by Annie Hauck-Lawson and Jonathan Deutsch (New York: Columbia University Press, 2009), 106.

10. Liu and Lin, "Food, Culinary Identity, and Transnational Culture," 136.

11. Ngai, *Impossible Subjects*, 10–11.

12. Martin Manalansan, "Immigrant Lives and the Politics of Olfaction in the Global City," in *The Smell Culture Reader*, edited by Jim Drobnick (Oxford: Berg, 2006), 41–52; Rick Bonus, *Locating Filipino Americans: Ethnicity and the Cultural Politics of Space* (Philadelphia: Temple University Press, 2000), chapter 3; and David E. Sutton, "Synesthesia, Memory, and the Taste of Home," in *The Taste Culture Reader: Experiencing Food and Drink,* edited by Carolyn Korsmeyer (New York: Berg Publishers, 2005).

13. Joseph Bernardo, "From Little Brown Brothers to Forgotten Americans: Race, Space, and Empire in Filipino Los Angeles" (PhD Dissertation: University of Washington, 2014); Laura Barraclough, "Contested Cowboys: Ethnic Mexican Charros and the Struggle for Suburban Public Space in 1970s Los Angeles," *Aztlan: A Journal of Chicano Studies* 37, No. 2 (2012): 95–124; Anthony F. Macias, "Bringing Music to the People: Race, Urban Culture, and Municipal Politics in Postwar Los Angeles," *American Quarterly* 56, no. 3 (2004): 693–717; Robert Self, "'To Plan Our Liberation': Black Power and the Politics of Place in Oakland,

California, 1965–1977," *Journal of Urban History* 26, no 6. (2000): 759–792; and Genevieve Carpio, Clara Irazábal, and Laura Pulido, "Right to the Suburb? Rethinking Lefebvre and Immigrant Activism," *Journal of Urban Affairs* 33, no. 2 (2011): 189.

14. A good example of this kind of work is Donna R. Gabaccia and Jeffrey M. Pilcher, "Chili Queens and Checkered Tablecloths: Public Dining Cultures of Italians in New York City and Mexicans in San Antonio, Texas 1870s–1940s," *Radical History Review* 2011, no. 110 (2011): 109–126.

15. Ronald Takaki, *Strangers From a Different Shore: A History of Asian Americans* (Boston: Little Brown, 1989); Sucheng Chan, *Asian Americans: An Interpretive History* (Boston: Twayne, 1991); Gary Okihiro, *Columbia Guide to Asian American History* (New York: Columbia University Press, 2001); Lon Kurashige and Alice Yang Murray, *Major Problems in Asian American History* (Boston: Houghton Mifflin, 2003); Erika Lee, *The Making of Asian America* (New York: Simon & Schuster, 2015); and David K. Yoo and Eiichira Azuma *Oxford Handbook of Asian American History* (New York: Oxford University Press, 2016).

16. Elizabeth M. Hoeffel, Sonya Rastogi, Myoung Ouk Kim, and Hasan Shahid, "The Asian Population: 2010," U.S. Census, March 2012.

17. This estimate is from 2006: Pew Hispanic Center, "Modes of Entry for the Unauthorized Migrant Population," May 22, 2006.

18. Christine Chiao, "Jet Tila Appointed Thai Cuisine Ambassador," *LA Weekly*, April 9, 2013, http://www.laweekly.com/restaurants/jet-tila-appointed-thai -cuisine-ambassador-2897096.

19. "Thailand: Commerce Minister to Revive 'Thai Kitchen to the World' Project.," *Asia News Monitor*, January 14, 2009.

20. Monica Luhar, "Community Marketplace Breaks Ground in America's Only Thai Town," *NBC News*, September 23, 2016, http://www.nbcnews.com /news/asian-america/community-marketplace-breaks-ground-america-s-oldest-thai -town-n653271.

21. Deborah Schoch, "Temple Tradition Bows to Neighbors' Pressure: North Hollywood's Wat Thai Suspends its Popular Weekend Food Fairs Over Parking Issue," *Los Angeles Times*, August 13, 2007.

22. A similar conflict played out at Wat Mongkolratanaram in Berkeley, California in 2009. Kristin Bender, "The Brunch at Berkeley's Buddhist Temple Will Continue—at Least for Now," East Bay Times, February 20, 2009, http://www .eastbaytimes.com/2009/02/20/the-brunch-at-berkeleys-buddhist-temple-will -continue-at-least-for-now-2/.

23. Anita Mannur and Martin Manalansan, "Dude, What's that Smell? The Sriracha Shutdown and Immigrant Excess," January 16, 2014, https://www .fromthesquare.org/dude-whats-that-smell-the-sriracha-shutdown-and-immigrant-excess/#.WLJVcyMrK2w; Niraj Chokshi, "'Taco Trucks on Every Corner': Trump Supporter's Anti-Immigration Warning," *New York Times,* September 2, 2016, https://www.nytimes.com/2016/09/03/us/politics/taco-trucks-on-every-corner -trump-supporters-anti-immigration-warning.html.

24. "Columbusing" refers to white people "discovering" something that marginalized communities have been doing for quite some time, but acting like it is new and then reaping benefits from it.

25. One of the more in-depth critiques can be found in Lorraine Cheun, "Food, Race, and Power: Who Gets to be an authority on 'ethnic' cuisines?," *Intersectional Analyst,* January 8, 2017, http://www.intersectionalanalyst.com/intersectional-analyst/2017/1/7/who-gets-to-be-an-authority-on-ethnic-cuisines.

26. Jonathan Gold, "Andy Ricker's Pok Pok Brings Genuine Taste of Thailand to L.A.," *Los Angeles Times,* December 25, 2015, http://www.latimes.com/food/jonathan-gold/la-fo-1226-gold-20151226-story.html.

27. Quincy Surasmith, "Acclaimed Mediocrity: On Pok Pok and Ricker," *Eat Kune Do,* January 9, 2017, http://www.eatkunedo.com/blog/2017/1/on-pok-pok-and-ricker.

28. Maria Godoy and Kat Chow, "When Chefs Become Famous Cooking other Cultures' Food," *NPR,* March 22, 2016, http://www.npr.org/sections/the-salt/2016/03/22/471309991/when-chefs-become-famous-cooking-other-cultures-food; Michael Russell, "Andy Ricker of Portland's Pok Pok wins 2011 James Beard for best chef Northwest," *The Oregonian/Oregon Live,* May 9, 2011, http://www.oregonlive.com/dining/index.ssf/2011/05/andy_ricker_of_portlands_pok_p.html.

29. Chef McDang, "Thais Don't Give a Damn About Thai Food," *CNN,* March 2, 2011, http://travel.cnn.com/bangkok/eat/chef-mcdang-thais-dont-give-damn-about-thai-food-919905/.

30. Uma Narayan, *Dislocating Cultures: Identities, Traditions, and Third-World Feminism* (New York: Routledge Press, 1997), 182.

31. Narayan, *Dislocating Cultures,* 182.

INDEX

Abarca, Meredith, 68
Abrahams, Roger, 13
acculturation, food practices and, 3. *See also*
   assimilation
Agency for International Development
   (AID), 30
Aikman, Bonnie, 77
Akins, Taylor, 187
American Field Service (AFS), 30
Americanization of Thai food, 108–10,
   177
American Society of Travel Agents
   (ASTA), 39–40
American University Alumni Association,
   30
Amornkul, Prakorb, 166
Anderson, Benedict, 67
Andrews, Colman, 92, 101, 104, 105–6
Animal and Plant Health Inspection
   Service (APHIS), 75
appearance of dishes, 45–46
Apple, Marianne May, 43
archives for historical investigation, 19–21
Arleta, 121, 124
Asalah Boucha, 122–23
Asia, U.S. expansion, post-World War II,
   5–8
Asia Foundation (TAF), 30
Asian-Americans: anti-Asian sentiment, 11;
   history narratives of, 183–84; immi-
   grant class divisions and, 142–43;
   "invisibility factor," 149; Los Angeles

riots (1992), 149–51. *See also* Thai
   Americans
Asian cuisine: U.S. fascination with, 51–53.
   See also Thai cuisine
assimilation: Americanization of Thai
   food, 110, 177; cultural pluralism and,
   11; food practices and, 3, 180, 181; suburbs, movement to, 17, 146, 181; Tang,
   Tommy, views on, 86; Thai American
   political engagement, 154–55; Thai
   culture, origins of, 48
ASTA (American Society of Travel
   Agents), 39–40
authentic ingredients, defined, 208–9n2
autobiographical narrative, cookbooks and,
   49–50
Ayuthya, Chumsai na, 31–32

Bangkok Market: as business incubator, 84;
   ingredient sourcing, 72–73, 78–82,
   81*map*; opening of, 56–57; Thai Ameri-
   can community formation and, 82–84,
   83*map*; trade barriers (1970s–1980s),
   73–78
Bao, Jiemin, 4, 132–33, 139
Bayless, Rick, 187
Bégin, Camille, 4
Benedict, Ruth, 29
Bernardi, Ernani, 134
Bhusiririt, Penny, 166
Bonus, Rick, 180
bounded solidarity, 217n16
Bourdain, Anthony, 171

Bradley, Tom, 11, 145, 153*fig.*
Brennan, Jennifer: appropriation of ethnic cuisine, 188–89; "authentic" Thai cuisine and, 45–46; autobiographical narratives of, 50; cooking classes of, 51; interpretation of Thai culture, 47–48, 49; Los Angeles Thai food boom (1970s–1980s), 94; power relationships, narrative about, 50–51
Brock, Sean, 187
Brooks, Charlotte, 6
Buddhism: Thai American Buddhist Association, 122; Thai food festivals and, 118–20; Theravada Buddhism, overview of, 123; Wat Thai, history of, 122–28, 127*fig.*
Buranasombati, Chow, 70, 90, 100–101
Burgos, Adrian, 177
Burma, 212n62
Burum, Linda, 107–8
Bush, George W., 173
Bush, Laura, 173
business incubator, Thai Town as, 166
business investments, Thai Americans, 89–90
Byer, Beverly, 98–99
Byrnes, James, 26

California: ingredient sourcing, California and Mexico, 79–82, 81*map*; Proposition 187 (1994), 149, 150–51; San Fernando Valley, 120–21. *See also* Los Angeles, California
California cuisine, 219n50
California School of Culinary Arts (CSCA), 172–73
Cantonese cuisine, 51–52
Carpio, Genevieve, 18
Carroll, George, 135–36, 140
Carroll, Phyllis, 136
celebrities: Los Angeles Thai food boom (1970s–1980s), 95–96
Chan Dara, 85, 95, 96, 100, 111, 112
Charuwon, Burt, 162
Cheng, Cindy I-Fen, 6
chili peppers: as key ingredient, 46, 47, 71, 72; sensory experiences, restaurants and, 102–10

China: influences in Thai food, 47; Thailand's Chinese population, 48–49
Chinese cuisine: *vs.* Thai cuisine, 103–4; U.S. fascination with, 51–53
Christianson, David, 133, 141, 143–44, 145
citrus hystrix (kaffir lime), 71–72, 76, 79–82, 81*map*
class divisions: suburban zoning and, 138; Thai Americans and, 115–17, 142–43
Coates, Peter, 214n93
Cold War: "Oriental" cooking, fascination with, 51–53; power relationships in Thailand, 48–49; Thai cuisine, exposure to, 1–2; U.S. expansion, post-World War II, 5–8
colonialism: cuisine driven multiculturalism and, 13; food, role of, 6–7; imperialist nostalgia, defined, 207n108; United States in Thailand, 24–32, 177–78; U.S. military bases, effect on Thais, 32–37
columbusing, 187, 238n24
Community Economic Development (CED), 164
Comprehensive Crime Control Act (1984), 214n92
cookbooks: author autobiography and, 49–50; Los Angeles Thai food boom (1970s–1980s), 94–95; by Peace Corp volunteers, 43; as romanticized version of culture, 49. *See also* Brennan, Jennifer; Wilson, Marie
cooking classes, 51; culinary appropriation and, 51–53; Los Angeles Thai food boom (1970s–1980s), 94–95
Cooking Thai Food in American Kitchens, 68
cookware, 46
Cooper, Susan, 33
Cornell Thailand Project, 29
Creating a Buddhist Community, 4
Crisp, James, 144
Croizat, Meda, 44, 94
cuisine driven multiculturalism, 11–15
culinary contact zones: defined, 2, 191n2; food festivals as, 132–33; in Los Angeles, 17–18, 87, 97, 116; Thailand's tourist economy, 7–8, 43, 54–55, 88–89, 177
culinary diplomacy, 3

culinary imperialism: culinary tourism and, 46–47, 177–78; culinary tourism and power relationships, 50–51; food, role in empire, 6–7; Thai cuisine, exposure to, 1–2

Culinary Institute of American (CIA), Napa Valley, 173

culinary tourism: Americans in Thailand, 7–8; cultural imperialism and, 46–47, 177–78; as neocolonialism, 42; power relationships and, 50–51; Thai Town and, 167–73. *See also* Thai Town

cultural contact zone, defined, 191n2

cultural food colonialism, defined, 46

cultural imperialism, 13, 46–47, 60–64

cultural producers, 10–11

culture: "academic diplomats," effect on culture, 60–64; Americanization of Thai food, 108–10; culinary tourism, Thai Town and, 167–73; food, transformative power of, 184–85; "food and culture" literature and, 3; food critics, shaping of race and ethnicity, 105–7; food festivals and suburban culture, 128–34, 133*fig.*; food festivals and white spatial imaginary, 134–41; Los Angeles Thai food boom (1970s–1980s), 94; melting pot, Thailand as, 47–48; metropolitan transformations and food culture, 182–83; power relationship in Thailand, 48–51; regional Thai identities, 107–8; restaurants, staging of, 97–101; restaurants and cultural pride, 91–92; Thai American identity formation, overview of, 1–5; Thailand, tourism development and, 38, 40, 41–42; tourism and idealized image of Thai people, 46–47; Wat Thai festivals, conflicts with, 141–42. *See also* food festivals; Thai Town

Curries and Bugles, 50

Davis, Mike, 15, 111, 138

defensive localism, 138

DeLaurier, Gregory, 34

demographics: East Hollywood (2000), 147; Los Angeles suburbs (1970s–1990s), 121–22

Desbarats, Jacqueline, 62, 93

dessert, 45

Dexler, Barbara, 44*fig.*

Dexler, Bob, 44*fig.*

Dhammakosacharn, Phra, 123–24

Dhirakaosal, Suphot, 160, 164

"dilemma of diversity," 14

dinner parties: culinary appropriation and, 51–53; Thai students, community building and, 69–70

diplomacy, culinary, 3

Dosti, Rose, 100, 102, 103, 105, 109

Dunlop, Fucshia, 187

Dwan, Lois, 97, 105, 106

East Hollywood: demographics (2000), 147. *See also* Thai Town

Eating Asian America, 3–4

economic issues: Bangkok Market as business incubator, 84; business investments, Thai Americans, 89–90; class divisions, Thai Americans, 115–17, 142–43; Community Economic Development (CED), 164; El Monte Slave Labor Case (1995), 155–61; ethnic *vs.* enclave economies, 215n119; food festival vendors, opportunities for, 130–31; foreign trade zones (FTZs), 79–82, 81*map*; immigrant job opportunities (1970s), 89; ingredient sourcing, California and Mexico, 78–82, 81*map*; Los Angeles as fragmented metropolis, 15–18; Los Angeles as immigration hub, 9; Los Angeles riots (1992), 149–50; Los Angeles Thai food boom (1970s–1980s), 93–94; NAFTA (North American Free Trade Agreement), 80; post–World War II, U.S. investment in Thailand, 27–28; service-based economy, Thailand, 53–55; suburban zoning and, 138; Thai immigrants, jobs for, 10; Thai Kitchen of the World campaign, 172; Thai Town as business incubator, 166; tourism, food service and, 7; tourist infrastructure development, 38–42; trade barriers (1970s–1980s), 73–78; U.S. military bases, sex industry and, 32–34, 36–37 education system: student visas and imperialism, 60–64; U.S. influence on Thailand, 29–31

El Monte Slave Labor Case (1995), 155–67

empire: definition of, 195n22; food, role of, 6–7. *See also* cultural imperialism

enclave economy, 215n119

Enloe, Cynthia, 36–37

ethnic economy, 215n119

ethnic groups and identity: cuisine driven multiculturalism, 11–15; ethnicity and class advancement, 230n125; food critics, shaping of race and ethnicity, 105–7; food festivals and suburban culture, 128–34, 133*fig.*; food practices and, 3; Los Angeles suburbs (1970s–1990s), 121–22; transnational identity, creation of, 179–82; Wat Thai of Los Angeles and, 126–28. *See also* race

exdocumented status: defined, 10, 58; social networks, formation of, 67

farongs, 26–27, 31–32

Farrer, James, 7, 191n2

FDA (Food and Drug Administration), 74–75, 77–78

feminization of labor force, 9

Ferraro, John, 162

fish sauce *(nam plah)*, 45

food: appropriation of ethnic cuisine, 187–89; authentic ingredients, defined, 208–9n2; colonialism, role in, 6–7; emotional memories and, 68–69; racial thinking and practice, 3–4, 178–79; transformative power of, 184–85; use of term, 2

"food and culture" literature, 3

Food and Drug Administration (FDA), 74–75, 77–78

food critics, shaping of race and ethnicity, 105–7

food festivals: community development and, 118–20, 145–46; private/public space debates and, 119–20; in San Fernando Valley, 120–21; suburban culture and, 128–34, 133*fig.*; Thai American class divisions and, 142–43; Thai Town, culinary tourism and, 167–73;

Wat Thai, a "right to the suburb," 141–46, 185–86; Wat Thai, history of, 122–28; white spatial imaginary and, 134–41

food service industry: cultural producers and place-makers, 10–11; food imports, 9; invisibility of workers, 189; racialized feminization of, 9; Thailand's tourist economy, 7–8

foodways: Bangkok Market, opening of, 56–57; cultural imperialism and, 46–47; defined, 191n3; development of Thai community and, 57–58; as gateway to Thai life and society, 47–53; imperialism, exposure to new foodways, 7; racial formation and, 178–79; as reflection of ethnic traditions, 3; Thai American community formation and, 82–84, 83*map*; Thai Kitchen of the World campaign, 185; Thailand's tourist economy, 7–8; use of term, 2. *See also* Thai Town

foreign (free) trade zones (FTZs), 79–82, 81*map*

Frank, Dana, 75, 213n84

Frug, Gerald, 137

FTZs (foreign (free) trade zones), 79–82, 81*map*

Fulbright, William J., 29–30

Fulbright Foundation, 29–30

garnishes, 45–46

GATT (General Agreement on Tariffs and Trade), 73, 76

gender issues: Cold War gender roles, 53; empire building and, 177; food festival vendors, 130–31; labor exploitation and, 159–60, 161; restaurants, staging of, 98–99, 100; restaurant working conditions, 110–17, 185; Thai American gender divisions, 88, 97–98, 132, 178, 179; Thai migration to Los Angeles, 58, 66–67; U.S. military bases, effect on Thais, 32–37; white spatial imaginary and, 136

General Agreement on Tariffs and Trade (GATT), 73

Giroux, Henry, 137

militourism, defined, 204n41
Milton, Richard, 65
Minor, Jerolyn (Jerri), 31
Modern Thai Cuisine, 109
Molina, Natalia, 82
multiculturalism: cuisine driven multiculturalism, 11–15, 186–87; "food and culture" literature, 3; in Los Angeles politics, rise of, 145–46; Thai Town and, 148, 162, 163–64

NAFTA (North American Free Trade Agreement), 80
nam plah (fish sauce), 45
Naraspo, Phramaha Singsathon, 122
Narayan, Uma, 6, 13, 132, 188
National Economic and Social Development Plan (NESDP), 74
neocolonialism: culinary tourism as, 42; imperialist nostalgia, defined, 207n108; student visas and, 60–64; United States in Thailand, 24–32, 177–78; U.S. military bases, effect on Thais, 32–37. *See also* cultural imperialism
NESDP (National Economic and Social Development Plan), 74
Ngai, Mae, 180
Ngan, Win Chuai, 155–56, 161
Nicholaides, Becky, 138
Nokham, Tim, 162
Noochia-or, Jintana, 142–43
North American Free Trade Agreement (NAFTA), 80
North Hollywood: demographics, 121; Wat Thai, history of, 122–28, 127*fig.*

Omatsu, Glen, 151
oral histories, 19–20
Orenstein, Dara, 80
"Oriental" cooking, U.S. fascination with, 51–53
The Original Thai Cookbook, 45, 50–51

Pacific Area Travel Association (PATA), 39–41, 52
Pacoima, California, 120–21, 124
Palms Thai, 164
Panorama City, 121, 124

PATA (Pacific Area Travel Association), 39–41, 52
Pa Thaan, 114–15
Pathomrit, Wandee, 112–16
Peace Corps, 30–31, 43, 58–59
Perry, Charles, 100, 102, 106, 109
Phayakarit, Somchet, 161
Phibunsongkhram, Plaek, 26, 49
Phillips, Carolyn, 187
Pinsuvana, Malulee, 68
Pin Tong Th ai Café, 99
Pinwatana, Suwattana, 128–29
place-makers, 10–11
Pok Pok, 187
political engagement, Thai Americans, 154. *See also* Thai Community Development Center (CDC)
Polynesian cuisine, 52
Pootaraksa, Kamolmal, 94–95, 100, 107
Portes, Alejandro, 217n16
Portugal, influences in Thai food, 47
power relationships, in Thailand, 48–51
Pramoj, Seni, 26
Pratt, Mary Louise, 191n2
Preserve America communities, 173
private *vs.* public, use of terms, 228n96
privatism, 137–38; political and community engagement and, 154–55
Proposition 187 (1994), 149, 150–51
public space *vs.* private space, 137–38; use of terms, 228n96
Pulido, Laura, 18
Purcell, Mark, 18

Rabey, Ed, 98–99
race: cuisine driven multiculturalism, 11–15; food critics, shaping of race and ethnicity, 105–7; Los Angeles riots (1992), 149–51; racial formation and foodways, 3–4, 178–79; suburbs, demographics of (1970s–1990s), 121–22; Wat Thai food festival disputes and, 143. *See also* ethnic groups and identity
Rachatawan, Somchua, 151
racialization of space, 15–17
racialized feminization of labor force, 9
racial nativism, 150–51
Raksasataya, Amara, 62

Sosothikul, Wichai, 124
Southeast Asia, xvi*map*; golden triangle, 212n62; U.S. expansion, post-World War II, 5–8
Southeast Asian Treaty Organization (SEATO), 27–28
space, racialization of, 15–17
spiciness, sensory experiences, 102–10; Americanization of Thai food, 108–10
Stadler, Donald E., 66
Stanonis, Anthony, 170
Stanton, Edward F., 27
student visas, 59–64; "Robin Hood" status, 64–67
Su, Julie, 158
suburbs: food festivals and suburban culture, 128–34, 133*fig.*; food festivals and white spatial imaginary, 134–41; localism, 138; Los Angeles as fragmented metropolis, 15–18; multicultural politics, rise of, 145–46; privatism and, 137–38; racial demographics (1970s–1990s), 121–22; San Fernando Valley, CA, 120–21; Wat Thai, a "right to the suburb," 141–46, 185–86
SukoThai, 103
Sun Valley, 121, 124
Surapol Mekpongsatorn, 70
Sutthiprapha, Sokanay, 155–56, 161
Sutton, David, 68, 180
Svast, Sirichalerm, 173
Sweatshop Watch, 158
sweatshop work, 155–61

T'ai, influences in Thai food, 47
Talésai, 91–92, 95, 101
Tang, Tommy, 85–86, 91, 100, 109
Tassananchalee, Kamol, 101
taste, sense of, 4. *See also* sensory experiences; *yum*
Tepparod Thai, 70, 100–101
Thai American Buddhist Association, 122, 123–24
Thai American Citizen's Alliance, 160
Thai Americans: anti-Asian sentiment, 11; archives for historical investigation, 19–21; Bangkok Market, community formation and, 82–84, 83*map*; Bangkok

Market, importance of, 57; business investment by, 89–90; class divisions, 115–17, 142–43; El Monte Slave Labor Case (1995), 155–61; food service economy and, 10; history of, 4–5, 183–84; "invisibility factor," 149; migration to U.S., history of, 58–64; movement to suburbs, 17; political engagement of, 154–55; racial formation, overview of, 1–5; restaurants, culture and identity, 86–88; in San Fernando Valley, 120–21; transnational identity, creation of, 179–82; use of term, 191n1; *yum*, pursuit of, 57. *See also* food festivals; Thai Town; Wat Thai of Los Angeles
Thai Community Development Center (CDC), 147; anti-human trafficking efforts, 159–61; El Monte Slave Labor Case (1995), 155–67; history of, 148–55, 153*fig.*; Thai Town, planning for, 162–67
Thai cuisine: Americanization of Thai food, 108–10; appropriation by white chefs, 187–89; authentic ingredients, defined, 208–9n2; as barrier to political mobilization, 154–55; *vs.* Chinese cuisine, 103–4; as culinary diplomacy, 3; culinary tourism in Thai Town, 167–73; food and emotional memories, 68–69; influences of other cultures in, 47; ingredient sourcing (1960s), 70–73; ingredient sourcing, California and Mexico, 78–82, 81*map*; Los Angeles, restaurants (1970s), 88–92; Los Angeles Thai food boom (1970s–1980s), 92–97, 93*map*; regional identities, 107–8; restaurant cooks and kitchen workers, 110–17; sensory experiences, restaurants and, 101–10; Thai American community formation and, 82–84, 83*map*; Thai American racial formation, overview of, 1–5; trade barriers (1970s–1980s), 73–78. *See also* food festivals; Thai Town
Thai Gourmet, 108
Thai Home Cooking From Kamolmal's Kitchen, 95, 107
Thai Kitchen of the World campaign, 172, 185

Thailand, xvi*map*; education system, U.S. and, 29–31, 57–58; El Monte Slave Labor Case (1995), response to, 160–61; golden triangle, 212n62; as melting pot, 47–48; National Economic and Social Development Plan (NESDP), 74; power relationships in, 48–51; regional identities, 107–8; service-based economy of, 53–55; support for Thai Town food festivals, 168–70, 172–73; Thai Culinary Ambassador, 184–85; Thai Kitchen of the World campaign, 172, 185; tourist economy, 7–8; Treaty of Amity and Commerce (1833), 25; U.S. expansion, post-World War II, 5–8, 24–32; U.S. military bases, effect on Thais, 32–37; U.S. tourism in, 37–42; U.S. trade barriers (1970s–1980s), 73–78; in World War II, 25–26

Thai Merchant's Association, 164–65

Thai New Year festival *(Songkran),* 129, 167–70

Thai Smakom, UCLA, 162

Thai Town: culinary tourism and, 167–73; metropolitan transformations and food culture, 182–83; overview of, 147–48; planning and development of, 162–67; Thai Community Development Center, history of, 148–55, 153*fig.*; urban renewal and, 185

Thanarat, Sarit, 40–41

Thepsophon, Phra, 133, 142, 144, 145

Theravada Buddhism, overview of, 123. *See also* Buddhism; Wat Thai of Los Angeles

Theravada Buddhist Center, Inc., 124, 125

Tilakamonkul, Jet: cooking demonstrations by, 168; interview with Anthony Bourdain, 171; on Pramorte's vision, 72, 79, 93; as Thai Culinary Ambassador, 184–85; on *yum,* 211n49

Tilakamonkul, Pramorte "Pat": Bangkok Market, history of, 56, 57; ingredient sourcing (1960s), 57, 72–73; ingredient sourcing, California and Mexico, 78–82, 81*map*; restaurants of, 90–91, 92, 95; Thai American community formation and, 82–84, 83*map*; Thai Buddhist

Center involvement, 125; trade barriers (1970s–1980s), 73–78

Tommy Tang's Siamese Cafe, 85–86

tom yum, 72

TOT (Tourism Organization of Thailand), 40–41

tourism, in Thailand: adaptations to U.S. tourist preferences, 42–43; infrastructure development, 38–42; prostitution and, 36–37; Sodsook, Victor and, 88–89; tourist visas, Thais use of, 65–67; U.S. tourism in Thailand, 37–42. *See also* culinary tourism

Tourism Organization of Thailand (TOT), 40–41

Trade and Tariff Act (1984), 214n92

trade barriers: (1970s–1980s), 73–78; foreign (free) trade zones (FTZs), 79–82, 81*map*; ingredient sources (1960s), 72–73; NAFTA (North American Free Trade Agreement), 80

Trader Vic's, 52

transnational identity, creation of, 179–82

Treaty of Amity and Commerce (1833), 25

UCLA (University of California Los Angeles), 151–52, 162; Department of Urban Planning, 166

United States: immigration policies, 59–64; military bases, effect on Thais, 32–37; neocolonialism in Thailand, 24–32; post-World War II expansion in Asia, 5–8, 176–78; Thai migration to, history of, 58–64; tourism in Thailand, 37–42; trade barriers (1970s–1980s), 73–78; Treaty of Amity and Commerce (1833), 25. *See also* Los Angeles, California

United States Customs Service, 71, 74–78, 214n92; foreign (free) trade zones (FTZs), 79–82, 81*map*

United States Department of Agriculture (USDA), 74–75, 76–78

United States Department of Commerce, 40

United States State Department: tourism, promotion of, 37–38, 39; visas from, 60–64

United States Treasury Department, 75

urban areas, Los Angeles as fragmented metropolis, 15–18
USDA (United States Department of Agriculture), 74–75, 76–78
Utopian Thought, 137

Van Oosten, Jan, 27
Vigoreaux, Ernesto, 163, 164
visas, student, 59–64; "Robin Hood" status, 64–67
visas, tourist, 65–67
Vongparansuksa, Somchai, 164
Vucharatavintara, Chutima, 165–66

Walmsley, Emily, 4
war brides, 66–67
Warren, William, 42
Wat Thai of Los Angeles, 84; food festivals and, 118–20, 185–86; food festivals and suburban culture, 128–34, 133*fig.*; food festivals and white spatial imaginary, 134–41; history of, 122–28, 127*fig.*; metropolitan transformations and food culture, 182–83; a "right to the suburb," 141–46; Thai American class divisions and, 142–43
Wat Thai of Silicon Valley, 139
Wells, Margo, 52
white as racial category, 224n17
white rice *(khao),* 45
white spatial imaginary, defined, 136, 199n52
Wilson, Marie: appropriation of ethnic cuisine, 188–89; as authority on Thai cuisine, 24–25, 44–45; cooking classes of, 51; ingredient substitutions, 70–71; interpretation of Thai culture, 47, 49; Los Angeles Thai food boom

(1970s–1980s), 94; servants, description of, 54
Wilson, Pete, 149
Win's Thai Cuisine, 155–56
Wolf, Alfred, 143
women: Cold War gender roles, 53; empire building, role in, 177; food festival vendors, 130–31; labor exploitation and, 159–60, 161; restaurant working conditions, 110–17, 185; role as culinary tourists, 177–78; staging of Thai restaurants, 98–99, 100; Thai American gender divisions, 88, 132, 178, 179; Thai immigration data, 66–67; U.S. military bases, effect on Thais, 32–37; white spatial imaginary and, 136
Wongskhaluang, Surasak, 60, 169
Woo, Michael, 162
working conditions, restaurants, 110–17. *See also* labor force
Wu, Frank, 13
Wygand, David, 134, 140, 141, 144

Yenbamroong, Kris, 91
Yenbamroong, Prakas, 91–92, 100, 101, 107
Yenbamroong, Vilai, 91–92
Yingyuad, Sawasdi, 126
yum: different preferences, 211n49; food and emotional memories, 68–69; ingredient sourcing (1960s), 70–73; sensory experiences, restaurants and, 103–4; Thai immigrant pursuit of, 57

Zhou, Min, 215n119, 217n16
zoning laws: Wat Thai, a "right to the suburb," 141–46, 185–86; white spatial imaginary and, 134–41

AMERICAN CROSSROADS

Edited by Earl Lewis, George Lipsitz, George Sánchez, Dana Takagi, Laura Briggs, and Nikhil Pal Singh

CPSIA information can be obtained
at www.ICGtesting.com
Printed in the USA
LVHW05s1127170418
573713LV00002B/2/P